D1446071

Renew iten
Customer
Items tha
Title:
Beyond t
the mem
ID: 3112
Due: Sa

Beyond *the* World *of* Pooh

SELECTIONS FROM THE MEMOIRS OF

Christopher Milne

✦ ✦ ✦ ✦ ✦

Edited by **A. R. MELROSE**

With an Introduction by **LESLEY MILNE**

Dutton Books · New York

*The publisher gratefully acknowledges permission
to reprint the following: portraits of Christopher and Daphne Milne
and Christopher with A. A. Milne: UPI/Corbis-Bettmann;
Poohsticks Bridge and Christopher Milne in 1971: Andrew Holmes.*

✦   ✦   ✦   ✦   ✦

CIP Data is available.
Published in the United States by Dutton Children's Books,
a division of Penguin Putnam Books for Young Readers
375 Hudson Street, New York, New York 10014
Designed by Adrian Leichter
Printed in U.S.A.
First Edition
1 3 5 7 9 10 8 6 4 2

Contents

PART TWO
THE PATH THROUGH THE TREES

PART THREE
FROM HILL TO OPEN GARDEN

Preface

Still with his eyes on the world Christopher Robin put out a hand and felt for Pooh's paw.

"Pooh," said Christopher Robin earnestly, "if I—if I'm not quite——" he stopped and tried again— "Pooh, *whatever* happens, you *will* understand, won't you?"

"Understand what?"

"Oh, nothing." He laughed and jumped to his feet. "Come on!"

"Where?" said Pooh.

"Anywhere," said Christopher Robin.

When Christopher Robin Milne died on April 20, 1996, newspapers throughout the English-speaking world ran obituaries; after all, he had been the most famous boy in all of children's literature.

Little boys grow up, and their teddy bears are put away in cupboards. Well, that is usually what happens. Once, though, there was a bear that instead climbed into a very small book, and the book became very famous, and the bear and all his friends became very famous. That bear was Winnie-the-Pooh, and he had a boy called Christopher Robin. But the boy was also a real boy, and like all boys he had to grow up. What kind of man he grew into makes for a very human adventure; he became a husband, a father, a soldier, a bookseller, and a writer. But let us start at the beginning, as books should and all adventures seem to.

Christopher Robin came into the literary world watching the changing of the guard in a book of poems by the unlikely title *When We Were Very Young*. To father and writer A. A. Milne, the two-barreled name was used for reasons of familiarity and rhyme—they "come very trippingly off the tongue." They did indeed, and soon they were tripping off the tongues of an ever-growing number of readers—readers who wanted more of Christopher Robin. A. A. Milne says in his own autobiography that "it was this Christopher Robin, not I, not the publishers, who was selling the book in such large and ridiculous quantities." But to the elder Milne, the fictional boy caused neither self-consciousness nor concern for the privacy of his family: it was all but an invented name. From an early age the real boy was called Billy, and his first attempts at trying to sound his full name had him labeled Billy Moon within the family throughout his childhood. As it was, Christopher Milne (as he would later write) suffered all his life from an "embarrassment of names." Yet the case of the mistaken identity grew in the telling: first with a book of poems, then with a book about a boy and his bear, then another collection of verses, and finally, another book about a bear and his boy.

But the trouble lay not in the confusion of names but in the fact that the real boy and the fictitious boy shared common toys and lived in a common landscape. There really were woods and hills that were wandered over and climbed. And there really were Floods and Blusterous Conditions that called for a certain amount of wonder and bravery.

Somewhere and sometime, the line between the real boy and the fictitious boy had to be broken. Billy Moon grew up . . . Christopher Milne reclaimed his own name and staked out his own life. And if fame followed him, then it followed the wrong man.

In 1974 Christopher Milne produced his first memoir, *The Enchanted Places*, aimed at an imaginary audience "of Pooh's friends and admirers."

✦ ✦ ✦ ✦ ✦

I have attempted a picture of Milne family life, the family life that both inspired and was subsequently inspired by the books. . . . I have tried to answer the sort of questions that I imagined friends of Pooh wanting to ask. They would want to know about the real Pooh and the real Forest and whether there really was an Alice. They would want to know something about the real little boy who played with Pooh in the Forest. . . . They would not be particularly interested to learn what happened afterwards: what happened to the little boy when he grew up. Yet the little boy did grow up and it is the grown up little boy who is writing now.

Critics' reviews were divided. One saw the book as an act of revenge against his father: a desperate jab at trying to correct misrepresentations of the real Christopher Robin. Another critic saw it as an exercise in narcissism. The British magazine *Punch*, A. A. Milne's original stamping ground, even ran a satirical interview with Pooh Bear about the book. But others recognized that Christopher Milne was trying to gently correct a wrong and that he didn't want to place any blame. *The Enchanted Places* was written by a man who understood his father's need to be creative, who had come to realize how his own fame had been created, and who decided to step out of a storybook and make his own life.

The Enchanted Places celebrates the very best of things. Sadness can be read into it, but only by those who have grown up, too. Christopher Milne, with a reserve and a sense of privacy that are not expected in the autobiographies of the famous, shows more than he says. It is to be wondered that he did not attempt novel writing. But it is a happy book for being what it is: a remembrance as well as a retelling.

And if I seem to write most happily about the ordinary things that boys do who live in the country it is because this is the part of my childhood that I look back upon with the greatest affection.

✦ ✦ ✦ ✦ ✦

When Christopher Milne turned sixty, in 1980, his second volume of memoirs had recently appeared, and he wanted now to say something else. He wanted to tell about the non-Pooh part of his life. *The Path Through the Trees* is about the "escape from Christopher Robin." His voice is more confident—no, his voice is more firm. The man is telling us about how he made his life, and into this comes the clear and resolute conviction that while life is never predictable, the paths chosen in life have their own certainty. And the more he writes about the non-Pooh, the more we discover about the joy behind and in the Pooh stories. It is a refreshing thing, but has a certain irony. A foresighted reviewer in *The New York Times* picked it up seventy years ago:

> When Christopher Robin grows up and recurs to the adventures of his childhood, he will find that a number of things have not changed and that the motivations of his infancy are also those in large measure of his grown-up life.

These motivations are the simplicity of being "side by side" with others, of doing things together, of doing Nothing for the sheer joy of it! These themes come straight from the Forest and are embedded in A. A. Milne's political views and Christopher Milne's own philosophy of life. Those early years in the English countryside have an indelible importance to him—the freedoms gained in breathing and wandering in a woodland, the satisfaction of just being where one stands. It is no coincidence that the happiness he enjoyed in his marriage to Lesley de Selincourt derived in large part from the pleasure the couple got from doing "nothing" together; they also worked successfully and happily side by side in the same business for many years.

Their daughter, Clare, was born disabled and required a lot of attention. Christopher adored her, and she appears in his memoirs as a confidante and friend as well as a daughter. They were coconspirators in enjoying the garden, the animals and creatures who shared it with them, and the English outdoors while others worked. Christopher Milne took pleasure in looking after Clare.

> I have already mentioned the satisfaction I had found in designing and making furniture and equipment for Clare. And it did seem to me that, financed perhaps by those royalties I was so reluctant to accept for myself, this was something I might do for others. I might also convince myself that it was something Clare and I might do together. "C. R. Milne & Daughter—Makers of Furniture for the Disabled." The idea appealed to me: a pleasant dream. But it was never more than a dream. I doubt if I could have turned it into reality.

Christopher Milne writes with a gentle stroke, and he doesn't write in Capital Letters. If it was Piglet who once shouted "Can't you see? Haven't you got eyes?" then it is Christopher Milne who knows the reader can see and does have eyes. The story of his life is one of everyday things that we all share. His philosophy seems incredibly simple: if we live, we encounter disappointments and sorrows, yet we live a successful life if it is lived without regrets. Mr. Milne is an ordinary man, and it is not his fame he wishes to celebrate.

And this leads to the two final books—*The Hollow on the Hill* (1982) and *The Open Garden* (1988)—which end the journey with a mature Christopher Milne expressing what he has learned from life. It may seem unfair that even in a book of memoirs in which he describes his escape from Pooh, he is still inextricably linked to the Forest and its animals. But there is the paradox: he was pushed onto a certain path, but his journey was his own. He discovered byways that became his and that he could share with those he loved. He saw things he would not have; he thought things he might not have.

Using the metaphor of the artist with the freedom to settle down at his easel "and paint whatever he sees," Christopher Milne presents in these two books "not a finished picture, but a few tentative sketches of some of the more interesting features that have caught my eye." But for those who have followed Christopher Milne's remembrances, the two series of essays—which were not published in America—provide a logical end. The boy has been seen, the man has developed and his story been told—and now is the time to breathe the unique and precious air of the evening. If the American philosopher Ralph Waldo Emerson is correct in saying that "a man is what he thinks about all day," then Christopher Milne is caught thinking aloud.

Indeed, this present edited volume of Christopher Milne's memoirs and essays has been shaped by the notion that Christopher Milne should be allowed to speak for himself, and no attempt has been made to rephrase or alter what he actually wrote. Material of course was omitted, but that is necessary for any anthology. Bearing in mind that Mr. Milne wrote the first title not expecting to write a second, nor a third and a fourth, there is a different "feel" to each. Readers would have had to judge each title in isolation, as it were, one from the other. Yet as a single entity we have the real pleasure of taking a quiet and reflective tour through a man's life drama—an autobiographical play in three acts.

This is not some sort of psychological study. It is a plain study in keeping things simple and in finding joy in those things so well represented by Pooh and Piglet (and even Rabbit): the idea of living "side by side" with others, the philosophy of living gratefully (and with happy expectation), and the notion of doing "nothing" for the sheer joy of it! These are themes straight from the Forest.

Christopher Milne is no everyman, nor is he just any man. He ran his own unique race, and we can take pleasure in the triumph.

A. R. MELROSE
Auckland, New Zealand

Introduction

It gives me great pleasure to introduce this collection of Christopher Milne's writings. It is high time that more people had the chance to get acquainted with the man who was famous for being a boy with a bear.

Fame can be counterproductive. Think of A. A. Milne: "the man who wrote *Winnie-the-Pooh*." Think of C. R. Milne: "the original Christopher Robin." In truth, A. A. Milne spent the latter part of his life regretting that most of his work as a playwright, essayist, and novelist was forgotten. Pooh made him rich, but not happy. C. R. Milne spent the early part of his life fighting for an identity separate from his father and those immortal playmates in the Hundred Acre Wood.

Christopher and Alan Milne had a curious relationship, as neither knew the other very well. It is difficult to imagine these days, when families are so close, how children were raised in an affluent middle-class family between the wars. A small child saw his parents only occasionally, however much they loved him in theory. A little boy or girl was more a pet than a companion: well washed, brushed, and dressed up to be brought out, cute and lovable, on special occasions. He might be asked to sing or recite for teatime guests to coo over. I doubt that Christopher's parents ever saw him throw a tantrum or encountered dirty diapers.

He was lucky indeed to share the nursery floor with his wonderful nanny, a warm, loving woman to kiss and cuddle, to keep him safe. They remained friends as long as she lived.

Mother was that distant woman who laughed a lot, and Father a large, remote godlike being—and they remained so for much of Christopher's life. To Alan, the extraordinary event of acquiring a baby was at first a shock, and a breeder of dreams and memories. A son reinvents a father and has the potential to become all those things that the father was unable to be. (Christopher was expected to play cricket for England, but he inherited his mother's weak eyesight and never made it beyond the school team. Being a writer was not part of the plan.)

In his child, Alan saw himself, and around that vision he created his books, seeing the lost world of childhood that every grown person retains a corner of in his heart. Little Christopher was a catalyst that released Alan's roseate memories.

After the nursery years came boarding school, it being the universal practice in those days to send children away from home when they were six or seven, so that their characters could be duly formed as proper Englishmen and women and their parents could get on with their lives uninterrupted. Christopher was a fine scholar. As his father had done, he won a scholarship to Trinity College, Cambridge, in mathematics. (Maths, as well as cricket and golf, was a passion that they were able to share.) Then came the war.

It is an odd phenomenon that so many men apparently unsuited to a military life look back on the war years with nostalgia. A less warlike man than Christopher it would have been hard to find: he was gentle, sensitive, and kind. But service in the Royal Engineers introduced him to the real world outside that highly artificial middle-class enclave within which he had been raised. He associated with all classes of men. He found a lot of good friends with whom he shared both pleasures and horrors. Nobody out there cared about Christopher Robin, in spite of Vera Lynn, "the Forces' Sweetheart," whose syrupy rendition of "Vespers" was a favorite on the radio among the troops. He was simply Chris, the young officer who swapped his cigarette ration for chocolate and could be trusted to dismantle a land mine or organize construction of a Bailey bridge under fire. It was during his war service that he developed a lifelong love of deserts and of Italy.

Afterward was another story. Six years in the army don't qualify a man for employment; being a storybook hero doesn't help, either. After a series of dead-end jobs, Christopher and I made our own careers as booksellers in Devon, very happily and with considerable success. If some people insisted on calling our Harbour Bookshop the Winnie-the-Pooh shop, we turned a deaf ear. We needed the money.

Christopher always had a talent for words. Among the gifts his father gave him were a love of literature; a skeptical, inquiring mind; and intolerance for the second-rate. Both writers honed and polished every sentence, but in such a way that their writings appeared simple and easy, like very good conversation. This is the hardest way to create work that is immediately satisfying to the reader.

He was unable to write during his parents' lifetime. Their shadows hovered over him too darkly. During the postwar years, communication with his father had deteriorated, and they met seldom. But there was a great deal Christopher wanted to say, and he needed desperately to untangle in his mind an unusually complicated father-son relationship, which could only be done by looking at the past, standing alone in it as an observer as well as a participant. *The Enchanted Places,* his first book, was published when he was fifty-four. It is impossible to say whether he might have been a great writer had he started on that path as a young man. That path was blocked.

Of course I wish that Christopher *had* been a professional writer. He could use words like an angel; he had a finely tuned, analytical mind, a wickedly observant eye, and an impish sense of humor. Supposing he had been able to break away from the shadows in his twenties; supposing he hadn't felt responsible for a wife and child. Could he have been a novelist? To do that he would have needed to be a different man. He wrote only from personal experience, and his chosen world was a long way from the complicated web of human relationships that a novelist must feed on.

He was an activist in environmental causes, and a passionate believer in social justice. Some of the campaigns he supported would have raised a few eyebrows among the admirers of that tremendously establishment little boy on his way to Buckingham Palace with his nanny. It was a lifelong regret to him that on occasions when he was interviewed by the media, the things he wanted to say—things that he cared about—never got printed. An hour's chat would be thinned down to five minutes about his father. In the long term, he became resigned to this belittlement and could laugh about it, but I always longed for the time when people would listen to what he had to say. He had a great deal to say that was, and increasingly still is, relevant to the strange, hostile world that we all inhabit.

The things that he knew and loved best, apart from his family, tended to be offbeat. Insects, for instance, rather than cuddly animals, and that went for caterpillars as well as butterflies. He had a tiresome habit of ignoring my garden flowers in favor of some lowly weed. There were numerous elderly, sick, lonely people to whom he regularly sent letters and made telephone calls. He loved trees best in winter, and quiet lonely places, where he could spend an hour just being and absorbing the immediate, finely detailed confines of his world.

He deliberately chose to live in a backwater where the greater world passed him by, with a few much-loved friends and creatures to share his gradually diminishing territory as age and illness invaded it.

When his last book, *The Open Garden,* was published, he said that he had no more to say. I can't believe this was true.

Please enjoy what you discover about Christopher Milne in this anthology. It would have made him happy to know you are reading it.

LESLEY MILNE
December 1997

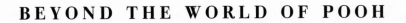

BEYOND THE WORLD OF POOH

PART ONE

The Enchanted Places

For Olive Brockwell
"Alice" to others
But "Nou" to me.
To remind you of those enchanted places
Where the past will always be present.

(Dedication from the original 1974 edition)

ONE

* * * * *

The Interview

Cotchford Farm on an August morning somewhere around the year 1932. The penstemons, the bergamots, the phloxes, the heleniums, the rudbeckias, the dahlias, and even the solitary coreopsis that had seeded itself so cleverly in the paving stones by the sundial had all been told the evening before that today they must look their best. But as yet—for it was barely ten o'clock—there was only one person in the garden to see how nicely they were doing it. He was a tall man, dark and handsome, wearing a brown suit and a brown homburg hat, and he was sweeping the brick path that ran beside the house. For it was Saturday.

George Tasker always swept the path on a Saturday, not because it particularly needed a weekly sweep (though today was different) but because Saturday morning was when he got paid. The shyness and embarrassment that this always caused him had led him to devise a sort of ritual to which my mother had learned to respond. He didn't like to knock on the door. He couldn't just stand around hoping to be noticed. Pulling up weeds from the beds by the house was her work, not his. While if he did anything more distant, he might never get seen at all. So he brought down his big brush and swept; and this made just the right amount of noise, not enough to disturb the Master but enough to remind the Mistress in case she had forgotten.

She had not forgotten. The side door opened and she emerged.

✦ ✦ ✦ ✦ ✦

"Good morning, Tasker."
"Good morning, Madam."

A brief conversation followed, for this too was part of the ritual. The Mistress said how pleased she was that it was all looking so pretty today, because someone was coming down from London specially to see it; and Tasker agreed modestly that it was looking quite nice. The Mistress said weren't we lucky with the weather; and Tasker said weren't we, though we could do with a drop of rain. And then the moment arrived and the pound notes were able to change hands and Tasker was able to sound slightly surprised as well as grateful, as if he had forgotten all about its being Saturday. A moment later the Mistress excused herself, as she still had rather a lot to do to get everything ready; and Tasker, after sweeping another yard of path to complete the ritual, shouldered his broom and went home.

Let us call her Miss Brown. Miss Brown was a journalist, and she was coming down from London to meet us, to be shown around, to ask a lot of questions, and then to write an article about us for a magazine. So my mother (after paying Tasker) was going around the garden tidying things away—golf clubs on the putting lawn, a fishing net by the stream, a pullover and a cushion in the Alcove, a copy of last week's *Observer* folded open at the crossword in the Garden House—things that my father and I had left lying about. My father was in his room working. And I was already beginning to feel slightly sick at the thought of having to meet someone strange. I had been told that I must: that she would expect to see me and that it would seem odd if I weren't there, but that I needn't do more than make an appearance, just be around when she arrived and then slide off. Would I have to change? Perhaps a clean shirt and a better pair of trousers and a comb through the hair wouldn't be a bad thing. My father wondered gently which side I usually parted my hair these days; and I remember thinking this odd, because I had always parted it on the left.

After lunch we retired to our various bedrooms to make ourselves presentable and to think our various thoughts. My mother's room was large and beautiful. It spanned the full width of the house at its narrow waist. So there was a window in the west wall that looked toward the dovecot and the azaleas (alas, now over) and away to the setting sun; and there was a window in the east wall from which you could see the big lawn, the Garden House, and the Six Pine Trees, and through which shone the early morning sun. As she got herself ready she was rehearsing once again the tour that she had planned: the rooms to be hurried by, the rooms where one could linger, the features that the eye could be directed toward, the route around the garden that would show it at its best, the places where one might pause, as if for breath, and wait (hopefully) for admiration. As she rehearsed, so she muttered to herself; as she muttered, so, now and again, she smiled. . . .

My father's room was small and dark, with a window that looked over the courtyard at the kitchen. He was brushing back his thin, fair hair. If Miss Brown liked the house and the garden, and if—which was really the point—she said so loudly and clearly; if she was a genuine Pooh fan and not just someone who muddled you up with A. P. Herbert; if she was young and pretty and gay and laughed in the right places; if all these things, then it might be rather fun. . . .

My room was next door, a large room with a high ceiling that went right up into the roof, and a floor so sloping it was an uphill walk to the window. I was trying not to think about Miss Brown at all, thinking instead of the things I was going to do when I had slipped away. In imagination I was already wearing again the clothes I had just taken off and was down by the river. It would be a good day for seeing if I could find any new crossing places. . . .

At last we were ready and waiting. Then came the sound of a car lurching in and out of the ruts along our lane, followed by the crunch of gravel as it turned into our drive. The Milnes trooped out to welcome their guest.

Nervous laughter. Introductions.

"And this is our boy."

"How do you do, Christopher Robin."

"How do you do."

There. It wasn't too bad. I had looked her bravely in the eyes and smiled my smile. And now we were moving toward the house. My mother led the way, my father and Miss Brown close behind. Gay chatter, in which I was not expected to join. So I tagged along at the back. A cat appeared and I stooped to reassure it, glad of an excuse to drop behind still farther.

A hasty glance into my father's room, then into the drawing room.

"Oh, isn't this wonderful! And you've done it all yourselves? How old did you say it was? Queen Anne? These beams look as if they were once ships' timbers. Oh, what gorgeous flowers. . . . " Miss Brown had been well trained.

Then at last through the French windows and out into the garden, my father and Miss Brown now leading the way. My mother dropped back.

"You can slide off now, Pip dear, if you like."

So I slid. First up to my room to get back into my comfortable clothes and Wellington boots; then, after a cautious glance through the landing window to see that they weren't still lurking by the house, quickly downstairs and through the front door. I didn't want to be seen. It would look silly to be caught sneaking off like this. By going out through the front door I could keep the house between us, and all would be well. I would have to go rather a long way around: up the lane and then turn down by the duck pond; but I'd be there soon enough.

Five minutes later I had my right boot wedged into an alder stump, right hand clutching a branch, left hand reaching out toward a willow, left boot dangling in space above the brown water. And there I paused to enjoy to the full the wonderful feeling of being alive. . . .

It was evening. Miss Brown had gone and I was back. My mother was in the garden quietly pottering, reliving those glorious moments, hearing again those wonderful, heartwarming words. Miss Brown had noticed everything *and* she had commented. She had specially remarked on the dahlias, Tasker's pride and joy. He must be told on Monday. . . . Gently muttering, gently smiling, my mother moved among her flowers, basking like a cat in the evening sun and in the memory of the praise that had been lavished on her and her beloved garden.

My father was on the putting lawn, pipe in mouth, stooping over his putter, deeply absorbed. One under twos and three to go. It looked as if it might be a record. He, too, still felt a glow from Miss Brown's visit. He, too, loved praise. True, there had been a moment when he had found himself wondering if she had ever actually read any of the books. But perhaps it had been a long time ago and she had forgotten. Anyway, she was a dear and very pretty and had said nice things, just as he had hoped. One under twos. He concentrated again on the ball; and as he hit it, the sun slipped behind one of the branches of the group of alders on the bridge and a tiny breath of cold air rustled the leaves of the poplar and made a tiny cold echo in his thoughts, so tiny at first that he could scarcely identify it. He watched the golf ball curving down the slope, but he had aimed too high and it was not coming down properly. Could it be jealousy? Today's Milne feeling jealous of the Milne that wrote those books five—ten—years ago? Could one feel jealous of one's self? Or was it something else? Something gone, something lost? She had asked what he was writing now. "A novel," he had said. "Will you ever write another book about Christopher Robin and Pooh, do you think?" Why do they always ask that? Can't they understand? He sighed and walked toward his ball.

I was upstairs in what was known as the Carpenter's Shop, my own private room at the very top of the house, a room whose floor and beams were so eaten away by woodworm that visions of it have haunted my dreams ever since. Yet it was a room I loved, because here I could be alone with my chisels and my saws. Each tool was labeled in my mind with the date and the occasion on which I had acquired it. Many of them had been bought four years before, one by one, out of my weekly pocket money, from the ironmonger's in London's Sloane

Square as Nanny and I walked home from my school. Many of them, complete with their labels, were to survive another forty years. I was busy perfecting a burglar alarm that I was planning to fit inside the door of the Secret Passage; and the evening sun, coming in through the window, was shining on my work. It would soon be dinnertime. After dinner there would be another chapter or two of Wodehouse— my mother reading, my father and I listening. Then, tomorrow being Sunday, I wouldn't be going riding, so might go exploring instead. How nice it was to feel that there was so much of the holidays still left.

And what of Miss Brown? Can we try and guess her thoughts?

She was in her car speeding back to London, in her handbag her notes, in her head her memories. She too was glowing. It had been an unforgettable day. She had been anxious and nervous, but it had all gone perfectly. She felt stimulated and pleased with herself, and she was already beginning to put together sentences to describe it, making a collection of appropriate adjectives: old-world, mellow, golden, peaceful. Her delight with the house and garden had been quite genuine. You could see how this setting had inspired the books—though it was an odd little room that Mr. Milne had chosen as his study. You would have thought a lighter, sunnier room with a view of the garden would have been better. But perhaps it might have been a distraction.

She thought about her notes. Had she got answers to all the questions she had planned to ask? More or less. The main point was that Mr. Milne took his writing very seriously, "even though I was taking it into the nursery," as he put it. There was no question of tossing off something that was good enough for the kiddies. He was writing first to please and satisfy himself. After that, he wanted to please his wife. He depended utterly upon doing this. Without her encouragement, her delight, and her laughter he couldn't have gone on. With it, who cared what the critics wrote or how few copies sold? Then he hoped to please his boy. This came third, not first, as so many people supposed. Did Christopher Robin or Mrs. Milne help him with ideas? Yes and no, it seemed. There was the Forest and the Five Hundred Acre Wood. These were real. Then there were the animals. They were real, too (except for Owl and Rabbit that he had invented). His wife and his boy (always his boy, never Christopher. Odd!) had, as it were, breathed life into them, given them their characters. What he had done was to write stories around them. The stories were entirely his own invention.

His books seemed to show a great understanding and love of children. Was he very fond of children? Silence. Then: "I am not inordinately fond of them, if that is what you mean, and I have certainly never felt in the least sentimental about them—or no more sentimental than one becomes for a moment over a puppy or a kitten. In as far as I understand them, this understanding is based on observation, on imagination, and on memories of my own childhood."

Another question she had put. "What does your son think about it all now?" (She had given up referring to him as Christopher Robin: nobody else seemed to.) "How has it affected him, being, you might almost say, a household name?" Mr. Milne had answered this question rather more slowly, rather more thoughtfully, perhaps rather less confidently. He hoped it had done him no harm, might even have done some good. His boy seemed perfectly happy and was certainly doing very well indeed at school and enjoying it all. He didn't think he would ever grow up to wish his name was Charles Robert.

Then she had asked what he hoped his son was going to be when he was a man. Mr. Milne had smiled at this. "At present his great interests are mathematics and cricket." "Does he show any inclination to take after you?" "He *is* taking after me. I was a mathematician and a cricketer when I was his age!" "I mean, as a writer?" Laughter. Then: "I don't know that I would specially want him to."

Now for some general impressions. Mr. Milne. An odd mixture of opposites: shy, yet at the same time self-confident; modest, yet proud of what he had done; quiet, yet a good talker; warm, yet with a thin lip and an ice-cold eye that might, if you said the wrong thing, be pretty chilling; sympathetic, yet unsympathetic to what he felt was stupidity; friendly, yet picking his friends with care. Next, Mrs. Milne. A certain hot and cold about her, too. You had to say the right thing. Obviously very proud of her husband and wrapped up in his work, though perhaps even more wrapped up in her garden. Lastly, Christopher. Didn't really get much of a chance to see him. Only managed a how-do-you-do and then he was gone. Clearly very shy indeed, painfully so. Probably his parents try to keep him out of the limelight, because, whatever his father says, it can't be too easy growing up with all this publicity. "Christopher Robin is saying his prayers." It can't be too pleasant to have that hanging round your neck when you are at school, however good you are at sums. Boys, after all, can be pretty beastly to each other when they try. There must be moments when he does wish his name was Charles Robert and he could be himself. And that long hair, too. Whose idea was that? His mother's or his father's? And when was it finally cut off? That was a question she never dared ask!

Some more thoughts. (The drive back to London would take an hour and a quarter, leaving plenty of time for thinking.) There were the books, four of them. You could read them and enjoy them. Behind them were the Milnes, three of them. You could meet them as she had and talk to them and see something of the reality that lay behind the books. And somehow that gave the books an added pleasure. Galleons Lap is Gills Lap, a real place, and she'd actually stood there and looked across the Forest to the distant rim of the world. The bridge where they had played Poohsticks was a real bridge, looking just like the drawing in the book. Yet that was not all. For behind what she had seen and had been shown lay who-knew-what that she had not been shown. She had seen the drawing room, but no one had opened for her that door halfway down the passage. She had glanced into Mr. Milne's study, but—well, naturally, of course—she had not been allowed to poke about among his papers. Yet what a gold mine lay there. The letters, the half-finished manuscripts, the jottings, even the scribblings on his blotting paper. What a gold mine for somebody, some day . . . perhaps. She had only seen what she had been allowed to see, a show arranged by the Milnes for her especial benefit. But what went on behind the scenes? What, for example, were they doing and saying right now?

But supposing she knew, supposing she were allowed to open every door and poke into every cupboard, supposing she could eavesdrop on every conversation, even listen to their silent thoughts. True, this might throw a new light on the books, lead to a deeper understanding of how they came to be written and of their inner significance. But would her search end there? The child is father to the man (as who-was-it said?). And the mother and father and attendant circumstances make the child. One would have to dig back, into Mr. Milne's childhood, meet his family, and then their family, and theirs. One would have to go right back to the beginning of the world to understand it all. And if one did, then what? One would understand, but would the books be any more enjoyable in consequence? Shakespeare was a great poet. Does it lessen our enjoyment of his plays that we know so little about his life, his parents? And anyway, fascinating though it is to see how every effect has its cause, fascinating though it is to track back along the endless chain of effect and cause, is one man's life chain all that more interesting than another's? Is a famous author's necessarily more interesting than that of an unfamous stockbroker?

With these thoughts spinning around in her head, Miss Brown reached Streatham Common. It was now dark. There was more traffic on the road. If she were to get her story back to her office intact, she would have to pay more attention to her driving. . . .

✦ ✦ ✦ ✦ ✦

TWO

Names

We had intended to call it Rosemary {wrote my father in 1939}, but decided later that Billy would be more suitable. However, as you can't be christened William—at least we didn't see why anybody should—we had to think of two other names. . . . One of us thought of Robin, the other of Christopher; names wasted on him who called himself Billy Moon as soon as he could talk and has been Moon to his family and friends ever since. I mention this because it explains why the publicity which came to be attached to "Christopher Robin" never seemed to affect us personally, but to concern either a character in a book or a horse which we hoped at one time would win the Derby.

I have suffered—if not all my life, then at least for the first thirty years of it—from an embarrassment of names. Let me now, with as much clinical detachment as I can manage, look in turn at each of the four mentioned above, together with their more common variants.

Billy · Survived to get itself into my copy of *When We Were Very Young*, which my father inscribed "Billy's own book," but died between there and *Winnie-the-Pooh*. It did, however, linger on among those friends of the family who knew me in the early 1920s, and so made occasional reappearances. But today it is totally extinct.

Moon · This was my early attempt at saying "Milne." Superseded Billy within the family around 1925 and thereafter remained my father's only name for me; used by him among his friends and acquaintances on every occasion when something more precise than "my boy" was required. Universally used among close friends and family, my mother only excepted, until after the Second World War. Still surviving here and there.

Billy-Moon · A rare variant of Billy. Now quite obsolete.

Christopher Robin · My official Christian names and so still appearing on occasional legal documents, but now generally superseded by "Christopher" even when "Christian names in full" are required. My formal name with acquaintances until about 1928, after which determined efforts were made by the family to kill it off. Today used only by complete strangers, some of whom think (or are charitably assumed to have thought) that Robin is my surname.

Christopher · Used by school friends and the like from about 1929. Used by my mother when introducing me to her friends from about 1938. Now used almost universally. The only name I feel to be really mine.

Chris · A variant of the above, used in the army and today only surviving at Christmastime on two or three Christmas cards.

C.R. · An acceptable variant of Christopher Robin, though not widely used.

Robin · Used only by the Hartfield Platoon of the Home Guard.

THREE

✦ ✦ ✦ ✦ ✦

Nursery Days

Billy made his appearance at 11 (later renumbered 13) Mallord Street, Chelsea, at eight o'clock on the morning of August 21 in the year 1920. He had been a long time coming, and this may partly explain why he never had any brothers or sisters. It is reported that Mrs. Penn, the cook, on seeing him, went downstairs to inform the Master that he was "tall, like Mistress"—an early promise that was to remain unfulfilled for another sixteen years. What Gertrude said was not recorded.

Gertrude and Mrs. Penn: they really have no more than walking-on parts in this story. But they must be introduced, if only to give today's reader the flavor of a middle-class household in the 1920s. Mrs. Penn is a hazy figure, for she left when I was about seven. I see her as small (so she must indeed have been small), round, grey, and elderly. Gertrude was small too, but thinner. My mother's family were well-to-do and had dozens of servants from butlers downward, and among them was Gertrude, my mother's personal maid; and when Miss Dorothy married, she was allowed to take Gertrude with her as part of the marriage settlement.

Domestic staff wore uniform. I imagine that in those days there was a department in Harrods that catered especially for their needs, and thither their mistresses would repair, armed with sets of measurements, to be shown the latest uniforms. "This style, if I may say so,

Madam, is greatly favored by the nobility." How little my mother would be influenced by the preferences of the nobility. How much more likely to choose something to match the curtains. Mrs. Penn I see in grey with a very large white apron; Gertrude was in bottle green with a small and elegant apron and a big black bow which she wore in the back of her hair. Mrs. Penn cooked and seldom left the kitchen except to go up to her bedroom, which she shared with Gertrude on the top floor. Gertrude did everything else. She cleaned the house before breakfast. She laid the fire in the drawing room. She served at meals. She made the beds. She polished the silver. She went around the house pulling the curtains when it got dark. And when it grew chilly, she would apply the match that lit the fire—though to be fair, this was something that my mother often managed on her own. And all this she did with quiet efficiency and great solemnity. I never once heard her laugh.

And what about me? Who was there to change my nappies and powder my bottom?

One can never be sure whether a very early memory is a real memory or just the recollection of something which you were told happened. My first memory—if indeed that was what it was—is of lying on a rug in the nursery. There was a screen around me. I looked up, and there above the screen was a round kindly face smiling down at me. So I smiled back at it. I was eighteen months old at the time. There had obviously been nannies before that, but either I hadn't taken to them or they hadn't taken to me. This was the one I had been waiting for.

In the domestic hierarchy, nannies come somewhere in the middle. There were times when they would join the servants in the servants' quarters and times when they would join the gentry. But mostly their place was with their charge, and that was in the nursery. They, too, wore uniforms. There were black-and-white nannies, grey nannies, blue nannies, and pink nannies. There were nannies with hats and nannies with veils. My nanny was grey, and she wore a veil when out in the street and a white cap and starched cuffs when indoors. We lived together in a large nursery on the top floor. We lived there, played there, ate there—the food being brought up from the kitchen on a tray—and then at the end of the day we retired, each at our appointed time, to the night nursery next door. So much were we together that Nanny became almost a part of me. Consequently it was my occasional encounters with my parents that stand out as the events of the day.

Our first meeting would be after breakfast, when I was allowed to visit the dining room. There was a large chest by the window, and this was opened for me and I climbed inside while my father finished his marmalade and my mother ate her apple. Our next meeting was in the drawing room after tea. In the drawing room I could play on the sofa or on my father's armchair. One day, climbing about on the back of his chair, I fell off. In exciting books people often give—as they never seem to do in real life—a "whistle of surprise." That's what I gave when I reached the carpet. And for weeks afterwards if I wanted to whistle, I had to climb on to my father's chair and fall off. Later, I found a simpler way. My final excursion was to the dining room in the evening. Here, on the floor under the table in the dark, I would play "boofy games" with my mother, getting more and more excited until the arrival of Nanny would bring it all to an end and I would be swept upstairs to my bath.

I enjoyed playing with my mother. This was something she was good at. There were plenty of things she couldn't do, had never been taught to do, didn't need to do because there was someone to do them for her, and she certainly couldn't have coped alone with a tiny child. But provided Nanny was at hand in case of difficulty, she was very happy to spend an occasional half hour with me, playing on the floor, sitting me on her lap to show me how the gentleman rides, reciting (for the hundredth time) Edward Lear's "Calico Pie."

My nursery was in the front of the house, facing the street. If I stood on the ottoman where I kept my toys, I could look through the bars of the window and see the whole length of Mallord Street below me. It was a quiet, almost deserted street: no cars, no people, no noise, nothing to look at. But if something of importance came, it would announce its arrival, and then I could run to the ottoman and climb up and hold on to the bars and watch. If there was a yodeling shout, that would be the log man leading a horse that pulled a cart loaded with logs. If there was the ringing of a handbell, that would be the muffin man with a tray of muffins on his head. If there was a roaring, rattling noise, that would be the coal man pouring sacks of coal through the little holes in the pavement that went down into the cellars. I even got to know the various clicks and creaks that announced the arrival of the organ-grinder, and so I would be all ready for "Tipperary" when it came. Organ-grinders always made me feel sad, and I used to throw them a penny. But the harp man made me feel sadder. He came on Friday evening and set up his stool just opposite my window. I never knew one organ-grinder from another, but the harp man was my friend. He had black hair, a small moustache, a dark grey coat, and an air of quiet melancholy. I was allowed to go downstairs and cross the road; and I would put two pennies into his little velvet bag.

But of all the noises, the most welcome was "Coooooo-eeeeee." And that was Anne.

Anne Darlington lived half a mile away in a flat in Beaufort Mansions. She was eight months older than I was and, like me, without brothers or sisters. So instead we had each other, and we were as close and inseparable as it is possible for two children to be who live half a mile apart. It was a closeness that extended to my parents, for Anne was and remained to her death the Rosemary that I wasn't.

Anne had a nanny who wore black-rimmed glasses and a black straw hat. When we were feeling wicked, we called her Jam Puff because she had so many chins, and she would pretend not to have heard. Anne also had a monkey whose name was Jumbo, as dear to her as Pooh was to me. When we were six, we left Jumbo and Pooh behind and went to Miss Walters' school in Tite Street, and one morning Anne, who always knew things before I did, told me there was no such person as Father Christmas. We sat next to each other in class while Miss Walters did her best to teach us this and that, and mostly we got it wrong.

"Christopher Robin, I'm afraid six from nine does not make five."
"No, Miss Walters. I'm not very good at easy sums. I'm better at them when they are harder."

I was better, too, at being Andrew Aguecheek and saying that Nay by my troth I knew not, but I knew to be up late was to be up late. I was better at singing.

> On the grassy banks
> Lambkins at their pranks
> Woolly sisters, woolly brothers
> Jumping off their feet,
> While their wooooo-leeeee mothers
> Watch by them and bleat.

After three years of this sort of thing I went onto another school and learned Latin, while Anne moved upstairs into Miss Hunt's class. But we continued to meet in the holidays. At Easter she came and stayed with us at Cotchford, and sometimes again in early summer.

> Where is Anne?
> Head above the buttercups,
> Walking by the stream,
> Down among the buttercups.

Those were the Buttercup Days, and there, in Shepard's picture, is Cotchford Farm. In late summer I used to join her (alone, while my nanny was on holiday) at St. Nicholas on the Kent coast. And finally we spent Christmas together at Mallord Street. She and I inevitably drifted apart as we grew older, but she and my parents remained devoted to each other, and until I was twenty-five my mother cherished fond hopes that one day we would marry.

"Cooo-eeeee." I ran to the ottoman, climbed up, leaned over the bars, and waved; and Anne and her nanny waved back. Where were we going? To the Albert Memorial in Kensington Gardens? To the Embankment Gardens by the river? Or across the Albert Bridge to Battersea Park? Were we taking our hoops or our skipping ropes?

> *When Anne and I go out a walk,*
> *We hold each other's hand and talk*
> *Of all the things we mean to do*
> *When Anne and I are forty-two.*

But the Christopher Robin who appears in so many of the poems is not always me. For this was where my name, so totally useless to me personally, came into its own: it was a wonderful name for writing poetry round. So sometimes my father is using it to describe something I did, and sometimes he is borrowing it to describe something he did as a child, and sometimes he is using it to describe something that any child might have done. "At the Zoo," for example, is about me. "The Engineer" is not. "Lines and Squares" and "Hoppity" are games that every small child must have played. "Buckingham Palace" is half and half. Nanny and I certainly used to go and watch the changing of the guard, but I must—for a reason that will appear later—disown the conversation. On the whole, it doesn't greatly matter which of the two of us did what: I'm happy to accept responsibility. But I must make two exceptions. The first is "In the Dark."

There was one great difference between my father and myself when we were children. He had an elder brother; I had not. So he was never alone in the dark. Lying in bed with the lights out, he could so easily be "talking to a dragon" and feeling brave, knowing that if the dragon suddenly turned fierce, he had only to reach out a hand

and there would be Ken in the next bed. But I could take no such risks. I had to keep reminding myself that the dragon was only a bedtime-story one, not a real one. I had to keep reassuring myself that all was safe by staring at the little orange strip of light that ran along the bottom of the night-nursery door, by straining my ears to hear the gentle but, oh, so comforting movements of Nanny in the next room. Sometimes she would call out, "I'm just going downstairs. I shan't be a minute": and then I would wait anxiously for the sound of her returning footsteps. Once I waited and waited until I could wait no more. Something awful must have happened. I got out of bed, opened the night-nursery door, crossed the deserted nursery to the door at the far end. And there was Nanny coming upstairs. "You naughty boy. What are you doing?" "Oh, Nanny, you were such a long time; I didn't know what had happened to you." She was cross, but only a little bit, and I didn't mind. It was so lovely to have her back.

I continued to have night fears for a long time. When, later, I went to boarding school, this was my one consolation when the holidays came to an end: there were no dragons in dormitories.

Once—I can't put a date to it, but I think I must have been about ten—my father, when he came to say good night to me, asked me an odd question. "Which side do you usually go to sleep on?" he said. I thought for a bit. I didn't really know. So I made a guess. "My right, I think." He nodded. "That's supposed to be the best side," he said. "You're supposed to be more likely to have bad dreams if you sleep on your left, because then you're lying on your heart." Bad dreams! BAD DREAMS! I did have bad dreams, awful dreams about witches. Now I knew why. I had been going to sleep on my left side. . . . In those days I used to lie on my tummy with one hand tucked under the mattress and the other under the pillow. I would start facing one way. After a while I would feel restless and turn over to face the other way. Then over again, and so on, until finally I was asleep. So I might end up on my right side, or I might equally well end up on my left. *I must never end up on my left side again!* Whenever I turned onto my left, I must keep my eyes open, wide open, staring, however much I longed to shut them. Then I must turn back onto the other side as soon as ever I could. And every night from then on, this became the way I had to go to sleep. For how long? For years, I believe.

> *I'm lying on my left side . . .*
> *I'm lying on my right . . .*
> *I'll play a lot tomorrow*
> *I'll think a lot tomorrow*
> *I'll laugh a lot tomorrow . . .*
> *Good-night!*

Before I come to the second poem that I must disown—and the reader may start guessing which one it will be—I must quote from something my father wrote in a "Preface to Parents" for a special edition of the verses, and which he later reprinted in his autobiography.

> In real life very young children have an artless beauty, an innocent grace, an unstudied abandon of movement, which, taken together, make an appeal to our emotions similar in kind to that made by any other young and artless crea- tures: kittens, puppies, lambs: but greater in degree, for the reason that the beauty of childhood seems in some way to transcend the body. Heaven, that is, does really appear to lie about the child in its infancy, as it does not lie about even the most attractive kitten. But with this outstanding physical quality there is a natural lack of moral quality, which express- es itself, as Nature always insists on expressing herself, in an egotism entirely ruthless. . . . The mother of a little boy of three has disappeared, and is never seen again. The child's reaction to the total loss of his mother is given in these lines:

✦ ✦ ✦ ✦ ✦

James James
Morrison Morrison
(Commonly known as Jim)
Told his
Other relations
Not to go blaming him.

And that is all. It is the truth about a child: children are, indeed, as heartless as that. . . .

Is it? Are they? Was I? I cannot pretend to know for sure how I felt about anything at the age of three. I can only guess that though I might not have missed my mother had she disappeared, and would certainly not have missed my father, I would have missed Nanny—most desolately. A young child's world is a small one, and within it things may have odd values. A teddy bear may be worth more than a father. But the egotism with which (I will admit) a child is born, surely very quickly disappears as attachments are made and relationships established. When a child plays with his bear, the bear comes alive, and there is at once a child-bear relationship which tries to copy the nanny-child relationship. Then the child gets inside his bear and looks at it the other way around: that's how *bear* feels about it. And at once sympathy is born and egotism has died. A poem in which my father really does express what I feel is the truth about a child is "Market Square," which ends up:

> *So I'm sorry for the people who sell fine saucepans,*
> *I'm sorry for the people who sell fresh mackerel,*
> *I'm sorry for the people who sell sweet lavender,*
> *'Cos they haven't got a rabbit, not anywhere there!*

How well I remember this feeling of sympathy—totally misplaced, of course—yet agonizingly sincere!

Undoubtedly children can be selfish, but so, too, can adults. By accusing the young of heartless egotism, are we perhaps subconsciously reassuring ourselves that, selfish though we still may be, there was once a time when we were worse. . . .

This brings me to the second poem I must disown—"Vespers." It is one of my father's best known and one that has brought me over the years more toe-curling, fist-clenching, lip-biting embarrassment than any other. So let me, for the first time in my life, look it clearly in the eyes and see how things stand between us.

The general impression left by "Vespers"—especially with anyone who has heard Vera Lynn singing it—is of a rather soppy poem about a good little boy who is saying his prayers. But if one reads it rather more carefully, one will see that it is nothing of the sort. It is a poem about a rather naughty little boy who is *not* saying his prayers. He is merely pretending; and to his and the author's surprise he has managed to fool a great many people. "Vespers," then, is not a sentimental poem at all: it is a mildly cynical one. But even so, nothing to get worked up about. After all, everyone is naughty sometimes.

So you might think. But it is not quite what my father thought. Let us see what he had to say in that "Preface to Parents."

Finally, let me refer to the poem which has been more sentimentalized over than any other in the book: "Vespers." Well, if mothers and aunts and hard-headed reviewers have been sentimental over it, I am glad; for the spectacle in real life of a child of three at its prayers is one over which thousands have been sentimental. It is indeed calculated to bring a lump to the throat. But even so one must tell the truth about the matter. Not "God bless Mummy, because I love her so," but "God bless Mummy, I know that's right"; not "God bless Daddy, because he buys me food and clothes," but "God bless Daddy, I quite forgot"; not even the egotism of "God bless Me, because I'm the most important person in the house," but the super-egotism of feeling so impregnable that the blessing of this mysterious God for Oneself is the very last thing for which it would seem necessary to ask. And since this is the Truth about a Child, let us get all these things into the poem, and the further truth that prayer means nothing to a child of three, whose thoughts are engaged with other, more exciting matters. . . .

"Vespers," it seems, is not just about what a certain little boy did on a certain occasion. It is the Truth (with a capital T) about a Child (with a capital C). And although I knew that this was my father's general feeling, I had entirely forgotten how uncompromisingly he had expressed himself.

It was at this point, while I was collecting my thoughts together, wondering how to go on, that I noticed the quotation from Wordsworth. It comes in the first of the two passages I have quoted:

Heaven lies about us in our infancy

This is a line from Wordsworth's "Intimations of Immortality." At first glance it seemed at home in its context. But on looking closer, I saw that this was far from the case. For the line had been given a new and altogether different meaning. Wordsworth had been saying that Heaven appeared *to the child* to lie around him. My father was saying that this was how it seemed to the *onlooker*. So then I read the whole poem. It is, of course, the Truth about a Child as Wordsworth sees it, and it is the complete reverse of my father's view. And at once it awakened an echo in my heart—as it must have awakened many another echo in many another heart.

> *Those first affections,*
> *Those shadowy recollections,*
> *Which, be they what they may,*
> *Are yet the fountain light of all our day.*

✦ ✦ ✦ ✦ ✦

In those days of splendor and glory I certainly felt myself nearer to God—both the God that Nanny was telling me about who lived up in the sky, and the God who painted the buttercups—than I do today. And so, asked to choose between these two views of childhood, I am bound to say that I'm for Wordsworth. Maybe he is just being sentimental. Maybe the infant William has fooled the middle-aged poet in the same way that the kneeling Christopher Robin fooled so many of his readers. Maybe my cynical father is right. But this is not how I feel about it.

Today it is fashionable to maintain that at the age of five a child is too young to be taught about God. The Divine is beyond his comprehension. One should wait until he is older. Dare I suggest that the reverse might be true: that the child of five is not too young; he is already too old.

I don't really want to get too involved either with Poetry or with Religious Instruction, nor do I want to spend too long on my infant knees. Furthermore, in a world heavily overpopulated with sociologists, psychologists, and research workers generally, I am reluctant to set up theories backed by nothing more than memory against the statistics and case histories of the opposition. However, this I must say. The Christopher Robin of that wretched poem is indeed me at the age of three. I retain the most vivid memories of saying my prayers as a child. They go back a long way, but I cannot date them. I well recall how I knelt, how Nanny sat, her hands around mine, and what we said aloud together. Did my thoughts wander? Were they engaged on other, more exciting things? The answer—and let me say it loudly and clearly—is NO. Would I agree that prayer meant nothing to a child of three? If the stress is on the last word, I must be careful: I may be thinking of a child of four. All I can accurately say is that I can recall no occasion when this was so.

At this point a picture floats uninvited into my mind. Nothing that ever happened, nothing to do with my parents, purely imaginary. Papa and Mama in church. Both kneeling. Mama's mind, disconnected from her ears, hovering around the Sunday lunch. Papa, squinting through his fingers, studying the hats in the pew in front. No, it's not only the three-year-old whose thoughts wander.

I said earlier that I was going to have things out with "Vespers." Partly, I must confess, I wanted to get my own back. But there was another reason. This seems the appropriate moment to give credit where credit was due.

And of course, credit lies with my nanny.

She had me when I was very young. I was all hers and remained all hers until the age of nine. Other people hovered around the edges, but they meant little. My total loyalty was to her. To the extent that I was a "good little boy," to the extent that my prayers had real meaning for me at a very early age and continued to have meaning for many years afterward, and to the extent that all this was something acquired rather than inherited, this was Nanny's doing. Was she a brilliant teacher? Not specially. She was just a very good and very loving person; and when that has been said, no more need be added.

It will now be apparent why, earlier, I disowned the conversation in "Buckingham Palace." This poem, too, gets mentioned in the Parents' Preface. " 'Do you think the king knows all about me?' Could egotism be more gross?" I'm prepared to let that go, but not the line that follows:

Sure to, dear, but it's time for tea.

Listen to Alice saying that: the daily routine clearly far more important for her than the child's question. You find the same thing in the poem "Brownie." Here are the last two lines of each verse. The child is speaking:

I think it is a Brownie but I'm not quite certain
(Nanny isn't certain, too)

and

✦ ✦ ✦ ✦ ✦

They wriggle off at once because they're all so tickly
(Nanny says they're tickly, too)

What Nanny actually says on both occasions—and you can hear her saying it, not even pausing in her sewing, not even bothering to look up—is "That's right, dear." Undoubtedly, this is the Truth about Some Nannies. But, as I hope I've now made quite clear, NOT MINE.

When I was eight years old, an odd little incident occurred. It is not strictly relevant, and I only mention it because it remains so vividly in my mind.

I was in bed, trying to go to sleep, but I couldn't, and as I turned from side to side so I got more restless and wretched. I didn't feel ill. It was something else. A very strange feeling. Something—someone— was stopping me from going to sleep, was keeping me awake. But who? And why? I struggled for an answer and gradually one began to dawn on me.

"Nanny!"
"What is it, dear?"
"Can you come?"
  She came at once.
"What's the matter?"
"I can't get to sleep."
"Are you feeling all right? Have you got a pain?"
"It's not that."
"What is it, then?"
  A pause. Then in a hushed voice:
"Nanny, I think I know. . . . It's God. I think He's cross with me."
"I'm sure He's not, dear. Why ever should He be?"
"No, Nanny; He is. And I think I know why. It's because of that Bible we bought for school. He doesn't like me having two Bibles."
"I don't think He would mind that, dear."

"No, Nanny: He does. I know He does. So can we give it away? Who shall we give it to?"

Nanny thought.

"We could give it to Farm Street. I think they might like it. I'm sure they would."

(Farm Street was a girls' school in Birmingham. The children had been writing to me over a number of years and I used to write back. In April I used to send them bunches of primroses.)

"Oh, Nanny, do let's. Can we do it now?"

"Well, dear . . ."

"Please start doing it."

"It's got your name inside. . . . It could be *from* you. I could write 'from' in front of your name. Shall I do that?"

"Yes, do do that. Do it now. Please."

So she did. She went next door and wrote; and then she came back and showed me, and told me that everything was all right now and that if God had been cross with me, now He had forgiven me, and I could go to sleep, and tomorrow we would post off the book.

Immediately the strange feeling left me and I went to sleep. The next morning the incident was all but forgotten. The Bible was never sent. I took it to school as usual. The "from" (in a different handwriting) always looked a bit odd, but I left it there.

A year later I went to boarding school and Nanny departed. Alfred was waiting for her. Indeed he had been waiting for her patiently for many years. Alfred! My rival! "Nanny, don't marry Alfred. Marry me." But in the end she did. And together they bought a bungalow, and they called it "Vespers." It was a nice gesture to my father. But only Nanny and I knew what the name really meant.

People sometimes say to me today: "How lucky you were to have had such a wonderful father!" imagining that because he wrote about me with such affection and understanding, he must have played with me with equal affection and understanding. Can this really be so totally untrue? Isn't this most surprising?

No, it is not really surprising, not when you understand.

There are two sorts of writer. There is the writer who is basically a reporter, and there is the creative writer. The one draws on his experiences, the other on his dreams. My father was a creative writer, and so it was precisely because he was *not* able to play with his small son that his longings sought and found satisfaction in another direction. He wrote about him instead.

FOUR

✦ ✦ ✦ ✦ ✦

Self-Portrait

HEIGHT: **Small for his age.**
WEIGHT: **Underweight. Needs fattening up.**

They did their best, of course, but it was really a waste of time, for no amount of eating has ever had any visible effect on me.

When I was a child, I was what grown-ups describe as a fussy eater. That is to say I ate what I liked well enough, and as much of it as I could squeeze in; but what I didn't like I divided up into little bits and pushed around the plate and said, "Need I, Nanny?" until she relented and I was allowed to leave it. I accepted that this was how it was with food: part pleasure, part penance. It never occurred to me that the penance part was unnecessary. I used to say that if ever I was sent to prison, I would at least enjoy the meals, bread and water being what I was specially fond of. And I said this, not sadly, not complainingly, but almost with pride—a criticism of nursery food all the more telling for being quite unintended.

Why were meals so unappetizing? We had a good cook. At the time I'm thinking of, Mrs. Penn had left us and been replaced by Mrs. Gulliver. I liked Mrs. Gulliver. She was as large and fat and jolly as Gertrude was small and thin and solemn, and she could produce the most wonderful meals, as I later discovered. Why didn't any of them find their way upstairs? Partly the reason was that nursery meals were served before dining-room meals. This meant that if Nanny and I had been allowed to share in the dining-room roast chicken and chocolate souffle, neither would have been looking its best when it reached my parents. So for us it had to be shepherd's pie and rice pudding. But this still doesn't explain why the rice pudding was quite so white, quite so stiff, quite so unlovely. This remains a mystery. It was not until I went to prep school that I learned what a proper rice pudding was like and developed an absolute passion for it that has lasted to this day, which is not the sort of thing one normally learns at prep school.

So there I was, not eating enough and not nearly fat enough. Something had to be done, and as I have said, they did their best. They tried strengthening medicine (which Tigger was so fond of). I was fond of it too, but it didn't make me any fatter. So then they tried gymnasium classes run by two Scotsmen called Munroe and Macpherson. On my first day, as we marched round the gym, horrible Mr. Macpherson shouted out: "Christopher Robin, you look like a camel. Hold yourself up, lad." But though I learned to climb a rope, I still didn't get any fatter. So then they tried boxing classes. I cantered across the floor and struck Mr. Macpherson on the nose, and he pretended it was a fly tickling him and said: "Harder, lad, harder." But though I was very proud of my boxing gloves, my muscles didn't bulge the way they should. So then finally they tried massage. I lay on the ottoman in the nursery while Mrs. Preston powdered me and then thumped and kneaded. But though I loved it, I remained resolutely underweight. And I have done so ever since.

APPEARANCE: **Girlish.**

Well, what can you expect? I had long hair at a time when boys didn't have long hair. One day Nanny went into the grocer's shop at the top of Oakley Street and left me lying outside in the pram. And while she was there, two people came and peered at me, and one of them said: "Oh, what a pretty little girl." That is not the sort of thing one forgets in a hurry. I used to wear girlish clothes, too, smocks and things. And in my very earliest dreams I even used to dream I was a girl.

✦ ✦ ✦ ✦ ✦

GENERAL BEHAVIOR: **Very shy and un-self-possessed.**

My father used to reassure me that he was shy too, that on the whole shy people were nicest, and that it was far better to be shy than boastful and self-assertive. But all the same I went a little too far the other way. When people asked me simple questions, like did I want another piece of cake, I really ought to have known the answer and not turned to the hovering figure at my side and said, "Do I, Nanny?"

GENERAL INTELLIGENCE: **Not very bright.**

There was a story—I think it was Anne who told me, many years later—that Miss Walters from my kindergarten was so impressed by my dimness that she got herself invited to tea at Mallord Street to see whether I was always like that or only at school. I don't know what her conclusions were. I don't know whether she came a little nearer to believing that I was not just being silly when I had said that I could do the difficult sums but not the easy ones.

GENERAL INTERESTS: **Good with his hands.**

Here at last was something I was all right at. I used to love making things. I sewed things (the Cottleston Pie that Pooh once sang about was an egg cozy I made), and knitted things, and made tapestry pictures. I had a Meccano set and made (among other things) a working grandfather clock. Or rather I made the works and a friend, older than I, came to tea one day and helped me with the case, the weights, and the pendulum. That night, however, I couldn't get to sleep. I lay awake, all restless and unhappy. Finally, I called out:

"Nanny, can you come?"

"What is it, dear?"

"It's the clock. I don't want to keep it. You see, I didn't do it all myself. Alec helped me with it. So can you take it to bits, please: just the stand part? Can you start doing it now?"

So she did: one of the odder things that nannies get called upon to do.

Then there were the things that I took to bits myself. Using a penknife, I once took a dead mouse to bits to see how it worked. But it was hard to tell exactly and really rather disappointing, and so I threw it away. I also took the lock on the night-nursery door to bits. I discovered how it worked but not how it went together again. So an ironmonger had to be summoned. What! Couldn't my father have mended it? My *father*, did you say? *Mend* something? Even at the age of seven I was already the family's Chief Mender. And mostly I succeeded. Admittedly the lock was a failure, and another failure was when I tried to run my six-volt electric motor by connecting it up to the electric light switch. Nothing happened. Even now, looking back on the event with greater electrical knowledge, I still can't understand why *nothing* happened.

It will now, I hope, be apparent why I said in an earlier chapter that the poem "The Engineer" was not about me. The poem begins:

> *Let it rain*
> *Who cares*
> *I've a train*
> *Upstairs*
> *With a brake*
> *Which I make . . .*

and it ends up:

> *It's a good sort of brake*
> *But it hasn't worked yet.*

I may have been a bit undersize. I may have been a bit underweight. I may have looked like a girl. I may have been shy. I may have been on the dim side. But if I'd had a train (and I didn't have a train), any brake that I'd wanted to make for it—any simple thing like a brake— WOULD HAVE WORKED.

FIVE

✦ ✦ ✦ ✦ ✦

In the Country

In 1925 my father bought Cotchford Farm and we became country-men, or, to be more accurate, half-countrymen. For we still spent most of our time in London, going down to Cotchford only at weekends and for the Easter and summer holidays.

Up to then we had paid only occasional visits to the country. There had been visits to my mother's lovely family home of Brooklands on the Hamble, visits from which survive the memories of a rocking horse and—annually reawakened—the color and scent of azaleas. There had been a holiday at Woolacombe, where I had first encountered what I'm told I called "the huge water" and where—if anywhere—I had got "sand between the toes." There had been a famous holiday in Wales where the first poems of *When We Were Very Young* had been written. And finally there had been visits to Decoy, a thatched cottage near Angmering in Sussex. At Decoy there was a lake. On the lake was a swan. And the swan's name was Pooh. There were woods and mead-ows, too, and I have hazy memories of these; but it is the little close-up things that a child sees most clearly. I remember beans, smooth, with pink and black blotches: holding them, arranging them, looking at them. I remember butterflies, cabbage whites and meadow browns, caught and held in the hand and examined. I remember daisies, wild daisies, not white as they seem to be to grown-ups, but pink; and I have only to pick one now and turn it over and look closely at the pink underside of its petals to see again the daisies of my childhood.

But Cotchford was different from all these. Cotchford was ours, and on an autumn morning in 1925 we climbed into the blue Fiat, my mother and father in the back, Nanny and I sitting next to Burnside in front, and drove down to take possession.

No. I have got it wrong. It was Cotchford that took possession of us.

My mother had been brought up partly in London, partly in the country. She knew what it was to live in a large country house and sit on lawns and wander past flower beds. London, no doubt, attracted her, especially as she grew older, with its gay parties and its pretty clothes, with its opportunity to escape from her wretched brothers and their muddy knees and everlasting sailing-talk. But at Brooklands her deep and abiding love of gardens was born, and with it her love of the peace and the solitude that you can find only in the country.

After the First World War she and my father had settled down in London, and she was happy there, being gay and smart and meeting exciting people. And no doubt to begin with this was enough. In any case it wasn't long before I turned up; and if I wasn't a full-time job, I was at least a part-time hobby. But it wasn't until we moved to Cotchford that my mother's talents knew that this was the moment for which they had been all this time quietly waiting. With memories of Brooklands to inspire her, with a succession of books by Marion Cran to guide her, and with seed catalogues and plant catalogues to hand in the bathroom for quiet after-breakfast study, she set to work. And as the money began to come in from the books, so, from time to time, Mr. Berrow appeared, with his horn-rimmed glasses, his plus fours, his bow tie, pencil, and paper to sketch out "proposed plans for terrace gardens, orchard, and summer house."

My mother in her garden. Trowel in hand, planting Darwin tulips by the hundred. Secateurs in hand, snipping at roses. Crouched down, weeding, weeding, weeding. Pouring jugs of hot water over the ants. Exhorting Tasker to ever greater efforts. Teaching me the names of the flowers—lovely names like salpiglossis and spiraea Anthony Waterer, difficult names like eschscholzia which were fun to spell. But mostly I remember her just quietly, happily, brooding over it all, alone in the half dark.

You can love the country in two quite different ways, as a cat loves it and as a dog loves it. My mother was like a cat. She responded to the beauty, the peace, and the solitude that it offered. She found this in her garden and she found it too in the countryside beyond. Solitude. She was happiest alone. Once, when she was going for a walk, I asked if I could come with her. "No," she said, "but come and meet me on my way back. I like best being met." And so we spent a lot of time meeting her. She would walk to the village, and half an hour later my father and I would set off up the hill and hope that somewhere before we reached the top we would see her coming around the corner. Or it might be the other way around, and she would meet us as we drove home (choosing the pretty way, of course), after spending the morning playing golf. At night, before going to bed, she would walk up to the forest, two miles along the road, until she was level with Gills Lap. On these occasions I sometimes accompanied her. It was different in the dark. You could be with someone and they would be there if you felt you wanted them, and if you didn't, you could forget them. Now and again, on our way, a car would come by: blinding lights, a roar, and a whoosh of wind that seemed to suck you out into the road in their wake. We clung to each other, standing against the hedge, until they were gone. Then on again. We both loved the country at night, the black shapes of the trees, the tiny spots of light from wayside cottages, the sound of the wind bustling about its invisible business. We scarcely talked, absorbed in our private thoughts.

If my mother was a cat, my father was surely a dog. He was a Londoner, a real Londoner with a deep love of London in his bones. For him the country had always been not where you lived, but where you went. Where you went on holiday. Where you went to do something—to ride a bicycle, to climb a hill, to look for birds' nests, to play golf. Like a dog, he couldn't just *be* in the country, sitting or strolling aimlessly. It had to be a proper walk, a walk with a purpose, planned beforehand, worked out on the map even. And you couldn't go alone;

you had to be with somebody; with me perhaps, or with the whole family, Nanny included. Like a dog, too, he was happiest of all when chasing a ball.

In front of the house a lawn sloped down to a ditch. It was virtually the only lawn that Cotchford possessed when we first arrived, and at once my father claimed it as his own private preserve and laid it out for clock golf. And as a clock-golf course it always remained, the only bit of the garden where my father reigned supreme. The ditch that bounded its lower edge was widened and turned into a moat, known as "the stream." A marshy bit in one corner was dug out to make a rather unpleasant pond. And eventually the russet apple tree in the middle died and was cut down. But otherwise the putting lawn remained unchanged over the years, and around and around it my father went, around and around and around. If I was at home, I joined him. "Just time for a quick record before lunch?" We played together, not against each other: more friendly that way. If I wasn't there, he played alone; and if he did a particularly good round, he would proudly tell me. When I was at school or away during the war, he would tell me in his weekly letter. He didn't tell my mother: she wouldn't have been specially interested, wouldn't even have known what "two under twos" meant. She never played. She hated all games.

So while my mother dug, my father putted. Does this sound like ant and grasshopper? In a way it was. But you can look at it another way. To each his trade. My father was a writer: this was his work. All he wanted from my mother was her encouragement and praise. My mother was a gardener, and praise and encouragement was all she wished for in return. No need also for a hand with the manuring: we had a full-time professional for that.

The stream was included in my father's domains. It had been hoped at one time that it might make an attractive feature with goldfish and water lilies. But all it seemed able to grow were dense mats of brown weed. Brown scum congealed on its stagnant surface, and strange creatures moved in its depths. So my father was allowed to keep it; and he and I shared it. We plunged nets and golf clubs into it, and piles of weed with their attendant black mud were landed on the bank. We stooped to peer closely. And gradually the various inhabitants would work their way up to the surface, flip-flapping if they were fish, wriggling if they were newts, crawling if they were dragonfly larvae. Each was examined before being put back. Sometimes golf balls came up in the catch, their brownness telling us how long they had lain submerged. Once or twice we caught what my father said was a triton, an extra-large, black, and nobbly newt, slow-moving and looking prehistoric. This was a great excitement. Sometimes a grass snake would slip into the water and take refuge between the stones that lined the bank. Grass snakes were even more exciting, but they were not welcome, for they ate the other creatures. And so they were pursued with putters until landed; and since landing a grass snake with a putter is not easy, we hoped it was also not too unsporting. They were then flung into the bullrushes and told not to come back.

So the garden for my father was where you sometimes looked for newts, but mainly where you putted and where you admired my mother's labors. It was also where, after lunch, you sought out a sheltered spot, and, armed with deck chair, cushions, rugs, and pullovers, retired there to reverberate gently until teatime.

These were the things you could do alone. But there were other things which needed two of you. There was cricket and there was catch: cricket could be played in the meadow, and catch with a tennis ball up against the wall. So my father was determined that, however much I enjoyed just being in the country, playing happily by myself, doing nothing happily by myself, however catlike I was, I was jolly well going to spend some of my time enjoying dog games with him.

l was not immediately enthusiastic. On my fifth birthday I had been given a shining suit of armor, and lived in it, almost went to bed in it, was in tears at the prospect of being unstrapped from it. "One day," said my father to his tiny St. George, "you will be thinking of nothing but cricket." I stared at him, aghast. My breastplate, my back plate, the wonderful things that protected my arms (even though slightly too long and rather scratchy round the wrist), my helmet with its red plume and the visor that I could pull down when danger threatened: how could I ever abandon these? "Nothing but cricket," I said in amazement. "Not armor?"

But my father was right. . . .

Putting, golf, cricket, catch, these were the things we did together—but not until Nanny had left us and I was at boarding school. Up to then I was much like any other child in the country. I took my toys out and played with them in the grass. I played in the hay, I played in the mud, played in the water, played with friends, played with Nanny, played alone, climbed trees, picked primroses in the spring and nuts in the autumn, went exploring, rode a donkey. To begin with, the country was very much for playing in. Later, much later, I began to enjoy long solitary walks. Or I would go down to the river and find a quiet place, secluded, hidden beneath the bank, and sit there for hours, watching the water as it gently twisted and eddied past me. Then perhaps I might see something: an eel, wriggling its way upstream; a grass snake with just its black head showing above the surface, moving gently from side to side; damselflies, their wings making a dry whispering sound as they came to investigate me; the plop of a water vole, and if you looked quickly, you might see it running underwater along the riverbed; a shy moorhen, a noisy mallard, a flashing kingfisher, whistling urgently. But never, though I waited in hope day after day, never the sight of an otter.

So of the three of us, I suppose it could be said that I was the one most totally captivated by Cotchford, for it gave me all the delight it gave my mother and all the delight—the very different delight—it gave my father; and it continued to do this, on and off, for thirty years.

On an August morning in the year 1942 I said good-bye to Cotchford. The penstemons, the bergamots, the phloxes, the heleniums, the rudbeckias, the dahlias, and even the solitary coreopsis that had seeded itself so cleverly in the paving stones by the sundial were still looking as lovely as ever. I said good-bye convinced, absolutely, that I would never return.

SIX

✦ ✦ ✦ ✦ ✦

Field and Forest

You must start with a map. We kept ours in the drawing room on the bookshelf by the window. You must start with a map because Cotchford Farm is on the map, and this was something we were all very proud of. Look. *Here!* And what is more, it is underlined. I used to think that it was the printer who had underlined it, but I realize now it was more likely to have been my mother or my father. And over the years, as countless proud fingers pointed it out to countless admiring visitors, so a sort of grey haze descended upon it, making it even easier to find. But as your map may be a new one, I had better help you.

The map you need is the 1/50,000 Ordnance Survey Sheet 183. Just off it, up in the top left-hand corner, is East Grinstead; and just off it, up in the top center, is Tunbridge Wells. The village of Hartfield is halfway between them, about eight miles from each. From Hartfield a road runs due south, the road to the coast. It goes up a steep hill and then down on the other side, and just before it reaches the bottom and crosses a little river, there is a lane off to the right. As we made our weekly journey from London, this was the exciting moment. The car slowed down, almost stopped, then swung into the lane, and our smooth motion changed into the familiar, welcoming, beloved bumping. For the lane was no more than a sandy track, well rutted by the wooden, iron-rimmed wheels of farm carts. In winter the ruts filled with water and we slooshed as well as bumped. I loved it. It was just how it should be: a proper country lane. My parents liked it this way, too: the bumpier it was, the less likely were people to want to build houses along it. Only Burnside grumbled. "Jolly old lane," he said.

Cotchford Farm is a couple of hundred yards along on the left, a steep gravel drive leading down to it. We never knew its history, just spoke vaguely of Queen Anne and of its having once been three separate houses now turned into one, which accounted for its odd shape. We never knew it as a working farm, though various outbuildings survived, owned by a neighboring farmer, and were still used in a half-hearted sort of way. It came to us through a man called Jervis, who had rescued it, done it up, and then sold it. And with it went two fields that took our boundaries up to the main road and along the river.

So there we were in 1925 with a cottage, a little bit of garden, a lot of jungle, two fields, a river, and then all the green, hilly countryside beyond—meadows and woods, waiting to be explored; and Nanny and I set out at once to explore them, bringing back reports of our discoveries.

First we set off toward the river. We called it the river, though it was really only a stream, to distinguish it from the stream (at the bottom of the putting lawn), which was really only a long, thin, almost stagnant pond. We were proud of our river. It was, we told our friends, a tributary of the Medway. This seemed to emphasize our remoteness from London. Not a tributary of the Thames: a tributary of the Medway; much grander, much more countrified. It was fringed all along by trees, mostly alders, and quite large ones, so that at a distance, looking toward it from the house, people could be excused for mistaking it for a wood. "Is that the Hundred Acre Wood?" they asked. You didn't discover that it was a river until you were right on top of it, for it had carved itself a deep channel through the red-brown, sandy-clay soil. If you climbed down to the water's edge, you were quite invisible from the meadow above you. Here the air was cool and richly scented. The water, brown and mysterious, moved with unhurried dignity. It was just the right width: too wide to jump, but where a kindly tree reached out a branch to another kindly tree on the opposite shore, it was possible to swing yourself over. It was just the right depth: too deep to paddle across but often shallow enough to paddle in and, in places, deep enough to swim.

This was the river that Nanny and I set out to explore, and immediately we made our first discovery: Dragon's Bridge. There could be no doubt about it; for there was the great, blunt snout raised above the bank; there was the eye—round, hollow, staring; there was the branching wing, ready to beat the air; there was the leg poised above the water; and there was the great, green, scaly back down which you could—("Do you think I dare, Nanny?" "Be very careful, dear.")— down which you could, if you were very careful, clamber until you were right across to the other side. Dragon's Bridge. This became and remained one of my favorite spots, the site of so many small adventures and happy memories. It was here that I built my hut of ash poles and bracken, here that I had my rope ladder (fastened to a giant oak tree that had perhaps sprung from one of the dragon's very own acorns), here that I launched my raft on its ten-yard voyage, and here that I swam with Anne. Four strokes was all we could manage before we ran aground or got mixed up with a bramble, and even on the hottest day the water was achingly cold. . . .

And it must have been here that, in the poem, "Us Two," Pooh and I

> . . . *crossed the river and found a few——*
> *"Yes, those are dragons all right," said Pooh.*
> *"As soon as I saw their beaks I knew. . . ."*

For on the other side of Dragon's Bridge was a chicken farm.

Two hundred yards or so upstream from Dragon's Bridge is the fence that marks our boundary. Who owned the land that lay beyond? Mostly we didn't know. Mostly we didn't care. As far as Nanny and I were concerned, it belonged to us, and we never met anyone to contradict us. We wandered freely from field to field, from wood to wood, and scarcely met a soul.

On the other side of our fence is a hazel copse where wood anemones grow and where a tiny stream—a tributary of the tributary of the Medway—could be dammed or diverted or made to turn a miniature waterwheel. Beyond the copse is a marsh, a tangled mass of rushes and bracken where only the gum-booted dare leave the path. It was here that, toward the end of one Easter holiday, to my enormous excitement, I finally tracked down the snipe's nest I had been searching for. At the end of the marsh the footpath crosses over the river above a weir, a plank spanning the water at the point where it curls smoothly over and crashes into the darkness, and a pole giving the nervous something to hold on to (and the daring something to swing on). On the other side is a good field for butterflies, where blues and coppers could usually be found. Here I once came upon a weasel family out for a walk and watched fascinated as mother weasel escorted her children to the edge of a little backwater and then, with much chattering and fussing, ferried them to the far side. The path follows the riverbank and soon enters a wood. This is Posingford Wood and is marked on the map. So just in case, map in hand, you are trying to follow me, I must remind you that the countryside I am describing is the countryside I wandered in as a boy somewhere between 1925 and 1940. It didn't change much in those fifteen years, but it may have done so since.

Posingford was a wood we often used to visit. It is about half a mile from end to end and runs uphill from the river at the bottom to the Forest at the top. It is a gay and friendly wood, the sort of wood you could happily walk through at night, feeling yourself a skillful rather than a brave explorer: a wood of hazels and willows and sweet chestnuts, with here and there an oak or a pine.

To the left of the path as it enters the wood is a lake. If you called our river a stream, then I suppose you would want to call this lake a bog. But for me it was a lake: in winter, when it froze over, it was possible to do some quite good sliding between the tussocks of rush. The path continues between lake and river until it is crossed by a larger track that has entered the wood over a bridge. This bridge still stands and still looks much as it did when Shepard came there to draw it: it is Poohsticks Bridge.

It is difficult to be sure which came first. Did I do something, and did my father then write a story around it? Or was it the other way about, and did the story come first? Certainly my father was on the lookout for ideas; but so too was I. He wanted ideas for his stories, I wanted them for my games, and each looked toward the other for inspiration. But in the end it was all the same: the stories became a part of our lives; we lived them, thought them, spoke them. And so, possibly before, but certainly after that particular story, we used to stand on Poohsticks Bridge—throwing sticks into the water and watching them float away out of sight until they reemerged on the other side.

Poohsticks Bridge was the way into Posingford if you came along the lane. The lane that takes you to Cotchford continues on to Upper Hartfield. Halfway along its length it bends round to the right, and at this point a track leads downhill to the left, and this is the track you want. This was certainly the easier way, the way Nanny and I used to come. The other way, boggier and bramblier, was the way I preferred when I was rather older, when Nanny had left and I was on my own, when I was on the lookout for wildlife and didn't want to meet people. Not that you were likely to meet many people if you did choose the lane. In fact, the only person Nanny and I would be likely to meet was Hannah, and we would probably be looking for her anyway. She was a little older than I and lived in a house near Posingford where her father kept a chicken farm. A small child needs another child to play with. In London I had Anne, and there were lots of other friends living nearby whom I could meet from time to time. It is true that Anne often came to Cotchford (bringing her nanny, but leaving her parents behind); but she couldn't be there all the time that I was, and so I needed someone else; and luckily there was Hannah, only half a mile away. I cannot remember either how or where we first met. Probably we just happened on each other on one of our walks up the lane, and Nanny—who was good at talking to the people we met—talked to her, and that was how it all started. Our meetings were almost exclusively out of doors. We never went into Hannah's house, except just to call for her, and she never came to ours. We played in the woods and in the fields. We climbed trees and pretended to be monkeys. We paddled in the river and dug a hole in the riverbank and called it the Channel Tunnel. We played in the barn and the stables that had once been part of Cotchford. We helped with the haymaking and rode home on the top of the hay cart. We helped with the apple picking and were allowed to eat the windfalls.

The barn was still in use. It housed, among other things, a swallow's nest, a farm cart, a chaff cutter, and a very original smell. And two cart horses lived in the stable. A little farther up the lane was the apple orchard, whose trees, old and bent, made wonderful climbing. It was here that I lost Roo. We had all—Nanny and I and the animals— spent the afternoon playing there; and on our return Roo was missing. We went back and searched and searched, but in vain. Opposite the orchard were the fields and woods we visited on our flower-picking expeditions. This wood for primroses, the ash plantation for orchids, the larger wood beyond for bluebells, the top of that field, along the edge of the bracken, for cowslips. Primroses, bluebells, orchids, cowslips, violets, and foxgloves: Nanny and I would gather whole basketsful. And it was here—more especially than anywhere else—I would find that splendor in the grass, that glory in the flower, that today I would find no more.

And so we worked our way down the lane, exploring farther and farther afield, until we came to the track down to the left, the bridge over the river, and Posingford Wood on the other side. And just as on our first visit to the river we had discovered Dragon's Bridge, so on our first visit to Posingford we met the charcoal burner. And while Nanny, good at talking to people, talked to him, I, good at listening, listened. And then we returned home full of our exciting adventure.

There can be no doubt which came first here.

✦ ✦ ✦ ✦ ✦

The charcoal burner has tales to tell
He lives in the forest
Alone in the forest . . .

A ten-year-old boy might well have asked what charcoal was—how it was made and what it was used for—might have asked to see the tools that were needed, and the pit where the wood was burned, might have gone home eager to try making his own charcoal. But I was only five, too young and too shy to ask. Old enough only to listen, and to remember indelibly one thing only. "And he told us he had once seen a fox!"

And rabbits come up and they give him good morning . . .
And owls fly over and wish him good night . . .
Oh, the charcoal burner has tales to tell . . .

There is a path through Posingford Wood—Nanny and I soon found it—that takes you up to the Forest. In fact this is the quickest way of getting to the Forest if you don't just go up the main road. (And who would choose a main road in preference to a path through a wood?)

If you look at Ashdown Forest on the map, you will see that it covers an area roughly triangular in shape, an equilateral triangle with sides about six miles long and with the towns of Forest Row, Crowborough, and Maresfield at its corners. The bit we knew best lay halfway along the side joining Forest Row and Crowborough. This was the bit we could reach on foot.

Perhaps at this point I should break off for a moment, to explain to those who today go everywhere by car that in those days we didn't. Cars had been invented—oh, yes, it wasn't all that long ago—and we had one and we also had a chauffeur to go with it. But they both lived in London and returned there after we had been deposited. So while we were at Cotchford we had to rely mainly on our feet. If we wanted to catch a train or if my father wanted to go golfing, we could always ring up Mitchell's, the garage in Upper Hartfield. If we wanted to go shopping in Tunbridge Wells (as we usually did around about my birthday), we could walk to Hartfield and catch a bus. Other than that, we walked. It was not until later that my father learned to drive (taught by Burnside) and we kept a car permanently at Cotchford.

So if we wanted to go up the Forest, we went on foot. And so did others: only those who could walk to the Forest went there. This meant that when we got there we had the Forest almost entirely to ourselves. And this, in turn, made us feel that it was *our* Forest and so made it possible for an imaginary world—Pooh's world—to be born within the real world. Pooh could never have stumped a Forest that was littered with picnic parties playing their transistor radios.

Anyone who has read the stories knows the Forest and doesn't need me to describe it. Pooh's Forest and Ashdown Forest are identical. We came there often, and since it was more of a walk than a ramble, these were frequently family occasions, the four of us in single file threading the narrow paths that run through the heather. For my father, as I have said, though a bad rambler, was a keen walker.

Cotchford lies in a valley. To the south beyond the river the land rises, steadily up and up, until you reach the Forest. Then up and up again until you reach the top of the Forest. And at the very top of the Forest is Gills Lap. I could see Gills Lap from my nursery window. You could see Gills Lap from a great many places for miles around—a clump of pines on the top of a hill. And of course you can see it as Shepard drew it in *The House At Pooh Corner*. In the book it is Galleons Lap, but otherwise it is exactly as described, an enchanted spot before ever Pooh came along to add to its magic.

A path from Gills Lap takes you to the main road. On the other side the Forest falls away to a valley, then rises again beyond to distant trees. At the bottom of this valley runs a little stream. It is only a very little stream, narrow enough to jump across, shallow enough to paddle across, but it twists and tumbles between steep stony banks. It was here that the North Pole was discovered. As you make your way down to it and continue up on the other side, you will be following the route Pooh took in an earlier chapter when he went "down open slopes of gorse and heather, over rocky beds of streams, up steep banks of sandstone into the heather again; and so at last, tired and hungry, to the Hundred Acre Wood"—only, of course, as your map will have told you, it is really the Five Hundred Acre Wood.

The Five Hundred Acre is very different from Posingford. It is a real forest with giant beech trees, all dark and mysterious. You would indeed need to be a brave explorer to venture into the Five Hundred Acre at night, and I never did. The easiest way to get to it from Cotchford is down the main road past the Six Pine Trees, over the bridge, and then, a little farther on, through a gate on the left where a path leads to a farm on the top of a hill. On the other side of the hill a field runs down to a little stream. A bridge crosses the stream, and beyond the bridge the trees begin. Perhaps, to be accurate, I should say "began," because these trees vanished during the war. And this was sad for me, because among them was a tree I was particularly fond of. It was only just inside the wood and the path ran right by it. So Nanny and I must have discovered it on our first visit. It was a huge and ancient beech tree, one of a group of about half a dozen. It looked as if over the centuries it had grown tired of holding its arms up to the sky and had allowed its lower branches to droop. One branch in particular came out horizontally, then curved downward to rest its elbow on the ground. And at this point you could sit on it. Or you could stand on it and walk a little way along it and then jump off into the soft carpet of dead leaves spread out below. You could practice balancing, then practice jumping. It was difficult to walk very far, for the branch was moss covered and slippery and soon got too steep, and there was nothing to hold on to. So then you could sit astride it and wriggle your way forward.

"Look, Nanny. Look how far I've got!"
"You mind you don't fall, dear."
"I'm all right."

I wriggled along the branch as far as I dared, until the ground seemed miles below me. If I had been braver, I could have gone right the way along to where the branch joined the trunk. But it was a bit frighten-ing. So I sat where I was, swinging my legs, then slithered back to safety. Then we went home to tea and to tell of our adventures and our discoveries.

"You must come and see it one day, come and watch me climb along it." And one day they did. One day all four of us visited the Five Hundred Acre to see the great tree: one to climb it, three to watch. And of those who watched, one perhaps to dream: to see the branch snaking to the ground and someone walking up it, walking easily, walking all the way, up the steep bit, along the level bit, right up to the trunk, finding there a door with a knocker and a bell, a door in the tree and someone living behind it. Who? Who? Could it be an owl? Could it be Owl that the visitor had come to see?

"And so at last, tired and hungry, to the Hundred Acre Wood. For it was in the Hundred Acre Wood that Owl lived."

I cannot swear that this was how it happened. It is only a guess. All I can say is that, though Owl was an imaginary character, invented by my father, his house was real. And this was it.

✦ ✦ ✦ ✦ ✦

SEVEN

Weathers

I̶t rained and it rained and it rained. . . . " In London, if it was raining, you took a bus instead of walking to wherever it was you were going. Or you put on a macintosh instead of a coat. If it was raining, Anne and I could spend the afternoon playing in the Natural History Museum instead of Kensington Gardens. It didn't make much difference to what we had planned to do. For if we didn't do it here, we could equally well do it there; and anyway most of the really exciting things were done indoors. But in the country it was quite different.

This was one of the things we discovered when we went to live at Cotchford. In the country, the weather matters. In London you only notice the weather when it is very hot or very cold or very wet. But in the country there is weather every day; and sometimes it brings new and exciting things you can do, and sometimes it stops you doing the exciting things you had hoped to do.

Take the wind, for example. In London it came only on windy days, gusting down the street, throwing dust in your face as it passed. Maybe, in the parks and along the river, the trees fluttered their leaves and nodded their heads to it. But in the streets the lampposts stood unmoved like guardsmen on parade, the houses stared unblinking at the houses on the other side, cars and buses went on their way. Only when it got really angry and sent an old gentleman's hat bowling along the pavement did people stop and look.

But in the country there was wind not just on windy days but every day, even though it might be so gentle that only the poplar behind the rose garden noticed its passing. There was the wind that played over summer meadows; the wind that brought the hot scent of hay or the cool sweet scent of bracken; the wind that blew the cherry blossom down like snow; the wind that sent dead leaves scurrying and dancing down the road; the wind that carried the sound of church bells over the hills on a summer's evening to fill me with a strange sadness. There was the biting cold east wind that came out of a blue sky early in the new year, so that from indoors it looked as if spring had arrived, and outdoors Nanny made me wear an overcoat. I hated wearing overcoats in the country, especially when it was so nearly spring. Overcoats were Londony things. Or there was the rollicking west wind, driving the clouds before it, roaring and tearing over the meadow, hurling itself at the trees, wailing in the telephone wires, hooting down the chimney, banging at the doors. "Come out, come out," it bellowed. And when I was out in it and alone in it, I could shout back: "Blow harder, blow harder."

Or rain. Rain falling from a grey sky, seen through my bedroom window just as it was getting light. Weather matters so much in the country, especially when you are young. I had been planning something special for today, something that needed the sun, and I had gone to bed the evening before all impatient with dull night, all eager for the morning. And now it was raining. I stood at the open window, staring up at the grey sky, staring and staring, trying to stare through the grey curtain to the blue that lay on the other side, trying to stare a hole in the curtain. "Red sky at night, shepherds' delight." Last night had been so lovely and clear, and there had been a red sky as the sun had gone down, flooding the courtyard and dining room with golden light. How could it be so different today? "Rain before seven, fine before eleven." My father had taught me that.

Well, it was raining now and it was not yet seven. So there was a hope, quite a good hope, really. I went back to bed, saying, "Rain before seven, fine before eleven," over and over again, to try and make it so.

But sometimes I liked the rain. "It rained and it rained and it rained," and little by little the level of the water in the stream rose until it was peering over the top. Then it began to creep up the putting lawn. . . . The stream that was really only a moat was now indeed a stream. The water was racing in through the little tunnel under the bridge at the top end, and piling up against the little tunnel under the other bridge at the bottom end. Perhaps I ought to put on Wellington boots and a macintosh and go and poke a stick through to clear it. Perhaps I might go down to the river to see what was happening. . . . Exciting! The river, which usually ran, brown and peaceful, between high banks, was now only a few feet from the top, and fairly swirling and frothing and bubbling and seething and roaring along. Alders which grew at the edge of the water were now marooned on islands in midstream, a fierce current racing between them and the mainland. The place where a tree root held back the river to make a waterfall—a sort of miniature, natural weir—could hardly be found, for the water below and the water above had both risen to the same level. I explored all along, then returned home to report. And still it rained. And it was still raining when I went to bed. And now I hoped that it would go on raining, and that when dull night was out of the way, I would wake up to find it coming down as hard as ever. Once again I rushed to the window as soon as I was awake. But I could hear the rain beating on the glass and knew before I got there that all was well. My bedroom window faced north. I would have to go to the window in the passage if I was to see what I wanted to see. And from the passage window I saw it. The water was over the top, over the top of the river and coming toward us across the meadow, over the top of the stream, halfway up the putting lawn, and already into the rose garden.

All morning I watched it—we all watched it—fascinated. And

every now and then I went out with a stick to mark the place where the tide had reached, a line of sticks getting nearer and nearer to the steps up to the path that ran outside the drawing room.

> Every morning he went out with his umbrella and put a stick in the place where the water came up to, and every next morning he went out and couldn't see his stick any more. . . .

But though it rained and rained and rained, and though the river and the stream joined hands and the entire meadow became a lake, and though the rose garden and the mauve garden disappeared, the floods never reached the house. The men who, centuries earlier, had chosen to build Cotchford at the bottom of the hill knew what the river could do, knew the highest point it could reach, and laid their foundations eighteen inches above it.

The wind roaring in the trees, roaring in the giant sycamore that grew in the lawn just outside my nursery window ("What would happen if the wind blew it down? Would it flatten the house, do you think?"). The rain beating on the water, and the river rising to meet it. The snow, a rare visitor, and so all the more exciting when it came. Misty days when Gills Lap vanished and it might be fun to see if you could get lost and then cleverly find yourself again. Sunny days when the trees were dark and heavy with leaf and the air was heavy with the scent of meadowsweet and the river was almost asleep. These were the Cotchford weathers, new and exciting to me; and for my father, perhaps, awakening memories of country holiday weathers when he was a boy. These are the weathers you will meet in the books.

I am often asked if I can remember when the stories were first read to me. Who read them? And where? And what did I think of them? Oddly, I can remember virtually nothing. One incident only survives.

My mother and I were in the drawing room at Cotchford. The door

opened and my father came in. "Have you finished it?" "I have."
"May we hear it?" My father settled himself in his chair. "Well," he
said, "we've had a story about the snow, and one about the rain, and
one about the mist. So I thought we ought to have one about the wind.
And here it is.

"It's called:

'IN WHICH PIGLET DOES A VERY GRAND THING.'

"Half way between Pooh's house and Piglet's house was a Thought-
ful Spot. . . ."

My mother and I, side by side on the sofa, settled ourselves comfortably, happily, excitedly, to listen.

EIGHT

✦ ✦ ✦ ✦ ✦

The Toys

I must now introduce the toys.

Pooh was the oldest, only a year younger than I was, and my inseparable companion. As you find us in the poem "Us Two," so we were in
real life. Every child has his favorite toy, and every only child has a
special need for one. Pooh was mine, and probably, clasped in my
arms, not really very different from the countless other bears clasped
in the arms of countless other children. From time to time he went to
the cleaners, and from time to time ears had to be sewn on again, lost
eyes replaced, and paws renewed.

Eeyore, too, was an early present. Perhaps in his younger days he
had held his head higher, but by the time the stories came to be written his neck had gone like that, and this had given him his gloomy
disposition. Piglet was a present from a neighbor who lived over the
way, a present for the small boy she so often used to meet out walking with his nanny. They were the three around which the stories
began; but more characters were needed, and so two were invented:
Owl and Rabbit. Owl was owlish from the start and always remained
so. But Rabbit, I suspect, began by being just the owner of the hole
in which Pooh got stuck and then, as the stories went on, became
less rabbity and more Rabbity; for rabbits are not by nature good
organizers. Both Kanga and Tigger were later arrivals, presents from
my parents, carefully chosen, not just for the delight they might

give to their new owner, but also for their literary possibilities.

So there they were, and to a certain extent their characters were theirs from birth. As my father said, making it all sound very simple, you only had to look at them to see at once that Eeyore was gloomy, Piglet squeaky, Tigger bouncy, and so on. But of course there was much more to it than that. Take bears, for example.

A row of teddy bears sitting in a toy shop: all one size, all one price. Yet how different each is from the next. Some look gay, some look sad. Some look standoffish, some look lovable. And one in particular, that one over there, has a specially endearing expression. Yes, that is the one we would like, please.

The bear took his place in the nursery, and gradually he began to come to life. It started in the nursery; it started with me. It could really start nowhere else, for the toys lived in the nursery and they were mine and I played with them. And as I played with them and talked to them and gave them voices to answer with, so they began to breathe. But alone I couldn't take them very far. I needed help. So my mother joined me, and she and I and the toys played together; and gradually more life, more character flowed into them, until they reached a point at which my father could take over. Then, as the first stories were written, the cycle was repeated. The Pooh in my arms, the Pooh sitting opposite me at the breakfast table, was a Pooh who had climbed trees in search of honey, who had got stuck in a rabbit hole, who was "a bear of no brain at all."

Then Shepard came along, looked at the toy Pooh, read the stories, and started drawing; and the Pooh who had been developing under my father's pen began to develop under Shepard's pen as well. You will notice this if you compare the early Poohs in *Winnie-the-Pooh* with the later Poohs in *The House At Pooh Corner*. What is it that gives Pooh his particularly Poohish look? It is the position of his eye. The eye that starts as quite an elaborate affair, level with the top of Pooh's nose, gradually moves downward and ends up as a mere dot, level with his mouth. And in this dot the whole of Pooh's character can be read.

That was how it happened. And when at last the final story had been written, my father, looking back over the seven years of Pooh's life, wrote his dedication. It was to my mother.

> *You gave me Christopher Robin, and then*
> *You breathed new life in Pooh.*
> *Whatever of each has left my pen*
> *Goes homing back to you.*
> *My book is ready, and comes to greet*
> *The mother it longs to see—*
> *It would be my present to you, my sweet,*
> *If it weren't your gift to me.*

In the last chapter of *The House At Pooh Corner*, our ways part. I go on to become a schoolboy. A child and his bear remain playing in the enchanted spot at the top of the forest. The toys are left behind, no longer wanted, in the nursery. So a glass case was made for them, and it was fastened to the nursery wall in Mallord Street, and they climbed inside. And there they lived, sometimes glanced at, mostly forgotten, until the war came. Roo was missing. He had been lost years before, in the apple orchard up the lane. And Piglet's face was a funny shape where a dog had bitten him. During the war they went to America, and there they have been ever since. . . .

If you saw them today, your immediate reaction would be: "How old and battered and lifeless they look." But of course they are old *and* battered *and* lifeless. They are only toys, and you are mistaking them for the real animals who lived in the forest. Even in their prime they were no more than a first rough sketch, the merest hint of what they were to become, and they are now long past their prime. Eeyore is the most recognizable; Piglet the least. So, if I am asked, "Aren't you sad that the animals are not in their glass case with you today?" I must answer, "Not really," and hope that this doesn't seem too unkind. I like to have around me the things I like today, not the things I once liked many years ago. I don't want a house to be a museum. When I grew out of my old First Eleven blazer, it was thrown away, not lovingly preserved to remind me of the proud day I won it with a score of 13 not out. Every child has his Pooh, but one would think it odd if every man still kept his Pooh to remind him of his childhood. But my Pooh is different, you say: he is *the* Pooh. No, this only makes him different to you, not different to me. My toys were and are to me no more than yours were and are to you. I do not love them more because they are known to children in Australia or Japan. Fame has nothing to do with love.

I wouldn't like a glass case that said: "Here is fame"; and I don't need a glass case to remind me: "Here was love."

NINE

✦ ✦ ✦ ✦ ✦

The Busy Backson

On January 15, 1929—the only date that has survived from my childhood unforgotten—wearing my new, bright red blazer and my bright red, rather large and loose-fitting peaked cap—with my hair of a length which, if not exactly boyish, was at least no longer girlish—at half past eight in the morning and accompanied by Nanny, I climbed onto a number 11 bus at the corner of Church Street, bound for Sloane Square and my first day at Gibbs. Four hours later I was home again and in my father's library, telling him all about it, telling him about the thing that had impressed and amazed me most.

"We have to call Mr. Gibbs 'Sir.'"

"Sir" was what Gertrude called my father, what servants called their masters, what people who worked called the people they worked for, not what boys like me had to call anybody, surely. I expected my father to be as amazed and indignant as I was, and was even more amazed when he wasn't. Gently he explained to me that schoolboys did address schoolmasters as "Sir," that he had done so when he was a boy and that now I must. Gently he reassured me. . . . And thus we reached a small landmark in our lives. For me it marked the full realization of the newness and strangeness of the world I had just entered; for my father, the first of many opportunities to help me on my way through it.

Gibbs was—indeed it still is—a boys' day school. It was then at the bottom of Sloane Street, and Mr. C. H. Gibbs was its headmaster. It took boys from the age of about six to the age of thirteen. I arrived at eight-and-a-half, stayed for four terms, then went on to boarding school. Gibbs for me was therefore a bridge between kindergarten and prep school, between Miss Walters's and Boxgrove, between Plasticine and raffia on the one hand and Latin declensions and simultaneous equations on the other. It was a bridge between childhood and boyhood, between the nursery world of Nanny and the drawing-room world of my parents, between the years in which I could identify myself with the Christopher Robin in the books and the years spent trying to escape from him. And since my arrival at Gibbs also marks the halfway point in this book {*The Enchanted Places*}, it is perhaps a good moment to pause and look back.

At Gibbs I was still living in the nursery. Nanny was still very much at the center of my life. She took me there every morning and was waiting in the hall to take me home at the end of the day. She came to the lantern lectures we had every Tuesday afternoon and helped me with the essays I had to write about them the following weekend. She prompted me with:

Lars Porsena of Cluseum, by the nine gods he swore. . . .

and

I stood tiptoe upon a little hill. . . .

She read me *The Heroes of Asgard* and *Great Expectations*. And, perhaps most important of all, she accompanied me on my visits to James Greig, the ironmonger in Sloane Square. For among the many new things I was learning at my new school—*mensa* and *amo*, the dates of George I, the shape of North America: none of them in later life to prove particularly useful—was one that was worth more than all the others put together. Once a week I did carpentry. Once a week I sawed and chiseled and sandpapered; and so once a week (or thereabouts) I told Nanny what it was I wanted, and together we went to James Greig to get it. Nanny did the asking (she was better at asking than I was), and I searched in my trouser pockets for the money. With Nanny's help and encouragement I became a carpenter, with my own private carpenter's shop in the attic at Cotchford. And I have remained a carpenter ever since.

But if Nanny was still with me, Pooh was moving into the shadows. For seven and a half years he had been my constant companion; now our ways were beginning to part. "GON OUT BACKSON BISY BACK-SON" said the notice on the piece of paper. I was now living in two worlds. In one of them we could perhaps still meet for a little longer, but in the other I was on my own. We had had a happy time together. The imaginary world we inhabited was very much the world you meet in the stories. Our real world was the sort of real world you would expect to find lying behind them. I loved my nanny, I loved Cotchford. If I cannot say that I loved my parents, it is only because, in those early days, I just didn't know them well enough. And if I do not say that I loved Mallord Street, it is only because I loved Cotchford so very much more.

I also quite liked being Christopher Robin and being famous. There were indeed times—as at pageants—when it was exciting and made me feel grand and important. But of the ripples of fame that came through my nursery door, each was judged firmly on its merits. A child loves getting presents at Christmas, loves opening parcels, but he becomes instantly critical once the brown paper and string are off. The double-barreled shotgun is wonderful and just exactly what he wanted; the large rubber ball is rather stupid. The rubber ball is left on one side and instantly forgotten (except by Nanny, who has thoughtfully noted down that it was sent by Aunt Mary); the shotgun is borne off to the nursery, and the instructions are eagerly read and puzzled out. It was the same with the Christopher Robin things. If, in the watercolor painting by Honor Maugham, I looked sad, this was because I was sad. The sun was shining; Hannah had come round to play with me and was hanging about outside waiting; and here I was indoors, having to sit still.

When I was about eight years old, being fond of animals, I was not surprisingly a Dr. Dolittle fan; and one day I wrote to Hugh Lofting to say so. Partly I wrote because Nanny encouraged me to; partly I wrote because I really did want to say how much I liked the books; and I suppose that partly I wrote because I hoped I might get a letter back. And I did; and I was thrilled when he asked me which of his books I had not read, so that he could send me copies. Kind Mr. Lofting to give a small boy so much pleasure. Was the small boy always as kind to those who wrote to *him*? Would he, as he grew older, become kinder or less kind? If the answer to the second question is "Less kind," this is because there is a difference between being an author and being a character in a book. The author remains the author always. The character may well grow out of his part. At the age of seven I was quite pleased when a large "Piglet" arrived in a box with his creator's best wishes. He was much more handsome, indeed frankly much more appealing and lovable, than my one (who was anyway by this time in a rather dog-bitten state). I christened him Poglet, and he and Pooh accompanied me on one of my visits to Littlehampton. But had he arrived five years later, his welcome would have been cooler. Anyone wanting to make toy Piglets to send to the little boy in the book had to study the back of the title page to be sure that the little boy was still a little boy. Miss B. was really too late. Miss B. produced a Pooh and a Piglet modeled in clay. Forty years later she discovered that she still had my thank-you letter and sent me a copy of it to ask if I thought it was worth anything. I replied that I hoped not; anyway, it wasn't to me. But on second thought I feel I may be mistaken. It is perhaps just worth printing as the only contemporary document that survives to give the true flavor of a Christmas holiday when I was twelve years old.

> Dear Miss B. . . .
> Thank you so much for Pooh and Piglet. I did love them so, and I love having them with me. They weren't too tired out with the journey although Piglet broke his arm; however he is all right now.

I am playing cricket (net practice) nearly every day here.
Every weekend we go down to the country: I can go on long
explores in the forest and up to Gills Lap (Galleons Lap).
We have four cats in the country, but although they are very
common they are awfully friendly and go to sleep on your
knee. Their mother who is about 7 or 8 years old has had at
least 60 or 70 kittens 50 of which had to be drowned. We
have in our country house two so-called secret passages.
Unfortunately I am the only one who can get into them but
I have great fun furnishing them, wall-papering them and
putting up electric bells and lights. This is very grand
because my room (or passage) is the only one which has
electric lights or bells.
My mother has just come back from New York. The boat
arrived a day late though and left her only two days for her
Christmas shopping.
I do hope you have a very happy new year
    with very best love from
    CHRISTOPHER ROBIN MILNE
P.S. Excuse bad writing.

It was not entirely Miss B.'s fault that she was five years late. Every
year brings its new batch of readers, meeting Christopher Robin and
Pooh for the first time, learning that maybe Christopher Robin is a real
live person and expecting him still to look like his picture. Even if you
are wise enough to realize that the books were written a long time ago
and that real live people grow up, you may still find yourself judging
them by today's standards. It is easy to see that some of the verses in
When We Were Very Young are now rather out of date. Nannies in uniforms are now more or less extinct. But attitudes as well as people
change. If today's reader detects an air of snobbishness and class con-
sciousness here and there, it would be unfair to blame the author for
this. My father was writing in the 1920s, about the 1920s, to entertain
people living in the 1920s; and these were the attitudes current at the

time. Yet if Christopher Robin seems a rather odd little boy, in one respect he is now less odd than he once was. Today his long hair and curious clothes are very much in fashion. But at the time, when other little boys had short hair, shirts, and ties, they were decidedly unusual. Was this Shepard's idea, or my father's—or whose?

First let me say that it had nothing to do with Shepard. It is true that he used his imagination when he drew the animals, but me he drew from life. I did indeed look just like that. And the reason I looked like that had nothing whatever to do with the books either. What the reason was I can only now guess. At the time I accepted it as I accepted nursery food. It was just part of life. And I was that sort of child: the sort that accepts things without question. Later on, when I was older, I might perhaps have asked; but a tactful moment combined with a sufficient interest in learning the answer never presented itself. And it is not really until today that I have found myself wondering. Too late now to know for sure, and so I must just try to piece together such clues as survive.

When a child is small, it is his mother who is mainly responsible for the way he is brought up. So it was with me. I belonged in those days to my mother rather than to my father. He was busy writing. It was she who gave the instructions to Nanny. And so it was she who found the patterns and provided the material (leaving Nanny to do the actual sewing). It was she who outlined the hairstyle (leaving Nanny to do the actual scissor-work). This I know. All the same, there could well have been consultation and discussion in the drawing room— while I was in bed and Nanny was busy with the ironing—before decisions were made and orders were given. This I don't know. But I suspect that the result appealed equally to both my parents—though for quite different reasons. I suspect that, with my golden tresses, I reminded my mother of the girl she had always wanted to have. And I would have reminded my father of the boy with long, flaxen hair he once had been. Each reason—as I hope to show—would have been in character. And the second provides the key that unlocks the secret of the Pooh books.

TEN

✦ ✦ ✦ ✦ ✦

Another Portrait

In May 1930 I said good-bye to Nanny. I was nearly ten years old. She had been with me for over eight years. Apart from her fortnight's holiday every September, we had not been out of each other's sight for more than a few hours at a time. Even when I had gone to hospital to have my tonsils out, she had come with me. I was also saying a temporary good-bye to home, for I was off to Boxgrove School near Guildford and would be spending the next three months in a strange place among strange people.

Life at a boarding school is so very different from home life that the only way some boys can cope with it is to become two boys. They split themselves down the middle and become a schoolboy at school, reverting to home-boy during the holidays. This, I suspect, is particularly true of introspective boys, such as I was. Indeed, in my case, the split was particularly deep. For it was now that began that love-hate relationship with my fictional namesake that has continued to this day. At home I still liked him, indeed felt at times quite proud that I shared his name and was able to bask in some of his glory. At school, however, I began to dislike him, and I found myself disliking him more and more the older I got. Was my father aware of this? I don't know. Certainly this must have been an anxious period for him. Up to now my mother had been mainly responsible for me. Now it was his turn. He had made me a name, more of a name than he had really intended. How much of a help would this prove to be? Or how much of a hindrance?

On the last day of the holidays the pattern was always the same. We were back in London. My father went to the Garrick Club in the morning. I lunched alone with my mother. After lunch she read aloud to me in the drawing room. At about three o'clock, my father returned. Burnside came in for my trunk and loaded it onto the car. I changed into my school clothes and said good-bye to my mother. She never came with me. The journey to school was always with my father alone. We did *The Times* crossword, then sat silent. School was all right when I got there, but home was so very much nicer, and these journeys, three of them every year for nine years, were as sorrowful for me as the three annual journeys in the opposite direction (by train) were blissful.

We said our good-byes while still in the car and while there was still a mile or two to go. We said them looking straight ahead. It was easier that way. The good-bye I said to my father was different from the one I had said an hour earlier to my mother. Hers was good-bye until the next holidays. His was only a partial good-bye; for part of him would be remaining with me, hovering over me, lovingly and anxiously watching me, throughout the term. It was he, not she, who got something done about the draughty classroom at Gibbs and the overcrowded changing-room at Stowe (and, many years later, about a military hospital at Bari). It was he, far more often than she, who used to visit me on visiting days; he who knew the masters; he who could chat happily and naturally to the other boys.

But first we had to get to know each other, and a vivid picture still remains with me of his first visit to Boxgrove during my first term. This was one of those rare occasions when my mother came, too. It was a Wednesday afternoon. There was a cricket match on, and I was watching it from the bottom of the field. Then a message came down to me: "Your parents have arrived"; and I hurried back up the hill toward the school. And then I saw them, side by side, coming toward me. How strange and unfamiliar they looked—how out of place in these surroundings. How little I felt I knew them. How little they seemed to be mine.

Maybe they felt the same about me. This quiet, small, serious-looking boy, wearing his curious school clothes, with his hair now so very short. Who is he? Are we going to like him?

During the next few years we were going to find out; and in the remaining chapters I am going to report what then, and later, was discovered. The first discoveries concern mainly my parents; the later ones myself. And we will begin with a very early—indeed a pre-school—discovery about my father.

How much does a child ever know about the adults he lives with? There are certain things they show him, either because they want to or because they can't help it, and there are certain other things they keep from him. Of all he sees, some he understands: of all he understands, some he remembers. And if what survives is worn and fragmented, he can, in later life, an adult now himself, do a little repair work. Now and in the chapters that follow I am not attempting more than this.

One of the first things a child discovers about a person is what he looks like—his face. My father's face was easiest in profile, and so that was how I used to draw it. He came up to the nursery and sat, smoking his pipe, at one end of the nursery table, while I sat at the other. He sat and smoked and thought. I sat and drew and occasionally rubbed out. We both sat in silence. This was something we did from time to time, something we could do together on our first shy meetings.

My father was not an artist. Nor was I, though there were hopes in those early days that I might eventually become one. My father was good at writing. How nice if one day I were equally good at drawing. Drawing, rather than writing. You wouldn't want to have two writers in the family; for then people might say that the son was not as good as the father, which would be sad for the son. Or they might say that the father was not as good as the son, which would be sad for the father. But if one wrote and the other drew, they could each happily tell themselves that they were both equally clever.

So from time to time I was given pencil, paper, and a profile, and set to work. The result was then slipped into the wallet to be produced later at the Garrick. "Oh, by the way, you might like to see what my boy did yesterday." Or: "I think I might have something of his in my pocket. Not too bad really, considering he has never had any lessons." And then the question of possible lessons might follow. Perhaps Munnings could give some advice. (He didn't, but he gave me a signed print of one of his paintings.) Perhaps George Morrow might come round one day. (He said he might, but he never did; and we made the obvious joke as we waited hopefully.) Anyway, lessons or no lessons— and it was beginning to look a little like no lessons—it was an enjoyable way of spending an evening.

And here I am, at the age of about eight, settling down to enjoy it. First, the bulging forehead, where all those brains were. Would I have a bulging forehead like that one day? I hoped so. Eating fish was supposed to help. I must eat lots of fish. I liked cods' roe and haddock. . . . Then the nose: large, beaky, and easy. Noses were easy in profile; not so easy if they came straight at you. . . . Now the mouth. "I'm doing your mouth. Could you possibly take your pipe out just for a moment?" The mouth always went wrong and had to be rubbed out several times. It always came too heavy. My father had a thin, delicate mouth, and a lot of the sort of person he was could be seen in it. So if you got it wrong, you had drawn someone quite different. . . . "Done it, but it's not very good. You can go on smoking now. . . . " The chin was a lot easier, and so was the neck with its large Adam's apple. . . . And that finished the right-hand side. Now for some bits in the middle. The eye first. The eye was even harder than the mouth. There was so little to it, yet so much of my father was in his eyes. They were blue, and like the blue sea they could be warm and caressing or icy cold. Mostly they were warm and kind and gentle and humorous and perhaps a little mocking, but always understanding. But how did you get all this into a few pencil lines? . . . I sighed and went on to the ear which, though full of intricate loops and curls, was easy once you were sure you were putting it in the right place. . . . Then the thin fair hair brushed back to cover the bald spot. . . . A few final touches: the curly line joining nostril to corner of mouth, the pipe to disguise some of the smudges round the mouth, back of head, collar, tie. . . . "Done it!" I passed it over. My father studied it. "It's not bad," he said. "Not at all bad." He tried covering the lower half with his hand, then the upper half. Was the top half better than the bottom, or the bottom better than the top? The eye wasn't quite right; the mouth a little odd. But the nose was quite good. It *was* hard to get a likeness. How did one do it? Perhaps George Morrow, if he ever came, would tell us. . . .

Well, if I failed, at least I failed in good company. Others tried— distinguished professionals—and they did no better. Only Spy in his full-length portrait really—triumphantly—succeeded. What was it about my father that made him so hard to draw? And why, when he was so hard to draw, was he so easy to photograph?

Not long ago I came upon a photograph of my father taken when he was about eighteen years old and showing him with his brothers, Barry and Ken. I had not seen a photograph of my father as a young man before; and as for my uncles, I had no idea at all what they looked like, either then or at any other time; for I never met them. I wouldn't have met Barry: my father never even spoke of him. And Ken had died when I was eight. I knew my aunts Connie and Maud well enough, and I knew my cousins; but of my uncles I knew only what my father's autobiography told me: that he had disliked Barry (though it was never made clear exactly why), and that—for reasons all too obvious—he had adored Ken. And now, seventy years after it had been taken, here was this photograph of the three of them. It was, in its small, private way, a dramatic meeting. It would have been that in any case, however indifferent the photograph. But the photograph was very far from being indifferent. It was eloquent beyond anything I had ever seen. It was not content to show me three young men. It told me all about them.

In a single snapshot, everything that I knew about the three brothers was confirmed, and much that I didn't know became clear. There in the middle is brother Barry. But can he really be their brother? Is he really a Milne? He looks so different. Everything about him is different from the other two. His hair is black and curly and parted in the middle. Theirs is fair and straight and parted on the side. Ken and Alan are dressed alike in dark suits and stiff white collars. Barry is wearing a Norfolk jacket and knickerbockers. And since there is only one chair, it is of course Barry who is sitting in it, leaving the others to stand on either side. They are clearly posing for their photograph, thinking it all a bit of a lark. "All right then, here we are, the three Milnes. Fire away and don't blame us if it breaks the camera." And you can see at a glance that Barry is Mephistopheles and that inside himself he is chuckling "Ho, ho, ho!" And Ken is St. George and inside himself he is laughing "Ha, ha, ha!" You feel you know both Barry and Ken, and that if you were an artist, your fingers would itch to put it all down on paper. But Alan? Alan is different. Alan is difficult. He is clearly Ken's man: dressed like Ken, looking like Ken, on Ken's side and so on the side of the angels. But Alan doesn't wear his heart on his sleeve as the others do. Alan's heart is firmly buttoned up inside his jacket, and only the merest hint of it can be seen dancing in his eyes, flickering in the corners of his mouth. You can see now why Alan has always been so difficult to draw.

Difficult to draw, yet easy to photograph. Artists failed. Photographers—even unskilled amateur photographers—succeeded. What about writers? What about an unskilled amateur writer? Well, I must just do my best. Luckily I shan't be attempting anything too ambitious, certainly not a full-length study, just a collection of snapshots.

My father's heart remained buttoned up all through his life, and I wouldn't want now to attempt to unbutton it, to write about the things he never spoke about. All I hope to do is to catch some of the overflow that came bubbling out and get it onto the page before it runs to waste. No more than that.

✦ ✦ ✦ ✦ ✦

ELEVEN

She Laughed
at My Jokes

Alan Milne married Dorothy de Selincourt in 1913. This, of course, was before my time, and since they didn't talk to me about those early days (why should they?), I have to rely now on my father's autobiography for information. Not that he gives much. However, two sentences are all I need for the present. The first is: "She laughed at my jokes."

Surely this is the one absolutely vital qualification for a professional humorist's wife: that she should laugh at his jokes. Jokes are delicate things, and my father's were especially delicate. Was it funny? Only someone's laughter would tell you. Only someone's laughter would encourage you to go on trying to be funny. It is true that a writer writes first to please himself and that his own satisfaction with what he has done is perhaps his greatest satisfaction. But writing is a means of communication. It is not enough to speak; you must also be heard. The message must be received and understood. Also a writer needs praise. At least my father did. He needed someone to say: "I loved it, darling. It was awfully good." Of course, anyone who is well trained can say that without really meaning it, and I know that on one or two rare occasions my mother did. You can pretend to admire, but, unless you are a superb actress, you can't pretend to laugh. Laughter is genuine or else it is just a noise.

So, if a marriage bureau had been trying to fit my father with a suitable partner, a girl who laughed at his jokes, who shared his sense of humor, would be at the top of the list quite regardless of any other qualifications. Did it matter that she couldn't play golf? Did it matter that she didn't enjoy watching cricket? Did it matter that she wasn't very brainy? Not in the least.

Of course, young married couples like doing things together, delight in sharing each other's pleasures. So perhaps in those early days there were moments of sadness, as when my mother discovered that my father didn't like rice pudding, or when my father had to admit that my mother would never be any good with a mashie-niblick. In fact, there were really very few things that they did enjoy doing together. So wisely, they did them separately, then met afterward and told each other of their adventures: and if something funny had happened to one of them, they could laugh together about it and be happy.

This meant that when, in 1930, I came downstairs to join them, I found that I was either doing things with my mother or doing things with my father; not very often with both. It all seemed quite natural. I wasn't expecting my mother to bowl to me at our net in the meadow, or come looking for birds' nests. And if she and I were engaged on some sort of redecoration in the house or work in the garden, I wasn't expecting more than just admiration from my father when it was done. So far as I know, both my mother and my father continued to enjoy in married life all the pleasures they had enjoyed when single. They had been enjoying them alone. Now they could enjoy them with me.

No. This is not quite true. There is one possible exception; one pleasure that I think my mother had to sacrifice.

This is guesswork on my part. For she never admitted it. Indeed she may never have been consciously aware of it. My clue is a remark she made. It struck me as surprising at the time and so I remembered it. And now, sorting through my jumble of memories, I have come upon it with its label, "Surprising Remark," and the date: 1940.

We were at Cotchford. We had left London for good, but my father had gone up for the day, as he did once a week, and I was alone with my mother. It was not a very nice day, not nice enough to be out of doors, and there was nothing special I wanted to do indoors. So I thought I would listen to a concert on the wireless. This was a thing I had never done at home before. We had a wireless but didn't use it for music—just for the news and perhaps also the Saturday night play (which my mother enjoyed up to the point at which she fell asleep, and which my father and I were more or less able to read our books through). It was a pity about music, a pity good music meant so little to either of them, not that our wireless was really much use if you wanted to listen to that sort of thing: for it had been chosen for its smallness and neatness and elegance, not for its voice. However, it was better than nothing. I was rather hoping that my mother was going to be upstairs in her bedroom, but she had come down and was now lying on one of the sofas reading. Bother! But it couldn't be helped. I took the wireless to the other sofa at the other end of the room by the window and turned it on not too loud. I loved music. I had discovered my love for it at school when I had discovered that I could sing. Since I can't sing at all now, and since I can look back on my boyhood self as someone quite different from me today, I feel that it is not being boastful if I say that I used to be able to sing very well indeed. The music cup at Boxgrove bore my name for three successive years. In fact my father was so impressed by my voice that he bought me a ukelele and had someone in to teach me to play it. "It's only a shanty in old shanty town," I crooned to him. "The roof is so slanty it touches the ground." When the music master at Stowe, searching for talent among the new boys, had shaken my top A out of his ears, he asked me if I also played any instrument. "A ukelele," I said proudly. "I don't call that an instrument," he answered. Nor, now, do I; but I was a bit hurt at the time. I wish now that I had learned to play something— some proper instrument—to replace the voice I lost when, a year later, it broke. But there it was, and I could at least enjoy listening. I had a gramophone at school. My parents had given it to me. They had chosen it for its neatness and elegance; but luckily my study companion had one too, and his had been chosen for its voice. So we listened to Sibelius on his.

And now I was listening to Elgar's viola concerto, and when it was over I turned the wireless off. I had been playing it quite softly. I hoped I hadn't disturbed my mother. She had been very quiet, perhaps reading, perhaps sleeping. And now came her remark: "I liked that," she said.

When my father made Rabbit say to Owl: "You and I have brains. The others have fluff," he might have been thinking of the de Selincourts. For there was no doubt that Uncle Ernest, the famous Wordsworth scholar, had immense brain, and so had brother Aubrey. And there is equally little doubt that Dorothy and brother Bob had fluff. But if there had been this unequal distribution of brain among the family, all, in their individual ways, were artistic. This turned the brainy ones into intellectuals, making them, in the eyes of the unbrainy, totally unbearable. They talked about Art in a solemn and learned manner which the others couldn't stand. One can imagine Uncle Ernest sweeping Aubrey off to the Tate Gallery or the Queen's Hall, leaving Dorothy, to whom "*chiaroscuro*" and "*allegro vivace*" meant absolutely nothing at all, upstairs in her bedroom, contemplating her wardrobe and humming her own private homemade hums. If only Beethoven didn't have to be surrounded by all this eyes-shut, lips-pursed stuff, this intenseness, this awful Uncle Ernest, she might have enjoyed him.

Then came Alan. And now comes my second quotation from his autobiography: ". . . And I, in my turn, had a pianola to which she was devoted, and from which I could not keep her away."

Go on: smile. You are meant to. It is a little joke. You don't really imagine girls can be devoted to pianolas, surely!

Alan was brainy, but Alan was not artistic. And so Alan mercifully was not intellectual. He disliked Uncle Ernest as much as did Dorothy. If Alan knew Tennyson by heart, this only meant that he could be relied on to do the Tennyson quotations in *The Times* crossword. Alan and Dorothy, as well as laughing at the same jokes, would laugh together at intellectuals. But, alas, Alan was not musical. The pianola led nowhere. Poor Dorothy! She could read her own books.

She could decorate her bedroom to her own taste. There were many things which she could do on her own, but listening to music was not among them: this was something that they had to do together. Together they enjoyed Sullivan and Jerome Kern. Together they went to *Stop Flirting; No, No, Nanette;* and *Music in the Air.* And if, on the following day, my father said: "That was a catchy little song at the end of the second act. How did it go?" —my mother would think a little, then try out a few notes, stop, shake her head, look up at the ceiling, smile, try again—nearly—once more—Got it! And she would be off, humming it all, perfectly remembered. She liked what she liked: that was something. But she might have liked so much more.

Sullivan, of course, was also Gilbert. Musical comedy was comedy as well as music. And so, sitting side by side in the stalls, listening to the music, they could also laugh at the words. And so, too, could I. And since so much of the holidays was going to be spent doing things either with my mother or with my father, how nice to start with something we could all three enjoy together. What shall it be this time? Hooray! Leslie Henson, Fred Emney, and Richard Herne were on at the Gaiety. This was my absolute favorite. Or perhaps it might be Bobby Howes. Or Arthur Riscoe. Once it was Jack Hulbert and Cicely Courtneidge, and I enjoyed myself so much that in the interval a box of chocolates was brought around for me. "For *me?*" "Yes, sir. It is from Miss Courtneidge. She said it was for the little boy who is laughing so loudly."

So you see, whether you are an actress or whether you are a writer, it is all the same. You *do* need someone to laugh at your jokes.

✦ ✦ ✦ ✦ ✦

TWELVE

The Enthusiast

Grandfather Milne was a schoolmaster. To be specific, Grandfather Milne was the headmaster of a boys' private school called Henley House. Among his more distinguished assistant masters he could count H. G. Wells, and among his more distinguished pupils his two sons, Ken and Alan.

Of Alan he once wrote, in the school magazine:

> He does not like French—does not see that you prove anything when you have done. Thinks mathematics grand. He leaves his books about; loses his pen; can't imagine what he did with this, and where he put that, but is convinced that it is somewhere. Clears his brain when asked a question by spurting out some nonsense, and then immediately after gives a sensible reply. Can speak 556 words per minute, and writes more in three minutes than his instructor can read in thirty. Finds this a very interesting world, and would like to learn physiology, botany, geology, astronomy and everything else. Wishes to make a collection of beetles, bones, butterflies, etc., and cannot determine whether Algebra is better than football or Euclid than a sponge cake.

As my father commented: "It is the portrait of an enthusiast."

Being one of the brightest pupils of a very good headmaster, and at the same time the fond son of a loving parent, gave my father an attitude toward schools and teaching not generally shared by other parents. He was once the guest at a dinner party of Preparatory Schoolmasters:

> They all, so it seemed, made speeches; two Public School Headmasters made speeches; and the burden of all their speeches was the obstructiveness of the Parent to their beneficent labors. I had disclaimed any desire to make a speech, but by this time I wanted to. That very evening, offered the alternatives of a proposition of Euclid's or a chapter of *Treasure Island* as a bedtime story, my own boy had chosen Euclid: it was "so much more fun." All children, I said (perhaps rashly) are like that. There is nothing that they are not eager to learn. "And then we send them to your schools, and in two years, three years, four years, you have killed all their enthusiasm. At fifteen their only eagerness is to escape learning anything. No wonder you don't want to meet us."

But if my father could stand up to schoolmasters and if he inherited some of his own father's gifts as a teacher, he himself could never have become one. He could teach and loved teaching. He could radiate enthusiasm, but he could never impose discipline. He could never have taught a dull subject to a dull boy, never have said: "Do this because I say so." Enthusiasm spread knowledge sideways, among equals. Discipline forced it downward from above. My father's relationships were always between equals, however old or young, distinguished or undistinguished the other person. Once, when I was quite little, he came up to the nursery while I was having my lunch. And while he was talking I paused between mouthfuls, resting my hands on the table, knife and fork pointing upward. "You oughtn't really to sit like that," he said, gently. "Why not?" I asked, surprised. "Well . . ." He hunted around for a reason he could give. Because it's considered bad manners? Because you mustn't? Because . . . "Well," he said, looking in the direction that my fork was pointing, "suppose somebody suddenly fell through the ceiling. They might land on your fork and that would be very painful." "I see," I said, though I didn't really. It seemed such an unlikely thing to happen, such a funny reason for holding your knife and fork flat when you were not using them. . . . But funny reason or not, it seems I have remembered it. In the same sort of way I learned about the nesting habits of starlings. I had been given a bird book for Easter (Easter 1934: I have the book still), and with its help I had made my first discovery. "There's a blackbird's nest in the hole under the tiles just outside the drawing-room window," I announced proudly. "I've just seen the blackbird fly in." "I think it's probably really a starling," said my father. "No, it's a blackbird," I said firmly, hating to be wrong, hating being corrected. "Well," said my father, realizing how I felt but at the same time unable to allow an inaccuracy to get away with it, "perhaps it's a blackbird visiting a starling." A blackbird visiting a starling. Someone falling through the ceiling. He could never bear to be dogmatic, never bring himself to say (in effect): This is so because I say it is, and I am older than you and must know better. How much easier, how much nicer, to escape into the world of fantasy in which he felt himself so happily at home.

Luckily for him, I was, as he had been, an enthusiastic learner, eager to sit beside him on the sofa and be shown how one solved simultaneous equations. It is true that mathematics didn't lead anywhere, neither in his day nor in mine. It had got him a scholarship to Westminster and an exhibition to Trinity College, Cambridge. It got me a scholarship to Harrow (by mistake) and another to Stowe (which was what I really wanted) and then, later, one to Trinity. But after that, with both of us, our enthusiasm burned itself out. The exciting road we had been following had come to an end: almost the only prospect open to the mathematician was to become a mathematics master; and neither of us could have faced that.

So as we sat side by side, it was not of my future career that my father was thinking, but of the immediate present. For now, at long last, Nanny was out of the way. Now at last he and I could do things together. Here, after ten years of waiting, was his opportunity to share with me his boyhood enthusiasms, to relive his own boyhood through me, and in the process to find my love.

How long would it last? How long does a son feel for his father that very special love that he knew so well? With him it had lasted until he was twelve, but with him it had started so very much earlier. Would I stay with him a little longer to make up for those lost years? Till fourteen, perhaps, or sixteen? He was lucky. We were together until I was eighteen: very, very close. He knew he was lucky, that he had got perhaps more than he deserved, and he was very grateful. And once, a little shyly, he thanked me. . . .

Father and son. What sort of relationship is it? Does the father look down to the son, the son look up to the father? Or does the father get on to his hands and knees so that they are both on the same level? Sometimes the one, sometimes the other; but in our case neither would do. We had to be on the same level, but we both had to be standing, for my father couldn't bend, couldn't pretend to be what he wasn't. We could do algebra together, and Euclid, and look for birds' nests, and catch things in the stream, and play cricket in the meadow. We could putt on the lawn and throw tennis balls at each other. We could do those things as equals. But what about those other moments, which adults pass in casual chitchat, which husband and wife can so happily share in complete silence content to be in each other's company? Mealtimes. Car journeys. After dinner in front of the fire. Conversation with a small child is difficult. Perhaps instead one might learn the Morse code. My father had learned it during the war when he was battalion signals officer. So now he taught me, and with hand squeezes we were able to pass messages to each other as Burnside drove us down to Cotchford. Then at lunchtime, mightn't I feel a bit left out if he and my mother discussed dull, grown-up things? So, "How about a game?" he would say, and we would play clumps, or go through the alphabet to see how many flowers we could name beginning with each letter in turn. And finally, after dinner, almost a ritual, there was *The Times* crossword, with my mother (to give her a slight advantage) reading out the clues and my father trying not to be too quick with the answers.

My father had a passion for crosswords. We shared *The Times*: this was the rule. It was fairly easy. It took about half an hour, and though he would get most of the answers (including all the quotations), my mother and I would be able to manage a few contributions. On Sunday we took the *Observer*, and so on Sunday evening we did the "Everyman" crossword. This left my father free to wrestle single-handed with his favorite crossword writer, Torquemada.

How many Torquemada solvers survive today? Any that do will surely agree that his were the most difficult crosswords and he the most brilliant composer of them all.

Solving crosswords is immensely satisfying. In a way it is the same sort of satisfaction you get from solving mathematical problems. Pencil, paper, and brains: that's what you need. And you wrestle away until at last the answer comes. Or you can describe it as fitting words into an exact, interlocking pattern of squares. You can't alter the pattern: that is fixed. You juggle with the words, juggle with the letters, until at last it all fits, until the last letter falls neatly, satisfyingly into place. "Got it!" and with a happy sigh you put your pencil back in your pocket. In this respect it resembles the writing of light verse. Does this sound surprising? Then I must get my father to explain.

Charles Stuart Calverley was born on December 17, 1831. He was the supreme master of one of the loveliest of arts: an art, even at its most popular, practiced by few and appreciated by not many more: now a dying art, having such exigent laws, and making such demands on the craftsmanship of its practitioners, that it has no place in a brave, new, unperspiring world: the Art of Light Verse. I propose to be so old-fashioned as to write in praise of it.

Light Verse obeys Coleridge's definition of poetry, the best words in the best order; it demands Carlyle's definition of genius, transcendent capacity for taking pains; and it is the supreme exhibition of somebody's definition of art, the concealment of art. In the result it observes the most exact laws of rhyme and metre as if by happy accident, and in a sort of non-chalant spirit of mockery at the real poets who do it on purpose. But to describe it so leaves something unsaid; one must say what it is not. Light Verse, then, is not the relaxation of a major poet in the intervals of writing an epic. . . . It is a precise art which has only been taken seriously, and thus qualified as an art, in the nineteenth and twentieth centuries. . . . Light Verse is not the output of poets at play, but of light-verse writers at the hardest and most severely technical work known to authorship.

Light verse started where almost everything else in my father's life started—with Ken. They were young men, Alan still at home, Ken articled to a solicitor, when they made the unexpected discovery that each had a talent for it. "Good Heavens," wrote Ken in answer to Alan's first effort, "you can do it too." So from then on they collaborated, and for two years they wrote light verse together.

Writing light verse in collaboration is easier than one would think {wrote my father}. I don't mean by "easy" what our fellow Westminster, Cowper, meant when he boasted of the ease with which he wrote *John Gilpin*. . . . What I mean is that light verse offers more scope for collaboration than at first thought seems possible. For a set of light verses, like a scene of stage dialogue, is never finished. One can go on and on and on, searching for the better word, the more natural phrase. There comes a time when one is in danger of losing all sense of values, and then one's collaborator steps in suddenly with what one sees at once is the perfect word.

But this is only true if the two collaborators are at the same level, as Ken and Alan were when they started. If one is a professional and the other only a beginner, the beginner has little he can contribute. So he and I did not collaborate as he and Ken had done. There were verses in his letters to me. There were, rather more rarely, verses in my letters to him. But there were no verses that were the joint work of the two of us. . . . You can't teach someone how to write light verse. You can tell him the rules, your rules, the rules of your generation. But even the rules may change. . . .

> In my day {wrote my father} poets said what they had to say in song. This song (poetry it was called) demanded rhyme or, at least, rhythm from its devotees, and in consequence was hard work. It was obvious, therefore, that if you were going to improve poetry you would improve it most comfortably by omitting the things which were difficult to manage—rhyme and rhythm—and concentrating on what might come to anybody, inspiration.

There was anyway not much point in teaching a dying art. Better stick to mathematics. After all, mathematics was where it had all started with him. Mathematics had led to light verse, to articles in *Punch*, to plays, to Pooh. Mathematics could in the same way start me off on the road to wherever it was I was going.

Where *was* I going? "The boy, what will he become?"

How easy if my father had been a publisher instead of an author; for then I could have entered the family business and taken over from him when he retired. But an author has nothing tangible that he can hand on to his son. Only a handful of talents. A mathematical brain, perhaps, a sense of humor, an aptitude for games. Where did that lead you? Perhaps it didn't really matter. Perhaps it didn't matter what you did in life, provided you did it as well as you were able to and provided you did it happily.

These, really, were his two great talents: perfectionism and enthusiasm. He handed them on to me—and he could have given me nothing more precious.

THIRTEEN

✦ ✦ ✦ ✦ ✦

Collaboration

In those early days my father liked to think of himself and my mother as collaborators. His book *Once a Week*, appearing in 1914, was dedicated to "my collaborator who buys the ink and paper, laughs, and in fact does all the really difficult part of the business." But of course this was not the collaboration that had produced the light verse that he and Ken had written together. My mother and father were not really collaborators at all in that sense: not in what my father wrote. Nor indeed in anything he did. Or rather only in one thing, and that was the work they jointly produced in 1920. ("In August of that year my collaborator produced a more personal work.")

About sixteen years after that event, I was standing with my father in front of the summerhouse at Cotchford when, thinking his thoughts aloud, he said: "You know, I often tell myself that everything we are is that way because that was how our parents made us. Every talent we have has been inherited. And this is something worth remembering if ever we feel ourselves getting a bit swanky. The credit is not ours: it is theirs. Not even theirs, really, but their parents'. And so on, back and back. And even if you say, 'I had this talent and he had it too, but he wasted his and I used mine. Surely that is to my credit,' the answer is no. For if we make use of a talent, it is only because we have another talent, a talent for using talents, a talent for hard work, if you like; and this too was inherited. . . . "

Perhaps one of the things I have inherited from my father is his attitude to pride. One is entitled to feel proud of something one has done if one genuinely believes one has done it well. One is entitled to feel inwardly proud of oneself for doing it well. One is even allowed to bask happily, though modestly, in the praise of others. But one is never entitled to be conceited, to be boastful, to display one's pride in public. It is conceit rather than pride that is the deadly sin. So that when we feel our pride bubbling up inside us, threatening to spill out into conceit, we must cork it down with the thought that, clever though we are, it is a cleverness that was given to us, not one of our own making. In this way we can perhaps look at ourselves dispassionately, with something of a Mendelian eye, seeing ourselves as the product of two people who have collaborated. Perhaps this thought may help us not just to suppress our pride but also to feel less unhappy about our failures; for if we have inherited all that is good in us, we have also surely inherited all that is bad. If our talents came from our parents, so too did our un-talents; and this thought is consoling.

Of course, inheritance is only where it starts; my father was well aware of this. Teaching played its part, and a very important part. A talent for cricket, a "natural eye," was not enough. Instinct won't tell you how to deal with an in-swinger on the leg stump. There must be coaching, long hours at the nets: "Head down, Milne. Nose over the ball." Teaching was vital if a talent was to be given its best chance. What brilliant son of a brilliant schoolmaster would not acknowledge that? Nor is it surprising that my father was himself a good teacher, and that I, like him, enjoyed learning.

First the talent, then the teaching. Lastly the luck. This, too, my father acknowledged, again and again. He had been lucky and he knew it. "My real achievement," he wrote, contemplating the fact that he had been made assistant editor of *Punch* at the age of twenty-four, "was to be not wholly the wrong person in the right place at the right time." Luck! Like the dropped catch that enables you to go on to score fifty and so get a trial for the First Eleven. . . . Or equally the catch that wasn't dropped and doomed you forever to the Third Eleven.

If in this chapter I take the stage again, dressed now in grey flannel trousers and tweed jacket, and with my hair at last mercifully short, I do so as the product of that collaboration that started in 1920, and for the light which I hope it will throw on those two collaborators, my parents.

"And do you write, too?" he asked.

"No," I said.

"You haven't inherited any of your father's great gifts, then?"

"No," I said.

"Well, now. Isn't that extraordinary!"

No, I thought. But I kept quiet.

Why should it always be assumed that it is talents that are passed on and not un-talents? If my father had a talent for writing, my mother had an un-talent. Why should people always assume that I ought to have inherited the one rather than the other? If talents always dominated un-talents, we should today be a world of Newtons, Shakespeares, Leonardos, and saints. Blessed are the untalented!

Writing (so it seems to me) is a combination of two separate skills: the ability to use words and the ability to create with words; rather in the way that building a house demands two separate skills: the bricklayer's and the architect's. A writer, in other words, is simultaneously a craftsman and a designer. If my father felt, as an undergraduate at Cambridge, an urge to be a writer, it was probably because he felt first an urge to create; and it was probably fortunate for him (and us) that this was an urge he could satisfy in no other way. Another man might have made things with his hands; my father made things with his imagination. If you haven't the creative urge or if it is satisfied elsehow, then, although you may be a skilled craftsman, writing the most delightful letters to your friends, the most lucid reports to your superiors, you will never produce a poem or a play or a story. You may make a journalist, but you will never make an author.

Armed with this thought, let us now look dispassionately at the object which Mrs. Penn described so memorably on that August morning long ago as "tall like mistress." It is lying in its cradle, wrinkled and ugly. Suddenly, unseen by anyone, a Fairy appears, stoops over the cradle, waves her magic wand, and casts her magic spell. "He shall have his father's brains and his mother's hands!" She speaks, then vanishes. The years pass by. The infant grows up. The spell begins to come true. Yes, she was a real Fairy, all right. The only doubt is: was she the Good Fairy or was she the Bad Fairy? At first it seemed a blessing to be good at algebra and equally good at carpentry. "Versatile" was our word for it. Later, we talked about "strings to the bow." In the end I think we all had to admit to ourselves, if not to each other, that what a bow needs is one really good string, not two fairly good ones.

But as I have already said, my father never wanted me to be a writer. An artist, perhaps. An architect, perhaps. But not a writer. This great talent was all his own and not to be shared. Anyway, a ten-year-old schoolboy doesn't need to be thinking about his career just yet. Other things come first. Cricket, for instance.

Cricket, like football, is a game you can either play or (equally happily) watch. My father did both. He did most of his watching at the Oval, and as soon as I was old enough, I accompanied him. I was about ten or eleven, and, if I remember, Woolley was batting at the time. . . . We lived in Chelsea and so should by rights have backed Middlesex, but my father's allegiance as a Londoner was always to Surrey. When we bought Cotchford, he transferred most of it to Sussex; and I was for Sussex, too, wholeheartedly. Yet I never saw Sussex play. We never went to Hove. We never even watched a match at Tunbridge Wells, though it was only eight miles away and we went there often to shop. Our cricket watching was confined to the first two days of the summer holidays while we were still in London. Once we had moved down to Cotchford, though we would listen to the Test Match on the wireless—my father in the garden suddenly remembering, looking at his watch, giving a shout, galloping indoors, me following, enthusiastic, but with my enthusiasm never quite matching his—and though we would excitedly follow the fortunes of Sussex in the papers, we would never watch another first-class match. Why was this? Partly, I think, it was because he didn't want to have more than his fair share of me. If I was with him, then I was not with my mother. I played golf with him in the morning, I putted with him, played catch with him, and then in the evening we bowled at each other in the meadow. This was already almost more than his ration; and so, much as he might have liked to take me up to London to watch Surrey playing Sussex, it would have been wrong to do so. This was one reason, but there was, I think, another. Our visit to the Oval was more than just an opportunity to watch a game of cricket, just as the Green Sweet at the end of a meal was more than just the taste of peppermint. It was a ritual.

When, I wonder, did it all start? When did their father first take young Ken and Alan to the Oval, and who were the great ones they watched and whose fortunes they followed? Did they, too, confine their visits to the first days of the summer holidays? Did Ken and Alan continue these visits when they were grown up? Did Alan try taking Dorothy, hoping to make her an enthusiast too? Vain hope! So in the end Alan would have gone alone, taking only his memories, until at last the day came when I was old enough to join him, and the ritual could be reestablished.

The turnstiles clicked as we went in. "Soft seats, sixpence! Soft seats, sixpence!" My father dug a shilling out of his pocket. "Match card! Card of the match! Match card!" From up here where we were sitting, the distant voice had its own peculiar and memorable resonance. My father gesticulated to attract attention and gave his attention-catching whistle, and the voice came nearer. . . . There's more to watching cricket than wondering who's going to win. Even the sparrows and the pigeons seem different here. Even the distant gasometers are lovely. Even the sky, palest blue patches showing between high, yellow-tinged clouds, is unique and unforgettable. And then, of course, there is the luncheon interval, and the battered leather attaché case can be put on the seat between us and opened. No need to wonder what is inside it: ham sandwiches, egg sandwiches, and a paper bag full of cherries. This was how it always was. This, I suspect, was how it had always been. And while I looked forward happily to eight whole weeks of Cotchford, my father, equally happily, looked back. . . .

Two days at the Oval and then down to Cotchford to try out some of the strokes I had been watching; to be C. F. Walters flicking his wrists and sending the ball past extra cover to the boundary; to be Frank Woolley sweeping a long hop over mid-wicket's head. If I never became a good cricketer (and I never became a good cricketer), no one could say it was for lack of instruction. In fact I suppose one might fairly say it was from over-instruction. My road to the Third Eleven began during the Christmas holidays when I was nine years old. The South African cricketer, Major J. A. Faulkner, was running a cricket school somewhere in South London, and thither Burnside drove us, my father and me, four mornings a week.

Here I was put in the charge of T. B. Reddick and shown how to make the forward defensive stroke. By the end of the holidays, I could play forward defensively, and I could also follow through with a flick of the wrists when the good length ball was a half volley. The following May, armed with these two strokes, I went to my new prep school and, to my slight disappointment, found them of only limited value. However, next Christmas I learned the backstroke. Subsequently, when Faulkner's closed down, we moved to a school run by Sandham and Strudwick, and I progressed to square cuts, late cuts, hooks, and glides. And I may say that I cut and hooked, glided and drove with considerable skill and elegance. So that if this was all there was to cricket, I felt fairly confident that one day I would be playing for England.

Unfortunately, however, there are other things: things like not getting out first ball and like making runs; even totally different things like fielding and not dropping catches. And here my skill deserted me.

Cricket, one might say, makes two requirements of its practitioners: a coordination of hand and eye, and the right temperament. I had the one but not the other. It was not just that I was content to be graceful and elegant without bothering about runs (though this was partly the trouble). It was that I trembled. And, as the cricket master at Box-grove once pointed out to me: "The Captain of the First Eleven, taking his stance at the wicket, just ought not to tremble." I also trembled when a catch came my way, so that I nearly always dropped it. Once I had got past the trembling stage, had scored half a dozen runs, and got my eye in, I might well end up with a creditable innings. And if, in the field, a ball was hit at me so hard that I hadn't time to start worrying, I might very well bring off a brilliant one-handed catch. Nervousness! That was what kept me in the Third Eleven at Stowe. Bad luck as well, of course, like that time I played slightly across my second ball trying to hit it past mid-on. . . . But mainly, I must now admit, just nervousness. Inherited, naturally, which is a consolation. . . .

Grandfather Milne was nervous. Not nervous or shy or awkward with boys; only with grown-ups. "His shyness became apparent to us," wrote my father, "when we went out walking together and met an acquaintance. As soon as the acquaintance was sighted, Papa would cut short his conversation, or ours, and prepare for the ordeal. The funny story, the explanation of the Force of Gravity, our answer to a catch-question had to wait. . . . He let my hand go and put his own up to his hat. 'Good morning, Mr. Roberts, good morning to you, good morning.' Mr. Roberts returned the greeting and passed, but Papa's greeting went on. His hand still went up and down to his hat in nervous movements, he still muttered 'Good morning to you.' "

Some of his shyness was passed on to my father, but not enough to make him awkward or embarrassed or unhappy; enough only to prevent him from being a ready mixer, the life and soul of the party; enough to keep him behind his *Times* on a train journey; and enough, fortunately, to make him sympathize with me. For if the Milne shyness retreated when it reached my father, it did so the better to attack when my turn came.

And what an opportunity it found! An only child, oddly dressed, odd hairstyle, odd name, the hero of a nursery story. "Hullo, Christopher Robin! Still saying your prayers?"

An only child needs someone to cling to. I began by clinging to my nanny. I clung so tightly that she became almost a part of me, so that when I was told one August afternoon that I was to spend a fortnight with Anne and her family on the Kent coast and that Nanny would not be coming with me, I lay down on the ground and howled: and the memory of that howling is still vivid.

But tiny children are often shy. This is quite natural and nothing to worry about. They grow out of it eventually. With such thoughts my parents no doubt reassured themselves.

When I was nine, Nanny left. I was still as shy as ever; worse, if anything. I still needed someone to cling to. So I clung to my father. For nearly ten years I had clung to Nanny. For nearly ten more years I was to cling to him, adoring him as I had adored Nanny, so that he too became almost a part of me, at first, no doubt, to his delight, later perhaps to his anxiety. "Do I, Nanny?" I had asked when I was a child, and Nanny had provided the answer. Now my father was providing the answer, not because I didn't know it, but because I couldn't say it. Around the age of eight—and not altogether surprisingly—my voice had begun to get itself knotted up. By the age of twelve, though I was fluent on occasions, there were other occasions when the words got themselves sadly jammed. By the age of sixteen the jamming had got worse, and my shyness wasn't helping things. Grandfather Milne could at least say "Good morning"; I would have stuck at the "G," and, aware of an insurmountable "G" approaching me down the road, I would have hurried up a side street to avoid it. What does a parent do in such circumstances? Does he (for example) say, "If you want it, you must go and buy it yourself"? Or does he say, "All right, let's go and buy it together"? Rightly or wrongly, it was the latter that my father did, and I blessed him for it and loved him all the more.

So there I was, very close indeed to my father, adoring him, admiring him, accepting his ideas, yet at the same time immensely sensitive, easily wounded, quick to take offense. An accidental word of reproof or criticism from him, and tears would stream from my eyes and a barrier of silence would descend between us, keeping us apart for days. So he had to be careful what he said. But provided he was careful, I was, I imagine, an easy child to teach. His knowledge, his opinions, his beliefs could be passed on to me, and I would eagerly accept them as my own. It was too easy, almost. In fact it was dangerously easy.

✦ ✦ ✦ ✦ ✦

FOURTEEN

Walking Alone

My father used to say that the third-rate brain thought with the majority, the second-rate brain thought with the minority, and the first-rate brain thought for itself. His was, and he wanted mine to be, a first-rate brain. There were facts that he could teach me: facts that were not in dispute, like how to bowl a leg break or solve a quadratic equation. But where there was uncertainty, where opinions differed, here I would have to think and decide for myself. And perhaps the largest, most fundamental, and most vital area of uncertainty lay in what one believed about God.

If you had talked to my father about his religious beliefs (and if he had been prepared to discuss them with you), you might have concluded that he was a Humanist. But of course he would have objected to the label as he would object to any label that seemed to put him among a class of people all thinking alike. He might have preferred to be described as an agnostic, since this was a purely negative definition, describing what he was not. As to what he was, as to what exactly he did believe, this, in the end, he recorded in his book *The Norman Church*. But *The Norman Church* was not written until 1948, when he was approaching seventy. Up to this, his views had been his own affair, kept almost entirely to himself.

As to my views, I have already boldly stated what I thought they were at the age of three; and they remained substantially the same for the next fifteen years. In other words, here was I, a Believer, and here was my father, an Unbeliever, and somewhere in between (and I never discovered exactly where) was my mother. An awkward situation? Not particularly. My father was quite happy that my religious education should be the conventional one (and my mother was no doubt only too happy to leave such difficult matters to him to decide). If my nanny wanted to teach me to say my prayers, she could. If at school one did Divinity and went to Chapel, then it was far better that I should join the others than be the odd one out. For I was quite odd enough already. So provided he did not have to compromise his own beliefs, and provided no irrevocable decisions were taken that might affect mine, he was prepared to let things take their course. This meant that, though I was given two Christian names, I was never christened. Nor (naturally) was I confirmed. I was too young to be aware of this first omission, but the second one puzzled me at the time, not really knowing the reason. Puzzled me and left me a little unhappy, but nothing more than that.

When is a young person old enough to make up his mind for himself? When is his mind sufficiently developed to be able to weigh up all the arguments and not merely fall for the one that is most persuasively put? Certainly not when he is only sixteen.

My father waited until I was twenty-four. The war was on. I was in Italy. From time to time he used to send me parcels of books to read. In one of them were two in the Thinker's Library series: Renan's *The Life of Jesus* and Winwood Reade's *The Martyrdom of Man*. I started with *The Life of Jesus* and found it quite interesting; I turned to *The Martyrdom* and found it enthralling. From the very first paragraph I felt myself seized and swept along on Winwood Reade's tumultuous prose, through War, through Religion, through Liberty, to Intellect, finding at every stage the answers to all my questions, the resolutions of all the doubts that, over the past five years, had begun to gather. Then, after so much had been explained, after so much had been destroyed, came the new picture. In Reade's words: ". . . The colors blend and harmonize together and we see that the picture represents

One Man." One Man! Mankind! There was no God. God had not creat-ed Man in His own image. It was the other way round: Man had creat-ed God. And Man was all there was. But it was enough. It was the answer, and it was both totally convincing and totally satisfying. It convinced and satisfied me as I lay in my tent somewhere on the nar-row strip of sand that divides Lake Comacchio from the Adriatic; and it has convinced and satisfied me ever since.

I wrote at once to my father to tell him so, and he at once wrote back. And it was then that I learned for the first time that these were his beliefs, too, and that he had always hoped that one day I would come to share them. But he had not wanted to put any pressure on me. For twenty-four years he had been willing to allow the Church a free hand to use all its influence and persuasiveness (though never its force, and that was why I had not been christened), while he himself had remained silent. But now, he had felt, the time had come for me to decide, for me to hear the other side and then to make up my mind. So he had sent me *The Martyrdom*. But even then he had wanted to play absolutely fair, and so he had added *The Life of Jesus*. And then he had been content to leave the verdict to me. Well, he said, the Church had done its best. It had had twenty-four years' start—and it had failed.

I read the letter many times. It joined the others in my battle-dress pocket and was in its turn joined by yet others, until the pocket bulged too much. . . .

If I had to compile a list of "Books That Have Influenced My Life," high on the list would undoubtedly be Winwood Reade's *Martyrdom of Man*. And it would probably be equally high on my father's list too. If you read a book and it influences you greatly, or even if you just enjoy it very much, you long to persuade others to read it too. A book is not just to be read privately in the evening in front of the fire. It is a plea-sure to be shared, it is the cement that bonds person to person in greater sympathy and understanding. It was, after all, their shared love of the light verse of C. S. Calverley and Owen Seaman that helped to bring my parents together. (Admittedly Seaman was both my father's editor and my mother's godfather, but their delight was genuine, and for years after he had relinquished these responsibilities they continued to quote from and laugh at his verses.)

You can learn a lot about people by running your eye over the books they keep in their bookshelves. There were books by the thousand at Mallord Street and Cotchford: gardening books that my mother loved, detective stories that were my father's passion, the complete works of this or that famous writer, Lord Edward Gleichen's *London's Open Air Statuary* (a puzzling one unless you knew the reason. During the First World War he was my father's divisional commander, and as near neighbors afterward, they had exchanged works. Equally surprising must have seemed the presence of *Winnie-the-Pooh* among the general's books)—and many, many more. Impossible to look at them all, so let us just glance at a small handful.

When I first made my appearance, Calverley and Seaman were of course beyond me and would have to wait. But I could make an early start with Edward Lear and Lewis Carroll. Of the two, my mother preferred Lear, my father Carroll. Carroll's verses are technically the better, and this partly accounts for my father's taste. But they are also happier, more lighthearted, and this was, I think, another reason. Lear, though funny, is at the same time deeply tragic. You can laugh but you can also cry at the Yonghy Bonghy Blò, the Jumblies, the Dong, and the Pobble, even at Calico Pie. My mother cried very readily, an easy prey to her emotions. She was emotional but not shy. My father, on the other hand, was shy but not noticeably emotional. I, inheriting from each, was both. This difference between my parents can be seen again in a book that we all greatly loved and admired and read aloud or alone, over and over and over: *The Wind in the Willows*. This book is, in a way, two separate books spliced into one. There are, on the one hand, those chapters concerned with the adventures of Toad; and on the other hand, there are those chapters that explore human emotions—the emotions of fear, nostalgia, awe, wanderlust. My mother was drawn to the second group, of which "The Piper at the Gates of Dawn" was her favorite, read to me again and again with always, toward the end, the catch in the voice and the long pause to find her handkerchief and blow her nose. My father, on his side, was so captivated by the first group that he turned these chapters into the children's play *Toad of Toad Hall*. In this play, one emotion only is allowed to creep in: nostalgia. And for as long as I knew him, this was the only emotion that he seemed to delight in both feeling and showing.

So it is not surprising that it was he who pressed *Treasure Island* into my hands, while my mother read me *At the Back of the North Wind*. And Wodehouse was something at which we could all three laugh happily together in the drawing room after dinner.

A schoolboy needs guidance on what to read. I remember, after my first glance at the school library at Stowe, writing home to say it seemed to consist almost entirely of the Works of Burke in about five hundred volumes. My father was only too glad to recommend something a little lighter, and I was only too glad to take his advice. I worked my way through Wells, through Dickens, and through Hardy, each leaving a very deep and enduring impression on me as, presumably, they had on him. If one were to say what these three writers shared in common, it might possibly be that all three wrote about dustmen rather than dukes, and wrote about them with understanding and compassion. The de Selincourts (dare I make this sweeping generalization?) liked to think of themselves as aristocrats who had fled from the Revolution. The Milnes were proud of the fact that Grandfather was poor and Great-Grandfather even poorer. In this I was a Milne, not a de Selincourt, and I and my father felt the keenest sympathy for Kipps, for young Copperfield, for Oak when he was penniless, for Henchard when he was ruined.

So, one by one, with my father as guide, I scaled the heights of English Literature. Only Poetry, that range that thrusts up some of the greatest heights of all, did we skirt around. I wonder why? Shall I make a guess?

When my father had reached an age when he could reasonably feel that it was not unbecoming to take himself seriously in public (he was then seventy), he had this to say of serious poetry:

> *I saw old Autumn in the misty morn*
> *Stand shadowless like Silence, listening*
> *To Silence*

Kipling (or a character in one of his stories) said that there were just five transcendent lines of enchantment in poetry; lines giving what Quiller-Couch called the Great Thrill. Two of these are known to everybody:

> *Charmed magic casements opening on the foam*
> *Of perilous seas in faery lands forlorn.*

The other three, not perhaps quite so well known, are:

> *A savage place, as holy and enchanted*
> *As ever 'neath a waning moon was haunted*
> *By woman wailing for her demon lover.*

On my own account {continued my father} I add to them the lines with which I began, together with those earlier ones from "Kubla Khan":

> *Where Alph the sacred river ran*
> *Through caverns measureless to man*
> *Down to a sunless sea*

and

> *While Ilion like a mist rose into towers.*

✦ ✦ ✦ ✦ ✦

If these five passages have anything in common, what is it? I think it is that they transport us immediately into an experience which we seem to have known, in fact or imagination, all our lives.

In other words, poetry for my father opened casements not on to new but on to old landscapes, reawakening old, dim, half-forgotten memories. In a single word, poetry was nostalgic.

Perhaps because one man's nostalgia is not another's, because the memories poetry stirred in him could never be the memories it stirred in me, and because his memories were his most private possession—perhaps it was for these reasons that serious poetry remained in our family no more than something that my father was good at when it came to solving the quotations in *The Times* crossword.

So, leaving poetry behind us, we come to the last book in my list. It was a list that began with a book that influenced my life very greatly in one sort of way. It ends with a book that influenced it equally greatly in a different sort of way. A book can be either a signpost pointing in a new (and hopefully better) direction, or it can be a companion keeping one company, year in, year out, through all life's twisting ways. The first sort of book one reads once, the second over and over again. For me *The Martyrdom* was the first sort, *Bevis* the second.

Bevis, The Story of a Boy, by Richard Jefferies, though still in print (and today in a very handsome edition with Shepard's enchanting illustrations), is not, alas, a book that many boys now read. So perhaps *Bevis* fans will forgive me if I explain to the others that Jefferies was a naturalist and that the book describes in fictional form his boyhood on a Wiltshire farm. Bevis and his companion, Mark, play at savages, soldiers, and explorers; explore rivers, woods, and islands; build a raft and a hut, make a matchlock gun, learn to swim and to sail, squabble and make it up, brood, dream, stare up at the night sky and down to the meadow flowers growing at their feet. In short, they do all the things that I was either doing or wanting to do.

Though this was a book that my father put into my hands (literally: I remember his doing it), he did so saying it was a present from my grandfather; that it was my grandfather who specially wanted me to read it and who hoped I was now old enough to get from it the pleasure it had given him. And having done this, he did no more; and *Bevis* became and remained always a personal and private pleasure that I have made almost no attempt to share with anyone else. The book was published in 1882, the year my father was born. So my grandfather must have first read it when he was already a father and must have then urged it on his sons. Did any of the three share his enthusiasm? Certainly my father didn't, nor really is this surprising. For though Bevis had Mark for his constant companion, and though Jefferies had a younger brother, this is really the autobiography of a solitary, lonely boy, and so makes its appeal to other solitaries. I have known only two other *Bevis* fans. I can see what they and I had in common, and I can guess what it is that gives this book its particular appeal to the likes of us. It is the author's relationship with the countryside, with nature. If there are two of you and you are really together, as Ken and Alan were together, then the country is your playground where you exercise your muscle. You plan walks and bicycle rides, and afterward you boast about the distances you have covered. You scramble up rocks in order to be able to report that you got to the top. But if you are alone, then the country is not your playground, it is your companion; and nature becomes Nature, a person, someone to whom you can almost talk. You do not only walk through measured miles; you sit, dreaming, contemplating, absorbing it all, through unmeasured minutes. Your eye does not only identify the snipe flying overhead or spot the whitethroat's nest, it notices and remembers the pink tips on the petals of the daisy.

I was shy, solitary, awkward in company, inarticulate in speech, becoming worse as I grew older. How lucky, then, I was to have parents who understood, who felt that, though perhaps what I needed for my own ultimate good was to be thrown in at the deep end, this was where, happily or otherwise, I was spending my term-time, so that during the holidays it was only kind to allow me to enjoy myself in the shallows. How lucky I was to have Cotchford for four blissful weeks at Easter and eight even more blissful weeks in the summer, and to have it almost entirely to myself. If someone came to tea—and sometimes someone came to tea—I need do no more than put in an appearance, then slide silently off, down to the river, to look for crossing places. . . .

Alone by the river, alone through the fields, alone in Posingford, alone in the depths of the Five Hundred Acre, alone on the top of the Forest. Sitting alone on the grass in the sunshine. Walking alone through the woods at night. Alone with myself. Alone—yet never lonely. What bliss this was!

· PART TWO ·

The Path
Through the Trees

To Lesley and Clare
and to the memory of
my Father

(Dedication from the original 1979 edition)

FIFTEEN

✦ ✦ ✦ ✦ ✦

The Road Not Taken

The road runs up the valley, and a little stream keeps it company. It is a narrow road—if two cars meet unexpectedly, one will almost certainly have to reverse—and the hills rise steeply on either side. After about a mile there is a gap in the hills on the left, and here another valley, another road, and another stream join the first. There is a bridge and a giant plane tree and then, twenty yards up this second road, a pink-walled, slate-roofed house. The house is at the foot of a slope, the land rising steeply behind it so that on the ground floor there is a door in the front onto the road, and on the first floor there is a door at the back into the garden; and if your shoes are not too muddy, this is often the best way from the one to the other.

At the back the ground goes on rising until it reaches the top. The top of what? Not really the top of the garden, because it is no longer garden up there. Not the top of the orchard, because the apple trees are lower down. The top of the estate? The top of the wood? The top of the copse? The top of the wilderness? None of these sounds quite right; so we just call it "the Top," because that's what it feels like when you reach it. But it isn't really even that, as you discover to your surprise if you cross the road and climb the hill on the other side. From here you can see that our Top is only about a third of the way up. You can also see why there are two quite separate ways there; for it lies at the junction of two slopes. There is the slope that faces the first valley. This is a gradual one, and the path on this side climbs between fruit trees and hazels, through daffodils, primroses, bluebells, campions, and knee-high grass according to season. The other slope faces the second valley and is steeper and rockier. Here the path climbs in a succession of steps and terraces, between oaks and blackthorns, through bracken and bramble.

All told it is a tiny area, no more than a quarter of an acre, but as you do the round, going up one path and down the other, pausing here and there (if you are unaccustomed to Devon hills) and spending a moment or two on each of the seats you find on the way, you will notice that at each point the view of your surrounding world is different. At one point you look down the first valley, at another you look up it, at a third you look across it, while at a fourth you look across the second valley. Nowhere can you see more than half a mile, and in places scarcely a hundred yards. It is a small world. But with such variety does one need a larger one?

I sometimes wonder about this. What is the advantage of size, of distance? Does the astronomer with his telescope see more than the biologist with his microscope? Does the man who travels see more than the man who stays at home? Is the distant view of a bank of primroses more beautiful than a single primrose held in the hand? I don't think so. To the eye, a beautiful view is no more than a pattern of light and shade, of this color and that. Distance and closeness are calculated by the brain, then judged by the heart. Each heart has its own preference, and mine has always been for the small and near, with the large and faraway providing the contrast.

So I live at the bottom of a valley. I have a small bookshop in a small town; and I seldom venture far afield.

There is a level terrace just below the Top, and here, one day, I am going to build a hut. Clare and I have already been to the sawmills to buy some of the wood, she in her wheelchair watching, while I picked out the three-by-three oak that I will need for the frame. And we have been up to the site to do some preliminary leveling—clearing away brambles and bracken and tidying up the rock face at the back. That was as far as we got last spring, and now it is summer and too hot for that sort of work, and besides there are too many flies. So we'll wait until the cool of autumn and then hope to finish it, so that on winter afternoons we can go there and sit there protected from wind and rain, and for an hour or so I can dream that I am Thoreau at Walden.

While I was clearing away loose stones from the rock, I came upon several little caches of empty hazelnut shells—the larders of a bank vole. And sometimes under a stone I found a slow worm and picked it up and let it twine itself around my fingers and then around Clare's. When I move in, the bank voles and slow worms will have to move out. This is always the way of it. But they needn't move far, and many other creatures will not need to move at all.

Willow warbler, chiffchaff, and blackcap will still come in the spring to sing to me. Longhorn moths will still be there in their scores to dance over the bracken on sunny summer mornings; and dor beetles will make airplane noises on summer nights. Up here I shall be one of many. For our different reasons we have all chosen this particular hillside. Some of us live here all the year round; others pay annual visits; others come one year, but not the next. Why, for instance, are there so many common blue butterflies here this summer? I have left a patch of grass unscythed for them. It is only a dozen paces across, and I have counted up to fifteen resting on the grass stems; and there are seldom fewer than six. Have they come here from farther afield because my grass is best? Or was it because some years ago their food plant, bird's-foot trefoil, suddenly blazed into flower below Clare's swing? Was it the trefoil that brought the blues? And what, then, brought the trefoil?

It is as if a multitude of invisible lines all converge on my hillside, and along these lines have come the creatures who now live here. There are the annual lines that bring the migrant birds, short in time but long in distance. Then there are the lines that stretch back through generations and that have brought the residents: the buzzards that circle overhead, the voles, the slow worms, the blues, the trefoil, the dor beetles. And among all these converging lines is my own. Was my coming as natural and inevitable as theirs? Could a scientist explain it as confidently as he explains the return of the swallow? My line twists and turns, sets off in one direction, then seems to change its mind. And along its course are many points where the way appears to diverge, many points where I might have chosen differently and gone somewhere else. Or was the choice only illusory?

> *Two roads diverged in a yellow wood,*
> *And sorry I could not travel both*
> *And be one traveler, long I stood*
> *And looked down one as far as I could*
> *To where it bent in the undergrowth;*
>
> *Then took the other . . .*

But was there really a choice even then, even for Robert Frost walking through a Vermont wood? He thought there was. The two roads were so alike, it was just that one of them seemed a little grassier, a little less worn. That was the road he took. But would he have been Robert Frost if he had taken the other?

> *Two roads diverged in a wood, and I—*
> *I took the one less traveled by,*
> *And that has made all the difference.*

This then is the story of the road I took on my journey from Cotchford Farm in Sussex to my hillside at Embridge. When one is a child, one has little say in the matter: one's parents decide. Mine chose Cotchford, and they chose the various schools I was sent to as I grew up. It seems appropriate, therefore, to begin my story at the point in time when the choice stopped being theirs and became mine. And if I were asked to pick an actual date when this happened, as good a one as any—and with the advantage that it is also a memorable one—would be September 3, 1939.

SIXTEEN

* * * * *

The Distant War

I was just nineteen and I was about to go to Cambridge. My father and I had been spending the last fortnight of August on Dartmoor, near the village of Harford on the Erme. But while we were watching buzzards circling in the blue sky, elsewhere the clouds had been gathering, and in the end the news had brought us hurrying home. On September 1, 1939, Germany had invaded Poland. It was now September 3 and we were awaiting—indeed all the world was awaiting—Great Britain's reply. He and I, side by side on the sofa in the sitting room at Cotchford, hunched over the wireless . . .

Four years earlier my father had published a book called *Peace with Honor.* In it he had written: "I think that war is the ultimate expression of man's wickedness and man's silliness." He had now just finished his autobiography. In it he had written ". . . It makes me almost physically sick to think of that nightmare of mental and moral degradation, war." He had been a pacifist before 1914; he was a pacifist again from 1919 until 1939. And he was now, it might seem, about to betray the cause of which he was one of the more eloquent champions. He who had written "A nation has no honor" was now about to thrill with pride that Britain was doing the honorable thing. He had served with an infantry battalion in France in 1916, and it needed little imagination to see me following in his muddy, bloody footprints.

And I? Of course I shared his views on this, as I shared his views on almost everything. I was too young ever to have labeled myself a pacifist, but I was certainly pacific enough. My only excursion into militarism had occurred at a Christmas party when I was about seven years old. Luke, who was larger if not older than I, had suddenly and unaccountably announced to those around him: "I fight with my fists!" Feeling—I don't know why—that this called for some sort of reply from me, I had answered: "Me, too." I had approached him, been struck on the nose, and been borne off by Nanny in a flood of tears. Since then I had been discreet rather than valorous. I may have spent hours poring over *The Times' History of the Great War* in the library at my prep school, tingling at the more dramatic pictures, but I kept well clear of the more pugnacious among my schoolfellows, and willingly agreed with anyone who told me that war was a bad thing.

So, for our different reasons, we were both pacifists—and now we were about to renounce our beliefs. Why?

My father gave his reasons in a small book called *War Aims Unlimited*. To put them very briefly, they were that Hitler was different: different from anything he had ever imagined possible; that, terrible though war was, peace under Hitler would have been even more terrible. I am not here going to elaborate on his arguments. Indeed I am doubtful if pacifism versus militarism, either in general or in any particular instance, is a proper subject for argument—any more than one can argue about love. War and love: they have much in common. You can theorize about them, but until you have experienced them you cannot know them, for the emotions that they engender are as complicated and as conflicting, as noble and as ignoble, as any that life has to offer.

So I will merely record that on that September morning he and I felt a flood of relief, a thrill of pride, when the news came through that we were at war. And no doubt thousands of others, hunched over their wirelesses, felt exactly the same.

✦ ✦ ✦ ✦ ✦

There were two immediate questions to be answered. Would I be going up to Cambridge? And would my parents be returning to London? The answer to the first came a few weeks later: yes. The answer to the second was no. Indeed, not only would they not be going to London, but Londoners would be coming to live with us. Evacuees.

Thus it all began, and at first it seemed very remote. On the BBC and in the papers we learned that England was doing this and Germany was doing that and Russia was doing something else. We read about German tanks and Polish cavalry and the cautious maneuverings of the Allied armies in France. From these generalities a few individuals emerged: Chamberlain with his butterfly collar and umbrella, Lord Halifax with his bowler hat, Hitler with his little moustache, Stalin with his big one. As that great cartoonist, Low, drew them, so I saw them and thought of them: puppets dancing on a stage, puppets whose activities did not as yet touch me very closely. If one day I might have to become a soldier, it seemed that I was going to have to be an undergraduate first. But I had no very strong feelings one way or the other.

Cambridge in October, 1939. The war had been on for a month; yet although it was front-page news in the papers, it had already—with so many other, more exciting things clamoring for my attention—receded to the back pages of my thoughts. As a Trinity scholar I lived in college—in P.1. Whewell's Court, to be precise—and there I found that I had been provided with a sitting room and a bedroom, together with the larger and more essential items of furniture. The smaller items I had to provide myself. I made a list: table lamp, some pictures, saucepan, kettle, china, cutlery . . . and at the bottom I added cigarette box and ashtray. For I was now grown up.

There are three small things that distinguish the grown-up from the boy: he can drive, he can drink, and he can smoke. Admittedly these were skills boasted of by many while still at school, and certainly with me nothing had been expressly forbidden. It was just that there had been no encouragement either; and when it came to growing up, encouragement was what I needed. My father drove, safely, unenthusiastically, and in total ignorance of what went on under the bonnet. When on one occasion my mother asked if I, sitting next to him, was ever allowed to change gear, he said no—and the subject was dropped. But he sometimes let me hold the steering wheel while he lit his pipe.

My father drank, in moderation and without much discrimination. He liked a glass of cherry brandy before lunch and a cocktail before dinner, and he celebrated special occasions with a bottle of hock. But none of these were the drinks of undergraduates in 1939. If we drank at all, we drank beer. My father did not drink beer. He said he didn't like the taste, and I was prepared to accept that I wouldn't like the taste either. So I stuck to bottled cider. This left smoking.

My father smoked a pipe. In fact he was seldom without a pipe in his mouth. I remember on one occasion he and I went for a swim together while on one of our Dorset holidays. We had just dressed and were preparing to spend an hour or so reclining on the beach, idly throwing stones into the water, when he felt in his pocket. "My God!" he cried. "I've left my pipe behind. Quick. We must go home *at once*." And he set off, *running. . . .*

I had never smoked. So now was the moment to make the experiment. Pipe or cigarette? The trouble with a pipe was that you had to start by buying one, and when you went into a shop it would be obvious to everybody that it was your first pipe you were buying. I doubted, too, if I could ever light it in public without everybody noticing how badly I was doing it. Cigarettes were easier. Provided I said, "Capstan, please," with sufficient confidence, no one would know that it was the first packet I had ever bought. I said, "Capstan, please," and bore my treasure home. In all I suppose I smoked about six cigarettes, and a friend or two helped me with the rest. That was the end of the experiment and I've never smoked since.

Luckily there were plenty of undergraduates in those days who neither smoked nor drank nor drove a car; so it didn't matter. Instead we rode bicycles and discussed politics, and both of these I enjoyed. My political life started when a smallish, darkish, spectacled, and rather spotty man came into my room, introduced himself, and asked if I would like to join the Cambridge University Socialist Club. Was I a Socialist? he asked. No, I said. Did I know what Socialism was about? Well, not really. "Then join the Socialist Club and find out!" he said cheerfully. So I did. After all, there was nothing to lose. It didn't change anything. I could still be a Liberal like my father if I wanted to. So I joined and met other Socialists and learned a lot of things. I learned, for instance, that the war in which we were engaged was an "imperialist" war. "But we're not fighting to enlarge our empire," I said. No, but we were fighting to maintain it. "No we're not. We're fighting for our freedom against Nazi aggression." "We are an Imperialist Power," they replied, "and therefore this is an Imperialist War." I was not convinced, but I continued to listen and to learn, to argue and often to disagree. Stalin and Russia were good, they said. England and Chamberlain, bad. But I didn't think it particularly good when Russia invaded Finland, and I found their explanations far from convincing.

It was, however, their attitude to India that finally disillusioned me with the Socialist Club. We were sitting round a gas fire in somebody's room drinking coffee, about eight of us, planning our next campaign. "We must put India over *big!*" said one of us; and the moment he said it I realized two things. First, that I was not the sort of person who ever wanted to put anything over "big"; and secondly, if I had been, India would have been at the bottom of my list, not the top. There was a war on, admittedly not yet a terribly exciting one, but things were happening in Europe that were surely of greater importance. I didn't walk out of the meeting in disgust. I didn't hand in my resignation. I just drifted away and spent my evenings doing other things with other people.

However, it was not to learn about politics that I had gone to Cambridge. I was there as a mathematician, having won a major scholarship to Trinity College the previous year. Perhaps if there had not been quite so many things to distract me, I might have remained a mathematician. Perhaps if I had seen mathematics as leading to some desirable goal, I might have remained a mathematician. Perhaps if I had been better taught, I might have remained a mathematician. But none of these things happened, and so it was at Cambridge that my love of mathematics perished. I left eight months later with no further interest in the subject. It was a first love that, as so often is the way with first loves, burned fiercely, then died suddenly. But though I lost my ability to solve differential equations, something remained: an attitude to life, a way of thought.

People sometimes confuse mathematics with figures, assuming that a person who likes the one will be good at the other. In my case they have assumed that I would be looking after the bookshop accounts. So I was—but only because I could find no one else to volunteer. And as soon as I was able to, I gave it up. I hated it. I did it abominably. And I detest figures.

I liked them once, of course, because mathematics begins with figures: adding and subtracting, multiplying and dividing. I used to get great pleasure testing my nanny on the eight-times table. But once you have mastered multiplication, you want to get onto something else. You don't want to spend the rest of your life just multiplying things together. It's like asking a mountaineer to spend his life walking around and around the base of a mountain. Mathematics has this in common with mountaineering: the proper direction is upward. As with mountaineering, each step upward can only be tackled when the previous steps have been achieved, and each step—each traverse, each chimney, or whatever it might be—poses its own unique problem, demands its own particular solution, and gives, when solved, its own peculiar pleasure. Fractions, decimals, algebra, geometry, trigonometry, calculus, mechanics: these are the steps up the mountainside. How high is one going to get? For me the pinnacle was Projective Geometry. Who today has even *heard* of this branch of mathematics? It came, it flourished for a brief while, and then it died; and I cannot now recall what purpose it served or what problems it solved, just that I loved it for its beauty.

But isn't this enough? Does one ask more of mathematics? Does one demand that it shall serve also some practical purpose? No. Mathematics is like music. Neither needs to be useful. It is enough that each gives delight to those who seek delight from it. And if, quite by chance, a practical man comes along wanting to measure the height of a tree or work out the best way of building a bridge, it is an added bonus, a happy accident, if he finds a theorem or a technique that will help him. So it is no criticism of a branch of mathematics to say that the only problems it seems capable of solving are those of its own creation. It is—to take a familiar example from the nursery slopes— no criticism to say that no one but a fool would attempt to fill a bath by turning on tap A and tap B without first making sure that plug C is firmly in position. The point of the problem is the beauty of its solution.

The first great glory of mathematics, then, is that it is always offering you something new; and its second great glory is that it offers you beauty. It is never enough to solve a problem, to get the right answer. One must find the simplest, neatest, most elegant solution. Elegance: that was a word so often used by one of my math masters at Stowe. Only the really elegant solution gave any pleasure: this was why I so loved Projective Geometry. Its problems called for no laborious calculations, no pages and pages of figures, merely (if you were clever enough to find them) half a dozen lines of ingenious argument.

Today I am down at the bottom of the mountain again. I can't even remember the binomial theorem. But I have not lost my delight in elegance. Today my problems are more practical—designing a new fixture for the bookshop, for instance. And if months go by and the fixture has still not been made (and if Lesley tells me that it really only needs a couple of nails and a bit of wood: lend her my hammer and she'd do it herself), my answer is that, yes, I agree, but that I cannot do it that way; and she must wait a little longer until I have hit on the right way of doing it: the simple, neat, and elegant way, the only way that will give lasting pleasure.

"Two roads diverged in a wood . . ." And so they do in the field of mathematics. One road is labeled "Pure," the other "Applied." Applied math led to such things as engineering, the chance—you might think—of combining the mathematical brain that I had inherited from my father with the practical fingers that I had inherited from my mother. What an obvious road to choose! Pure math led—if it led anywhere—only to teaching. My grandfather, despite his shyness, had been a brilliant teacher, but I knew that I could never teach. So surely this was the road to reject. Yet I took it. For Pure Mathematics lured me with a beauty and elegance that I found totally lacking in Applied Mathematics. Where did it lead? Did it matter? The Piper played and I followed the music. In any case, at that particular time all roads led to war.

And then at Cambridge the tune changed, and notes became harsh; the siren song no longer enticed me. Mathematics and music: they have this also in common—each needs skillful interpretation. Music must be well played, mathematics well taught. And just as the great composer is seldom also a great player, so is the great mathematician seldom also a great teacher. . . . We took our seats in the lecture hall. Our lecturer swept in, spent forty minutes in private communion with the blackboard, then swept out. Our task was to take notes. It was an exercise in handwriting and nothing more.

So, mathematics having failed me, it was indeed to music that I turned. I hired a wireless and listened to concerts as often as I could. And if today a theme pursues its way through my head and if I can attach a name to it, it will almost certainly be from something I met for the first time in P.1. Whewell's Court.

On May 10, 1940, Germany invaded the Low Countries, Chamberlain resigned, and the Local Defence Volunteers were formed. The war was much closer now. I remember walking down Trinity Street with the captain of the Trinity Cricket Club. He was trying to visualize what he had just read in the papers—dead French troops piled up, one on top of the other, along the Maginot Line. He was a year older than I, due to enlist very shortly. Was he soon to see dead bodies piled up? Would he himself end up on one of those piles? The Germans flooded into France. Stukas dive-bombed troops and refugees alike. Parachutists floated down from the sky, and Fifth Columnists were on the ground to greet them.

At Cambridge the exams came to an end, the sun shone, and we waited, enjoying to the full our last moments of a world, unreal at any time, but doubly so now. Then, a few days later and a fortnight before the official end of term, we were sent down. Coming back in October? Some were: those in reserved occupations—scientists, engineers. Mathematics had been listed as a semi-reserved occupation, meaning that one was allowed an extra year as a civilian. So—yes—I would be coming back in October.

And so we said our good-byes and wished each other good luck; and I caught the train to King's Cross and then another to Hartfield, and thus back to Cotchford. And with me I brought two very precious, very particular memories.

The first concerns a cricket match.

My father had always hoped that one day I would be a great cricketer, captaining the School Eleven perhaps, or perhaps even playing for Cambridge. But at school the tender plant that had been so devotedly nourished hour after hour at the nets during the holidays drooped and faded: I got no further than the Third Eleven. So when I went to Cambridge I might well have given up cricket in disgust. After all, there were plenty of other delightful ways of spending a summer afternoon. But I didn't. Some residual keenness made me answer yes when asked if I played—perhaps because the question was put in January, when snow was on the ground and summer was a hundred miles away; or perhaps because I knew my father would have been disappointed if I had said no. So my name was put down, and I duly turned up for net practice.

I must make it clear—before I come to my particular memory— that in England a College First Eleven isn't quite the same thing as a Public School First Eleven. The games, which are played against

other colleges, are played in a much more friendly, much more casual manner than were those epic battles with rival schools. It doesn't
really matter who wins, and so no one feels that the Great Batsman is
letting down the side if he spends his afternoons on the river, preferring to save his energies for more testing bowling. Nevertheless, we
fielded a team whose variously colored blazers told of past glories,
and among them was a solitary figure, unblazered, uncapped, modestly clad in a plain white jersey. . . . I was invited to play, and
among my various innings was one of complete perfection: a late
flowering, a final, glorious bloom, before the whole plant withered
and died and I gave up cricket altogether. And in this inning, two
shots in particular, an off-drive and an on-drive. How trivial it seems
written down! How trivial it will seem to most readers! A year at
Cambridge, and almost all he has to set against his failure as a mathematician is a couple of shots in a cricket match! Quite true. And
I will hurry on to my second memory in a moment. But may I just
be allowed to say to anyone who understands about these things,
that the off-drive was a half volley just outside the off stump and
shot to the boundary between mid-off and extra cover. The on-drive
came in the same over, a full pitch, quite fast, on the leg stump, and
I was only just able to get my weight across in time. And never has
a ball hit so gently buried itself in a distant hedge so shortly
afterward.

On to the second memory: a concert at the Guildhall within a few
weeks of the end of term. It was given by the Women's Symphony
Orchestra and was the first public concert by a professional orchestra I
had ever been to. My seat—I must have booked late or been feeling
poor—was at the back of the orchestra, facing the conductor. The pro-
gram? Coriolanus Overture, memorable chiefly for the conductor's
expression, so visible to me, at each recurrence of the main theme;
a Beethoven concerto with Myra Hess at the piano, memorable for
the fact that I could hear *her* as well as her piano; and finally, most
memorable of all, Beethoven's Eighth Symphony. Today if I hear
something new, I must listen to it maybe ten times before I can recall

any of it, and even then the themes do not always come when they are bidden. Perhaps it is different when you are young. I had never heard the Eighth Symphony before, and indeed I have scarcely heard it since; yet in the weeks that followed, as I paced through the Cotchford fields and the German bombers flew overhead on their leisurely way to bomb London, back it all came, theme after theme, movement after movement. The music, the Sussex countryside, the German bombers: fitting accompaniment to the arguments and emotions that were turning themselves over and over in my head, and which were awaiting only one tiny incident to crystallize into a decision that I could announce in public.

The incident belongs to the next chapter. The decision can be anticipated in this. "I'm not going back to Cambridge next year," I said. "I want to join the army."

SEVENTEEN

✦ ✦ ✦ ✦ ✦

Preparations for War

On May 29 came the evacuation of Dunkirk. On June 14, German troops entered Paris. German bombs were already falling on London. A German invasion across the Channel seemed almost a certainty. So it is not really surprising that I had by this time lost my enthusiasm for Cambridge. Yet, almost inevitable though the decision was, it was not one I could quickly or easily make. It took several days of tramping across fields and through woods to mature, and it needed that final incident to tip the scales. The incident was trivial in the extreme. It was not the destruction of an army, not the corpses that littered the roads of France, but the death in a flying accident of a single airman. Flying Officer E. J. Kain, returning to England on leave, attempted a "victory roll" before landing—and crashed; and Flying Officer Kain, known to everyone as "Cobber" Kain, was our first Air Ace. So here was a death that seemed to touch me personally, the death of someone whose photograph I had seen in the papers, someone I felt I almost knew.

It is not abstractions—"Liberty," "England"—that stir the imagination, but people: not even people in the mass, but individuals. It is the drummer boy that we march behind. It is to the ensign waved aloft by the ensign bearer that we rally. How often in the past, I wonder, has it been the ensign bearer or the drummer boy who has determined the great issues of peace and war?

My father received my announcement as I would have wished. He gave me his fullest support and encouragement, both then and in the months that followed. And when I say this I don't just mean that he said, "Your decision receives my fullest support and encouragement," and then left events to take their course. He never left events to take their course if he could help them on their way; and helping them on their way meant going straight to the top. Sir James Grigg was Under Secretary of State for War. My father wrote him a letter.

We had already decided that I should try to get into the Royal Engineers, and I had joined the engineers' section of the O.T.C. {Officer Training Center} while at Cambridge. But, even if it had been possible for me to get an immediate commission, it was very firmly my wish now to start in the ranks. My reason for this was simply lack of self-confidence. If I was ever going to be an officer, I needed the assurance that it was because I was a good enough soldier, not because I had been to university.

How did one become a sapper? That was the question. And you may well think it was not one worth bothering an Under Secretary of State about. Indeed, you might well think that a greater problem might have been how to *avoid* becoming a sapper. However, this was what I had set my heart on, and we just didn't know whether we could trust the War Office not to post me instead to an infantry battalion. In any case, there was little enough else that a middle-aged author could do to help win the war, so my father probably welcomed this opportunity to exert himself on behalf of his son.

I can't remember now what was the outcome of his letter. But I do recollect another string he pulled, producing a reply from an engineer colonel in which he said how much easier it would all have been if I were skilled in some suitable trade. Was I by any chance an amateur bricklayer? And then it was that we suddenly saw that my one great qualification was not mathematics but carpentry. "So if the Engineers need a keen carpenter," wrote my father, "he's your man." "And," he added to me, "while waiting to see where that gets us, you must jolly well make yourself as expert as you possibly can, so that when Lord

Gort wants a bridge over the Rhine, Milne is the sapper he sends for. I wonder if there is a helpful book we could get. . . ." And, going once more to the top, he wrote to Christina Foyle, the bookseller, to find out.

Two books are now sitting on my table beside my typewriter: large, hefty volumes, both of them. The older, in spite of a new hessian-covered spine, is beginning to look its age, which is seventy. They are both by George Ellis and were published by Batsford. The first, the book Miss Foyle kindly gave me in answer to my father's plea, is called *Modern Practical Carpentry;* the second, which I ordered from Foyle's shortly afterward, is *Modern Practical Joinery.* And as I turn their pages now, I can see myself turning their pages so long ago, absorbing every word and every drawing. Did I learn how to bridge the Rhine? Well, I learned that the Mohawk River Railroad Bridge was a fine example of the arch-rib, trussed-frame type of construction much used in America. And on the opposite page I could study the intricate crisscrossings of stringers, strainers, braces, ribs, struts, posts, and beams—all made of wood, of course—and each dovetailed, housed, scarfed, halved, cogged, or saddled into its neighbor.

Bridges and roof trusses; coffer dams and caissons; splayed, cant-ed, and bevelled work; stairs, windows, and doors: page by page, I learned the elaborate, painstaking way the Victorian carpenter went about his trade. Utterly fascinated, I followed him into every mortice, every rabbet, every quirk, round every bullnose, down every birdsmouth, up every spandrel and every scarf. And I have remained a Victorian carpenter at heart ever since, refusing to equip myself with power tools, despising butt joints and skew nails when a stopped lap dovetail was the way Mr. Ellis did it.

Thus I set about preparing myself for the day when I would be called up. But meanwhile, Hartfield itself was threatened.

It is hard to believe now that we were quite seriously expecting the Germans to land on our Sussex coast, possibly somewhere around Bishopstone where our friends, the Darlingtons, lived; that we were quite seriously expecting to have Panzer columns roaring down from the Forest, over the bridge and up the hill past our house, with parachutists landing in our meadow to welcome them. But it had happened in France. So what were we going to do about it? The important thing was to do *something*, no matter how futile; for only by doing something could we keep up our morale during the months of waiting. And no doubt most of what we did *was* futile. No doubt the invader, had he come, would have swept past our concrete pillboxes, our dragon's teeth, our barbed-wire roadblocks, brushing them aside as if they had never existed.

But something would have survived from all our preparations, something which was not so easily destroyed: our determination to resist. So we each of us did our modest bit. My mother and I went out into the fields, gathered a harvest of nettles, gave them to Mrs. Wilson to cook, and ate them with resolution if without much pleasure. My father and I collected all our Ordnance Survey maps and buried them in the garden. And I, for my part, found a length of wire, tied one end to a tree by the main road, and coiled the other end ready to tie to a tree on the opposite side just before the first German motorcyclist made his appearance. And then of course I joined the Local Defence Volunteers; and of course I didn't do it the obvious way—walking down to the village and enrolling at the village hall. My father did it for me, if not actually writing to the Commander in Chief Home Forces, most certainly writing a letter to somebody. . . .

I spent about eight months in the LDV (or Home Guard, as it was later called) beginning with an armband and finishing with a full denim uniform. It was not my first introduction to a soldier's life, for my O.T.C. unit at Cambridge had already taught me how to slope a rifle; and the additional military knowledge I acquired defending Hartfield was only slight. However, there were two other things I learned—two new experiences—that were to be of the very greatest value to me.

The first concerned people. The England of those days was much more sharply divided into two classes than it is today. "Good morning, Smith," said the one. "Good morning, Sir," replied the other. Even when the two met as equals, a certain inequality remained. Thus at Lords Cricket Ground they made their appearance through two separate gates, one labeled "Gentlemen," the other "Players." Hitherto I had passed my life in a Gentleman's world, a world in which the Players existed only to serve our needs. Now, for the first time, I was to become a Player myself. In the scout hut at Hartfield the author's son would be lying down beside the cowman, he Jack, I Robin. It was a tremendous experience for me, an experience that seemed to be epitomized by my new name. Robin. No one had ever used it by itself before, and I scarcely recognized it as mine. It was the name they had chosen for me, and they couldn't have chosen better or done a kinder thing. With it they welcomed me across on to their side; and, oh, how gladly I went, and how happy and proud I was to be among them, listening to them, learning from them.

I learned much that I hadn't known before. I learned, for instance, that not all Players were contented with their lot. "You see, Robin," said Cherry, "it's Them as makes the laws and We as have to obey them. Now we've got only two pleasures in life, you might say: our beer and our baccy. And when They want more money, you'll find it's always beer and baccy that they tax. And it's not fair on the Working Man." I learned quite a bit from Cherry. He was something of the odd man out, the only one of us who seemed to bear life a grudge, who questioned and argued and said he didn't think it was right. A muscular man, he drove the coal lorry.

My other experience was of the night—dark, outdoor night. Hitherto when it got dark, I had come indoors and turned on the light. It was the obvious thing to do. My parents and I would read, perhaps, for a while, sitting before the fire, then, one by one, go upstairs to bed. But now, while others slept, we in the Home Guard were watching, awake and alert, rifle in hand, scanning the skies for enemy invaders. And it was during these vigils that my love of night was born. When not on Home Guard duty, I started going for night walks after dinner, up the road or along the lane, and occasionally even through Posingford Wood and so to the Forest. And I was delighted to find it neither frightening nor difficult, even without a torch. It was not that I could see in the dark especially well, but that I seemed able to sense my surroundings and so could move easily and confidently. I still feel this way about night, loving to be out in it, alone, the darker the better. Sight has gone. Sound now becomes all important, sound and a sort of sixth sense. The friendly hoot of an owl. The gentle munching of cows, or perhaps no more than their soft breathing coming from the other side of the hedge. Even the wind has its special night voice, a voice that seems to tell me that it is not just blowing, but up and *doing*, moving things around like a scene shifter on a darkened stage.

Walking at night I like to come upon the lighted windows of a wayside cottage, and to feel that behind the curtains is another world, a world bounded by four walls, a world of sight. I long to peer through the windows, and I know that even the dullest scene within would to me become high drama. I love, especially, returning home, to see the lights of my own house shining. So, I am sure, did the astronauts feel returning from the moon, traveling through black space toward a waiting world. Soon they will once more be a part of that world. Soon I will be home, part once more of the indoor world of light and warmth. Such is a dark night.

But there is another sort of night, the night of the full moon, a winter's night, of course, for only in the winter does the moon ride high. And now you can see. Indeed, you can almost distinguish colors. Trees cast shadows, and their leafless branches make intricate patterns on the roadway. There is a special oak near here that I like to visit when the moon is full. I like to look up and see the pattern of twigs against the sky, and then down to see the pattern repeated at my feet. When the night is dark my world is small, no farther than I can reach with my hand, and I prefer to keep to the valley bottom. On moonlit nights I like to climb out of my valley and stand on a hilltop and reach up to the stars and feel myself part of a larger world, a world that embraces moon and stars—and all Creation.

Guard duty over. Back to the scout hut. And now for the bread and drippings sandwiches that Mrs. Wilson has prepared for me. No, nothing to report. A quiet night. The Germans hadn't yet launched their assault on the Sussex beaches. . . .

So, as that long summer turned to autumn and then toward winter, we waited. We waited for the German army; and we waited (we Milnes) for a certain buff envelope. The German army never came. The envelope did; and its contents informed me that I was to join a Royal Engineer training battalion in November.

The posting (it went on to say) was of course conditional on my passing a medical examination; and a further buff envelope instructed me to report for that purpose to a drill hall in Brighton.

I went. I arrived. I gave my name, age, and other bits of information to a man at a desk, then perambulated the various medical booths within the hall, being measured at one, tapped on the knees at another, made to jump up and down at a third, and so on, until I had done the round and could return to the man at the desk. I was all keyed up, all excited, fairly *trembling* with excitement in fact, for I was now very nearly a real soldier. The man at the desk passed me a slip of paper. I read it. It was my certificate, and it told me—and anyone else who might be interested—that, having been duly examined by such-and-such a board at such-and-such a place on such-and-such a date I had been placed in . . . the words dissolved as I stared at them: *Category C.*

Even now at the memory my fingers become moist, for it was without doubt the most terrible moment of my life. But . . . but . . . but . . . I could hardly speak. But what's supposed to be wrong with me? The man answered sadly that it was not for the board to say. I must ask my doctor at home. "But what do I do now?" Just go home, he said. The army wouldn't be needing my services for the moment. I blundered out, blind with tears. . . .

What does a father do when he learns that his son is not fit for military service? Does he heave a sigh of relief? Maybe mine did, but it would have been a sigh quickly stifled by an understanding of how I felt about it, and by the thought that here was yet another opportunity for him to do something to help.

"We'll make a start by ringing up Dr. Thornton tonight," he said. It was almost as if he welcomed the challenge. If there really was something the matter with me, he would have it put right. On the other hand, if the medical board had made a mistake, he would jolly well see that I went before another board. Now then: who would be the best person to fix this?

Lord Horder, physician to the king, adviser to the government, and chairman of innumerable medical committees, was at that time probably the most influential doctor in the country. My father wrote him a letter.

To our relief, if not to our very great surprise, the medical board *had* got it wrong. They had, quite understandably, mistaken my excited trembling for something rather more serious. It might have been only nervousness, but equally it might not. Better, as far as they were concerned, not to take a chance. Better to lose an able-bodied sapper than to have to nurse a sick one. They were naturally reluctant to give me a second look over, and but for Horder's intervention, might well have refused. And the fact that all this wasted only a bare three months of my military career (but of course gave me an extra three months in which to perfect my carpentry) shows how fast things can happen if you pull the right strings.

So, on a February afternoon, behold a young man in a train speeding north. He is tall and thin, nervous and excited, and very, very happy. Behold also a middle-aged man in a Sussex garden. He too is happy, though in not quite the same sense. Content, rather. If the young man in the train is looking ahead to what might lie in the future, the other is probably looking back to what lay in the past. For the one, a new world is just about to unfold. For the other, a world is just ending.

He would write to me, of course, and I would write to him. He would be with me, or rather just behind me—as close behind me as the distance between us would allow. He would always be ready to advise if advice were sought, to help if help were needed. He would always understand.

He went indoors, found an atlas, and opened it at a map of England. Newark in Nottinghamshire: here it is, on the River Trent. Here's where his next letter would be sent. To Sapper Milne, C. R., the Second Training Battalion of the Royal Engineers, Newark, Nottinghamshire.

EIGHTEEN

◆ ◆ ◆ ◆ ◆

Reflections on War

My training completed, I was posted to the 56th Division: the division was mobilizing for service overseas. This entailed, among other things, a sorting out of the troops and equipment that were to go, from those that were to be left behind. For each unit would be leaving behind a rear party—consisting of the less young, the less fit—whose main task before being disbanded would be to tidy up. Here was a job just waiting for a supernumerary officer. Second Lieutenant Milne would take charge of one of the tidying-up parties.

So why didn't I? I was never told, and I shan't now attempt to guess. I shall just record the fact that one morning after breakfast the C.R.E., Lt. Col. Keane, said to me, almost casually: "By the way, Milne, would you like to come with us?" and I nearly passed out with pleasure.

At this point I must pause. You can, if you like, imagine the pause as taking place during my embarkation leave at Cotchford. During those seven days there would have been plenty of time for contemplation, for going through my thoughts and feelings and trying to understand them. And this is what I would like to do now.

So far, the war had been for me no more than a succession of newspaper reports on the one hand, and a sort of continuation of school on the other. Battles were being fought in Africa, in Malay, on the Atlantic, even in the blue sky over Cotchford, but the reality of war had not yet touched me. I had seen a bombed building or two on my rare visits to London—but it could have been the work of a demolition company. I had seen the remains of a German bomber lying in a Sussex field—but it was no more alarming than a piece of rusting farm machinery. I had been taught how to use a bayonet, jabbing it into a straw-filled dummy—but the dummy didn't jab back or cry out in agony. I had yet to experience the real thing firsthand. I had yet to come face to face with fear.

This meeting was now not so far away. What would it be like? How would I react to it? Would I indeed survive? These were the three questions I was asking myself as I walked around and around the garden and then across the meadow, along the river, through Posingford and up to the forest. I was saying good-bye to it all. Forever? Yes, forever. For of my three questions, it was only the last that I could answer with absolute certainty. I would not survive. The thought didn't particularly bother me; for I had no very special reason for not wanting to die. The other two questions were much more important.

I can answer them both now; and to some extent I must try to do so.

If I were merely writing an account of my adventures, then the first question would be the one to engage my attention. Thus I did, and thus and thus and thus. But too many war stories of this kind have been written for me to want to add to their number. And in any case, compared with those epics that still tingle the blood, my story is tame and unexciting. So I turn rather to the second question: how did I react to it all? This is far more interesting.

Dare I suggest that it is not just more interesting, it is also more important? For if we are to prevent war, we must first understand it. And in particular we must understand how it is that, while all reason is against it, yet instinct and emotion may draw us toward it, so that even someone who before 1941 and after 1946 could hardly have looked less like a soldier yet managed to find in those terrible years something of lasting value, something which, in its curious way, gave and still gives immense satisfaction.

War is like the application of heat to a chemical process: it speeds

things up. It speeds up the progress of science, the march of civiliza-
tion. This, I think, we all recognize. It also speeds up the development—especially the emotional development—of the individual. In a
single year of war we can experience all the emotions of ten years of
peace. They come fairly bubbling up within us. Indeed they may even
come bubbling over, and in extreme cases the whole apparatus may
explode. But if the bubbling is under control and is not excessive, the
outcome for the individual is not necessarily bad. I say this with great
reluctance, hating to put forward anything that might seem a recommendation of war. Nevertheless it is, I think, generally true that good
and bad can never be entirely separated from each other, that although
at times the one may dominate the scene, the other will still manage to
put in an occasional appearance. And this is true even of war. War is
like strychnine. A poison, yes, and one wouldn't recommend that it
should be put on sale in all grocers' shops. Yet this is not to deny that
sometimes, in very small doses, there are certain ailments that it may
help to cure.

Like so many of my contemporaries, I experienced all the familiar—if today somewhat tarnished—emotions. The rallying cries of our
leaders, the valiant deeds of our warriors, stirred me profoundly. I had
no doubts: the war in which we were engaged was a crusade against
the forces of Evil, a conflict in which I must play my part. My King
and Country needed me. So here I was, eager to offer my services,
proud that my offer had been—despite that first terrible visit to
Brighton—accepted. *Dulce et decorum est . . .* oh, yes, all that sort of
thing. Not expressed so crudely, of course, but felt, very deeply felt.
The emotions that had stirred our fathers and our grandfathers before
us, that had stirred young men from the beginning of time, were still
alive. Even as recently as 1940, even after all the disillusion of
1914–1918, war still had that power over us.

The process of growing up is in part a process of getting to know
oneself. Who am I? There is no one to tell us. We must find out for
ourselves, and we can only find out by trial and error. This is often
painful and the lessons discouraging. So the happy man is he who

learns quickly and who then makes the best of it. I had already learned a number of things about myself. I knew that I was shy, emotional, young for my age, unadventurous, and that while others were covering themselves with mud and glory on the rugby field, I preferred more peaceful surroundings. Frankly, I was not the warrior type, not the stuff of heroes. Nor were these my only disqualifications. There was something far more serious, something that had dominated my life as a schoolboy and now seemed likely to dominate it in the army: my stammer. Even today it is painful to recall the pain—indeed, the agony and the misery—that this used to cause me. There are some who can take what seems a grim pleasure in spluttering their way from word to word, leaving only their listeners to feel uncomfortable. But not I. And the memories of those battles with words, battles fought and lost, are with me still. At school I learned Greek. Today only a dozen words survive, one of which is *fronimos.* Its meaning is gone; its claim to immortality dates from the day when it took my tongue what seemed like half an hour to negotiate its "comparative" and "superlative" forms. And there were plenty of other, similar occasions, and would indeed have been more if I hadn't always done my utmost to dodge them when I saw them approaching. I knew my limitations. I knew when I was at my worst: reading aloud (which ruined Shakespeare for me), using the telephone, making polite conversation to grown-ups. And when I could, I ran away.

So although, when contemplating my future military career, I might allow myself delightful Walter Mitty–like dreams in which single-handed I defied the enemy while bullets whistled past me and shells pattered around like hail, in more sober moments I well knew there were certain things that were quite beyond me. I might just possibly be capable of brave deeds, but brave words were out of the question. And so if, back in June of 1940, I had attempted to assemble all my thoughts on paper, this is what I might then have written:

1. I want to do something as heroic as possible.
2. I can't attempt anything that is going to involve

much talking, particularly if it means talking into a
microphone.

3. If I can't fly a Spitfire myself, I wouldn't want to be the
    man who just oils the propeller for someone else to fly it.
    For this would make me miserably jealous.

4. I don't really like being a member of a team. I'm happiest
    on my own.

5. Does being nervous mean you won't be any good in battle,
    that you will go all to pieces?

6. I don't think it does.

7. And I'm jolly well going to prove that it doesn't.

To what extent did such thoughts point toward the Royal Engineers?
Certainly to some extent they did, but equally certainly instinct and
chance came into it. I did not know and I could never have guessed
how unerring was that instinct, nor how, as a sapper officer with the
56th (London) Division, I was to find exactly what I was looking for—
in Iraq, in northern Africa, and in Italy.

NINETEEN

✦ ✦ ✦ ✦ ✦

War—The Horror

In war you may be killed or wounded. But people are killed and wounded every day on our roads, and we don't talk about the horror of driving. The horror of war is not what it does to the human body (which anyway it probably does only once, if at all), but what it does to the human spirit. It is the sight (and sound and smell) of the dead and the injured, the fear that what has happened to them will happen to you, together with all the feelings of revulsion and despair aroused by the human carnage and general destruction that go to make war's horror.

In this respect we were luckier than our fathers. Our war was infinitely less horrible than theirs. At no point in the Italian campaign did we lose faith in our cause or in ultimate victory. At no point did we feel that our lives were being uselessly sacrificed by an uncaring High Command. Though at times our spirits may have been low, at no point did they reach total despair. And this I say loudly and clearly, because I cannot begin to write about the horrors of the war in Italy, still less about the horrors of my particular part in it, without first making it absolutely plain that, though the same word may be applied (for lack of another) to the Battle of the Somme, its meaning is totally different.

A small incident comes to mind. It was during a bridging course at Capua. One evening after supper the officer in charge was talking to a group of us, recounting his experiences during a training exercise at Aldershot. With sparkling eyes and obvious relish, he was telling us how live rounds had been fired over his head. Oh, yes, he too knew of the excitement of coming under fire. He too had his story. And I remember so vividly my reactions both at the time and later, discussing it with a colleague: amazement, almost indignation, that he should have offered this to us, who had just come in from a battle! That is why, ever since, I have always been so reluctant to talk about my own bloodcurdling adventures. And if I attempt to do so now—because I must—it is with the full realization that they are very small stuff compared with what others suffered. I say this mainly to excuse what follows. But it is also an opportunity to record what are, I suspect, fairly general reactions to our own personal war experiences: pride and a sense of superiority if the hardships and dangers we had to undergo were greater than the other man's; humility, sometimes amounting almost to feelings of shame, if they were less.

The horror of war has two components: revulsion and fear. The two are quite different and could be encountered quite separately, and when separate they were not too hard to bear. It was when they were together that they became so formidable. For then Death was tapping us on the shoulder saying, "Look! What I have done to them I can do to you. What I have done here I can do again." Sickened at what we saw and at the same time sick with fear, we did indeed feel more than doubly sick.

I remember my first corpse with that clarity that is reserved for all firsts. He was Sapper Pockett, and I even remember his name, though I have no cause to, for he was not one of our sappers, not even in the division but from a construction company. I had never known him alive and saw him dead for only half a minute. There he lay, alone by the roadside. Someone passing by had chanced on him and, seeing him to be an engineer, had come to us; and Major Lake had sent me to cope. But what did one do? I really had no idea. Have a look, for a start, anyway: so I had a look. A shell had landed just in front of him and blown him over, so that his head was broken and spilled like an egg that has been dropped on the floor. I wondered what would happen if I tried to get him into my truck, what sort of mess it would make of us all; and I recoiled at the prospect. In the end I left him and went to find a Burial Unit. Here I met an officer whose stammer was even worse than mine—which helped to restore my morale. He asked only one question. "Is he in one p-p-p-p-p-piece?" Good for Sapper Pockett. Apart from a missing arm, he was at least that.

Sapper Pockett was fresh. The corporal—whose name I forget, if indeed I ever knew it—was stale. He had been wedged in the iron ladder at the top of a water tower for several days before I was told to try and get him down. The ladder, originally vertical, had been bent and now overhung at its upper end, making it anyway unpleasant enough to climb. But far worse than this was the smell and the dripping that came from the object at the top. Let me forestall the anticlimax: I did not succeed. It was the Caserta fire brigade that got him down in the end—and the weight of his crashing body broke their ladder. On my own, with only a rope, I could never have done it. But at least I tried. I got right up beneath him, tied myself to the ladder, and then, with both hands free, tied a rope to his ankle. Drops of clear pink liquid were coming off him all the time, but I had fastened a handkerchief over my nose and mouth, wore a gas cape over my head and shoulders, and my glasses protected my eyes. Then I untied myself and returned, weak and trembling, to the ground. We pulled the rope. But he had been dead too long, and his decaying flesh was moist and slippery. Boot and sock came off and fell uselessly at our feet.

Thus my initiation; and how fortunate for me that both incidents occurred when there was no danger and no fear. It was only revulsion I had to face, and to my great relief I had faced it well enough. They were only small ordeals, but most valuable in the self-confidence they gave me.

To some extent, I suppose, the mind protects itself automatically from what it fears to contemplate. A doctor can look upon a battered body and see it only as a medical problem. My corporal was a problem in engineering. When a mine exploded beneath a jeep one night on the Garigliano, my attention was so riveted by the banshee wailing that came—I eventually realized—from its horn, that it was not until I had stopped the horn by ripping out its flex and then put out the fire that followed, that it occurred to me to wonder what had happened to its driver. And then I remembered the torchlike object that had been tossed up into the air by the explosion. Presumably that was he, in which case what was left of him was now lying in a minefield. There was only one thing I needed to do: make quite sure he was dead. I blessed the darkness and I blessed the minefield, for I would not now be inspecting the tattered remains of a human being, I would be spending the next few minutes trying not to trip over unseen trip wires or put my foot on unseen igniters, which was quite sufficient to occupy all my attention. And when that had been done, I could return to my ferry and forget the whole incident.

If there wasn't a particular problem to distract the attention, my mind would fasten onto minor details. A line of dead Fusiliers on a hillside, and it was their boots that I found myself thinking about. Socks and boots were such homely, ordinary, personal things, so much a part of everyday life. You put them on in the morning and took them off at night, and the socks had holes in the toes, and the boots were worn down at their heels. Somehow it seemed incongruous that you should continue to wear them when you were dead. . . . And on another occasion, when my corporal, Bob Whalley, was hit in the throat and collapsed on top of me and bled to death all over me, what struck me as interesting was that even in his dying gasp, "Oh, oh, oh," I could still detect his North Country accent.

But on the whole I didn't meet death too often. Today one pictures the crowds that gather around a road accident eager for a sight of the victims. It was not like that during the war. Nobody concerned himself with what was not his concern and, as engineers, our concern was with things, not people. So the dead we ignored. In any case, it needed only one person to put on a bandage, two to carry a body. More than that just got in the way.

Thus was a thoroughly untough soldier gradually toughened up, until in the end he was able to cope with fear and horror simultaneously. I remember on one occasion in northern Italy seeing a wounded man being helped out of a tank. It must have been at least 150 yards away, and I have no particular recollection of the shell or whatever it was that hit him. I just have this very clear picture of two figures on top leaning down and then lifting up a third figure, and that third figure was—or seemed to be—red. The incident concerned me not at all; the sight was far too distant to be in the least horrible: had the man in the middle sprained his ankle and been wearing a red jersey, he would have looked no different. The reason for my sudden wave of nausea was because of what had happened five minutes earlier.

I had been near a farmhouse that had suddenly come under very heavy mortar fire. I ran inside, took refuge in what turned out to be a stable, lay on the floor, and hoped for the best, while the shells came crashing down outside. It was fairly frightening while it lasted, and it seemed to last ages. A small distraction was that I found I was sharing the stable with a cow and so was able to wonder what would happen if the cow suddenly started charging about. Since this would have made my position even less comfortable, it was a distraction of doubtful value. However, the cow seemed remarkably placid. . . . Eventually the storm came to an end, and I was able to go outside and look around. Apparently not much harm had been done: none of the machine gunners who were occupying the farm had been hit. The only casualty, so they told me, was the Italian farmer himself, who had tried to make a run for it. Silly man; he should have stayed put. So I left the farm, slightly shaken, but with lightheartedness once more surging back. "Can't catch me!" I had gotten away with it again. . . . And then I saw the man in the tank. And the message was plain. "War is not a Game. War is real. Shells can kill. Next time it might be you." And immediately I felt awful.

But however unpleasant it was to see death or injury, fear was our worst enemy: fear of our own death. It was fear that made us go to pieces. If we ran away, it was because we were afraid.

"I would it were bed-time, Hal, and all well." Thus Falstaff to Prince Henry before the battle of Shrewsbury. And if I were asked to give my reasons for believing that Shakespeare himself had on some occasion taken part in a battle, these ten words would be my proof. How deceptively simple they sounded, yet what a chord they set reverberating! How well I remember this yearning for bedtime as, cold and frightened ("But it's not really cold, so why am I shivering?"), I set out on an enterprise I knew was going to be unpleasant. Bedtime! All the bedtimes of happier days, right back to my childhood, came in a great procession before my eyes, and I reached out toward them—almost literally, for I could feel the muscular spasm—as if I were trying to grasp them and heave myself through the next few hours to the security that lay on the other side.

It was like this at Teano. It was like this on a number of other occasions, too. But in one respect Teano was (thank goodness) unique, and that is why I would like to say what happened there.

It was just before I left the Field Park Company, all eager for the more adventurous life I would surely find in a field company. My bridging platoon was in among some olive trees just north of the Volturno. The rest of the company was still in the Caserta area south of the river. The division was pushing ahead against increasing resistance toward Cassino. That night a bridge was to be built at Teano.

I should have been excited. I might well have felt jealous that once again I would just be a spectator while another officer did the work, had all the fun, and got all the glory; but at least I should have been excited that here was something happening and that I was taking part in it. Better surely than sitting under an olive tree feeling frustrated. I had felt excited enough on all the previous occasions. There had been the division's first-ever Bailey bridge at Battipaglia. I had been there. We had built it in daylight and the Germans had shelled my lorries—

not seriously, I must admit, but enough to boast about afterward. And there had been several more bridges after that as we crossed the Plain of Naples, all of them built at night, all of them uneventful, uninterrupted. There may have been moments of jealousy. There may have been moments of acute boredom as, with nothing to do, I stood idly watching while others worked, or wandered off on my own into the dark and paced up and down, and thought about this and that, and looked at my watch and wished time would go a little faster and that I didn't feel so sleepy. But at least I was up near the front doing important work; and so, all in all, life was good and I was happy, and the more bridges they wanted the better.

So why didn't I rejoice tonight? Why did I suddenly feel afraid? I had never felt afraid before. Why now?

Was it because the officer who was to be in charge was himself afraid, and his fear was catching? Or was it instinct, the instinct one has that thunder is in the air, that a storm is about to burst. One did seem to develop a sort of subconscious barometer that warned of danger. Mine had been high for so long. Now it was suddenly falling. . . .

It had always seemed the natural thing to accompany my lorries to the bridge site, even though there was so little for me to do when I got there. I suppose that if something had gone wrong, it might have been useful to have an extra officer around. But normally there wasn't anything that one of my corporals couldn't do equally well. So if I went, I went because I wanted to, not because I had to. I wanted to see what was happening, and I wanted to be with my men. After all, that was my rule: an officer's place is where the work is most exciting.

So what good reason was there for not going tonight? None. But equally there was no good reason why I *should* go; and I began to produce arguments for staying behind. I had always been in charge in the past: well, why shouldn't someone else be in charge for a change? Why shouldn't Corporal Quick take the lorries up? He could do it equally well. And the experience and responsibility would be good for him. There was nothing special about this particular bridge, no reason really for supposing that it would be any different from all the others. So why should I have to spend a boring, wearying night doing nothing, when I might just as well be in bed?

I went to Quick and gave him his orders. And then, to show how little I had been persuaded by my own reasoning, I told him not to wait until all the lorries had been unloaded so that they could return in convoy—as we had always done in the past—but to send them back one at a time, as soon as they were ready to leave. "Don't hang around up there," I said. "They can easily find their own way back."

Thus I hoped I had covered myself, whatever happened. My conscience could now rest easy.

Away they went, and I retired to my tent and lay on my bed and tried to convince myself that I had not been a total coward, that the night would be peaceful and all would be well. I lay awake listening. Yes, as I thought, not a sound to be heard. They had already been gone some time, and the first empty lorry would be due back any minute. The minutes dragged by, but no lorry came. The hours crept slowly toward midnight, then even more slowly onward, onward toward another day. Did I sleep? I doubt it. What time did they get back? I can't remember. What happened? What I had known would happen, only worse. They had been shelled continuously; a number of sappers had been killed; Quick had been wounded; there were two dead bodies in one of the lorries; the bridge had been abandoned.

Pathetically, I tried to sound surprised. . . .

Fear of what might happen: that was one sort. Fear when it was actually happening: that was another.

There were many varieties of bangs, some more unpleasant than others. An approaching shell is a little like an approaching dog. One dog in a thousand may bite, one in a hundred may growl, the rest wag their tails. If you've met the dog before, then however uncertain its temper and even if it growls a little, you'll have learned how to treat it and you'll probably not get bitten. If it's a stranger, you are rather more apprehensive. "Good doggie, good doggie," you say, hoping to convince it that it is one of the well-behaved nine hundred; and if it then growls, you fear the worst. So it was with shells. Very few actually did any harm. Most would approach with a not unpleasant singing sound, wagging their tails in a friendly way, and once we were used to them they were not particularly frightening. A few came tearing at us like an express train and were much more alarming. And a few were fitted with ingenious devices. After all, if a shell isn't going to hurt you, it is at least something if it scares you. Better a dog that barks than one that wags its tail, where burglars are concerned. So there were the "moaning minnies," fired in batches of six, and which, as they approached us, sobbed crocodile tears at the havoc they were about to create. And there were the air bursts—shells that exploded in midair, and, whether or not they were more lethal, certainly both sounded and looked much more menacing. But even those that sang could on occasion bite, and so we searched for additional reassurance. "Good shell, good shell," we said. "It's not us you're after, is it? It's those poor devils over there." And we could thus feel ourselves to be, not intended victims, but spectators, which was much less frightening. And if an accidental one came close and made us duck, we could tell ourselves it was a mistake, not meant for us at all, and we could almost forgive it.

When you were up and about, it was never too bad. For it was not expected that we should work when a storm was raging. The infantry could make a dash for it and risk getting wet. Tanks had their armor to keep them dry. But sappers worked in the open, slowly, carefully, often in quite large groups, and with nothing to protect them. So when a storm broke, we took cover and waited until it was over. After all, the German guns only had a limited number of shells. Even if they could see us, they could never afford to fire at us all the time. There were other, more important targets.

But in bed at night it was very different. "I would it were bed-time, Hal. . . ." Yes, indeed; but only if all were well. It usually was. Nights were usually quiet—but not quite always; and then bed could be the most miserable of places, with nothing to distract one, nothing to do but lie awake and atremble, waiting wretchedly for the next explosion. And oh, how close and menacing they always seemed on these occasions. No chance now of persuading myself that they were being aimed at someone else: they were being aimed at me, and I knew it! If I could have gotten up and gone out and looked around, I might have convinced myself that this was not so; but it needed more determination than I possessed. And so I lay there waiting and waiting for the nightmare to come to an end. . . .

Thus our encounters with fear passed through three stages. In the first, we barely noticed it: war was an adventure, and excitement dominated our emotions. In the second stage, the excitement had worn off: fear was present, but we were able to control it. In the third stage, the strain began to tell. War was now no longer a game, nor could we fool ourselves that it was a party. It was just thoroughly stupid and thoroughly bloody. At the start, filled with confidence, we had walked upright, chin up, chest out, like soldiers on parade. Later we had developed a permanent stoop. We walked with knees bent, eyes to the ground, measuring the distance to the nearest hollow, ready for an instant spring. In the end we didn't bother. It wasn't worth it. If you're going to hit me, do it now, for heaven's sake, and get it over. . . .

It was October 1944. We were down in the Lombardy Plain. We had fought our way from bloody ridge to bloody ridge, up and down, up and down, with always another one ahead of us. And then at last we had fought our way through to the Promised Land, only to find it no Promised Land at all but another, even nastier battlefield.

We were down in the Plain of Lombardy, and my platoon was in a farmhouse and just outside was a field of aubergines. We were preparing our midday meal, cooking it in a German field kitchen.

This field kitchen didn't really belong to us. We had taken it over from a platoon of a field company in the 78th Division back at Taranto four months previously. They were leaving Italy for the Middle East. We had just arrived back; and so we were inheriting all their vehicles and equipment. But the field kitchen was a little different: they had captured it, and so it was their very own and only lent to us on the understanding that they could reclaim it on their return.

They were now back, and a message had just come that their platoon commander was at Company HQ, all eager to bear it away.

I went round, feeling thoroughly cross and uncooperative.

"I'm sorry," I said, "it's in use at the moment. It's got my men's dinner inside it, and I'm not handing it over until they've finished with it."

"But I've got to get it back at once," said the subaltern. "I must have it right away."

"I'm sorry. You can't. You'll just have to wait—or come another day."

Three officers, standing in a group, arguing irritably, all a little on their dignity: a nice target. A ranging shell landed nearby.

When dogs are on their dignity, nothing less than a direct hit with a bucket of water will break up the argument. So it was with us. In my case, it was partly the argument, partly that the honor of the division demanded that I not make the first move, and partly that I was past caring anyway; and I expect it was much the same with the others. "Wounded" and "killed in action" were familiar words in those days, and to those who saw them day after day in the newspapers, they recalled perhaps those pictures of battles in which men are firing guns at each other at point-blank range, horses are rearing, swords are flashing, and it seems unlikely that there will be a single survivor. How different is modern war! At times how unglamorous! One might be wounded charging the enemy with a tommy gun, but one was just as likely to be struck down while sitting on the latrine. Indeed, in our case, more likely. For it was the odd and the unexpected shell, catching us when we were least expecting it, that so often did the damage. Nearly all my platoon's casualties occurred in circumstances that were far from glorious, and I was no exception.

The other shells had landed with a crash. The one that finally settled our argument made, so it seemed to me, no sound but a puff, a sort of buffet somewhere behind my head. I scarcely heard it. I never saw it. And, luckily, I never even felt it.

His lips curling in a cynical smile, the god Mars distributes his rewards. For some they are appropriate—for after all, he must retain the respect in which men hold him, retain his authority over their lives. And so for some it is the well-earned medal or the hero's death in action. But for others . . . One by one we come before him, and hopefully we hold out our hand.

When my turn came, he saw before him someone who, for all his attempts to look like a soldier, yet remained a faintly ludicrous figure. And so, being in one of his kindlier moods, he gave me what I wanted just when I wanted it. He took me gently and he pressed his thumb into the back of my head, not too hard to hurt, not too deep to leave more than a small but permanent dent.

A few days later, my parents learned that I had been wounded and placed on the "seriously ill" list. But by that time, I was feeling nothing but a deep sense of happiness and pride.

TWENTY

War—The Lesson

I have often looked back on my five years in the army, on my four years with the 56th Division, on my two and a half years in Italy; and sometimes I have felt that they were five wasted years, years that could have been better spent qualifying for some profession, years that put me at a disadvantage compared with those who, younger than I, had missed the war and gotten ahead: sometimes I felt that I was one of war's casualties. But that mood passed. At other times I looked back with private pride and satisfaction on what I had done. It had not been much, really. But I was proud that I had started in the ranks, proud that I had spent so long overseas, proud to have been in the 56th, serving in Italy throughout the campaign, proud to have achieved my ambition of commanding a platoon in a divisional field company, and very, very proud that I had been wounded. At other times I was grateful that during those four years abroad I had seen so much of the world: Cape Town, Bombay, half a dozen different deserts, and Italy. Italy in particular. At other times I just felt how lucky I had been to have found so much that was good, so little that was bad: that those five years had provided me with a foundation stone, strong and lasting, on which to build my adult life. And at times—and especially at this very moment—I looked back with an agonizing realization of the price that had been paid. It is this realization that has made this such a difficult chapter to write: for how could I describe my many blessings, when others had known only the curse of war. If I had received, they had paid. That I might come home, they had stayed behind. . . .

So I must end with two small memories, both from Anzio, both from the time when we were pretending to be infantry. Yes, pretending. For let me make it quite clear that we were never the real thing. We never did what they did. We never suffered what they suffered. We couldn't: we weren't good enough. We just occupied reserve positions behind their front line. And when that line was dented, it was not we but the real infantry who had to counterattack to restore the situation. And one evening, as the sun was setting, we watched the counterattack go in.

We had been warned to expect it, and now here it came: men carrying rifles, men dragging Bren guns, half walking, half running, hurrying up the hillside. We could hear them panting, see their grim faces as they came hurrying and stumbling by. Then they dropped to the ground, while another group came up and passed them. Thus they moved up the hillside, taking turns, one group hurrying forward while the other group lay on the ground ready to give covering fire. At the top of the hill was a gate onto a road. They had to go through this gateway, and they did it as they had been taught, fanning out, slipping through one at a time, careful not to bunch. And so they passed out of sight—but not out of memory. Shortly after they had disappeared, the German "defensive fire" came down all around us, and it was very heavy indeed. Later I helped some of the wounded back. Had they achieved their objective? I don't know. But I do know that every objective that the infantry was ever set had always to be paid for: that of those who set out in the evening, not all would have breakfast the following morning. The question was not: "Should a price have been paid?" but "Was the price too high?"

With the engineers it was never like this. If we paid, it was with sweat, not blood. Blood was never part of our bargain, for our objectives could not be achieved—our bridges not be built, our roads not be cleared—if we got ourselves killed. It was our duty to stay alive; theirs, not ours, to die. Loose coins in a pocket, they were, loose change. How much? One lieutenant, two corporals, and ten men? Fair enough.

Let no one ever recall his exciting, his heroic, or his funny adventures in the war without remembering the infantry. There is nothing exciting, nothing heroic, nothing funny about struggling up a hillside lugging a Bren and then getting yourself killed as you reach the top.

My other memory is of four Spitfires. They came in a line, flew over our heads, wheeled to the left, and then, one at a time, dived and dropped their bomb. Up they came, one at a time, surfacing; and now they were in a circle, flying around, and each, as it came again to the target, dived. They had dropped their only bomb; so now they fired their machine guns. Four identical planes flying around and around, but with one great difference. The leader, when he dived, dived steeply, almost vertically, dived so low that he almost vanished behind the trees; the other three made shallow dives. One deep, three shallow. One deep, three shallow. One deep . . . and as I watched the leader go down for the third time, I noticed that he was wearing a red carnation in his cockpit, a carnation that grew and grew. . . . That was all— except for a splash of dark grey smoke coming up from behind the trees to mark the spot where he had landed. . . .

And I remembered J. F. Roxburgh preaching a sermon at Stowe. It was the first time I had heard him preach, and it was on Armistice Sunday, 1934.

"In war," he had said, "it is always the best who die. . . ."

✦ ✦ ✦ ✦ ✦

TWENTY-ONE

Changing Heart—Hedda

I stood at the top of the steps and watched her go—a great white moth fluttering away into the darkness—down, down, down, between walls afoam with wisteria. I stood there until the darkness and the town had swallowed her up, then turned to climb the hill, the first stage of a long journey that would take me across Europe, across the Channel, back to England, back to Cotchford, back to civilian life again.

But I would return. We had agreed to that. I would return in the spring. And meanwhile there would be her letters and the feeling that I was getting things ready—qualifying for a job, finding a job, finding a home—getting things ready for the day when I could invite her to come and join me. If our ways were to part, if seven hundred miles were to come between us, it was only for a little while.

Yes, it was not only war that I had found in Italy. It was love— and that too for the first time. Love and war and all the complicated, conflicting, tumultuous emotions that each engenders; both were there waiting for me. The one had claimed a piece of my head; the other, less literally, now claimed a piece of my heart.

Hedda was one of a group of Italians whom Harry—in ways known only to people like Harry—had managed to organize. There were about eight of them in all, two married couples and four unattached females. Hedda was the youngest, a year younger than I. The others were quite a bit older, somewhere between late twenties and mid-forties, I would guess. And to welcome them to our villa on the hill above Trieste were the seven of us, the officers of 221 Field Company. And thither they came on Saturday evenings, to eat, to talk, to dance, perhaps to listen to some music, or swim in our swimming pool.

I was not present on their first visit. I forget now what particular excuse was given—headache, pressure of work, calls of duty. If Harry wanted to import a gang of popsies, that was okay and just the sort of thing Harry would want to do, but count me out. I don't dance, thank you very much, and I don't particularly enjoy female company, thank you very much, and I don't fancy spending my evenings necking with signorinas who don't speak my language. This was my reaction. And so my heart sank when I was told that the party had been a success and that they would be coming up again next week.

"Oh, and Chris, there was one who would have been just right for you. We told her all about you and she wants to meet you. She's at Venice University, studying English."

Then I hope you told her that I don't dance.

"That's all right, Chris, she wants someone to help her with her English. You ought to be good at that. She's quite a smasher, by the way."

Oh, shut up, Harry.

One of the blessings of being an engineer officer was that dancing didn't need to be one of our accomplishments. This was because of our domestic arrangements. As I have already explained, each company lived on its own, and so, if we ever had an officers' mess, it never held more than seven of us; not enough, mercifully, to justify the appointment of an entertainments officer eager to keep us all entertained. Only once did one of our colonels attempt to bring his officers under a single roof, and that was when we were in Palestine. The attempt was resented and was a failure, but before we broke up and went our individual company ways again, he did manage to organize one dance for us. Attendance was more or less obligatory. 220 Field Company was allotted seven young ladies from Tel Aviv. One of them was to be mine.

"But I don't dance. I can't dance. I just don't know how to."

So Jack took me in hand and taught me the two-step, and together we had two-stepped round the company lines after dark the night before, until I thought I had mastered the quarter- and half-turns. Thus my armory when I was presented to my partner consisted of the two-step as taught by Jack and the waltz as vaguely remembered from my prep school days. But when the band struck up I lost my nerve and had to confess that the waltz was all I could manage; so we sat side by side until a recognizable waltz turned up, then took the floor. This was it. We stood opposite one another. I clasped her. I knew what to do with my hands. Now for my feet. I looked down at them, hopefully, encouragingly, and they began to tremble and make little spasmodic movements. Oh, I knew how to do it perfectly well, really. One-two-three, one-two-three; it was easy once you got going, and I could whirl her around the floor until we were both giddy. It was just knowing how to begin, which foot and when, and getting her to do it too so that we didn't collide. The dance was now in full swing, carefree couples were spinning by, but we were still motionless, locked together, paralyzed. . . . In the end I said, "Sorry. We don't seem to be getting on very well," and she said, "No we don't, do we?" and we returned to our seats. . . . I was naturally reluctant to repeat that sort of fiasco again.

Luckily, dancing (said Harry) formed only a small part of the evening's activities; and so on the second occasion I agreed to be present.

Looking back on it afterward, I had to admit that I had quite enjoyed it. The Italians had been a jolly, friendly lot, and some of them had been able to speak a little English. Hedda had been there and she was indeed most attractive, and being in her company had given me a pleasing and quite new sensation. It was all rather exciting, and to my surprise I found myself looking forward to the following Saturday when they were due to come again.

So it all began. My fellow officers were either married, or engaged, or at the very least, had girls waiting for them in England. Only I had never had a girl in my life. Only Hedda was the right age for me. And so it was natural that we should be paired together, and not surprising that the others should take a delight in watching and encouraging our progress. So it all began, at our villa on the hill; and Saturday was the day that I lived for.

Then, with approaching exams making a convenient excuse, another day was added. The place this time was her home in Piazza Garibaldi. And after work (and with a message that I would be out to supper, but might like something to eat when I got back), I slipped off and made my way down into the town. Oh, well-worn track! How much happiness in anticipation did I carry down you, how much happiness in retrospect carry up, and how many hopes and fears did I turn over and over in my head, as my feet, left to themselves, followed the familiar route! Today, looking back on those springtime years, I can't help feeling a little sad that most people now do it all so differently. Were we innocent? Were we immature? Were we old-fashioned? Probably all three. But how fortunate for us that this was so, and that we were thus able to share together those incredibly happy months and leave behind no regrets. Our lives came together, ran side by side, then separated; and mine most certainly and hers too, I am prepared to swear, were vastly the richer for the experience.

I rang her bell, then climbed her stairs, and usually it was she—though sometimes her grandmother—who opened the door to me. And then we were alone together in a little room furnished with a settee, where we could sit together side by side. How did we spend our time? As innocently as anyone could wish, more boringly than anyone would have thought possible, yet as pleasurably as any courting couple ever had since the world began.

In between visits we wrote each other letters, each in our own language; and thus we learned about each other and about those things that are in any case often easier to express in writing, and especially so if conversation is difficult. And in between visits and letter-writing, and with the help of a *Teach Yourself* book, I set out to learn Italian.

Already, as I have said, I had fallen in love with the land of Italy. Now, in Hedda, through Hedda, and because of Hedda, I began to love and understand the people of Italy. To the troops who had landed at Salerno they had been Wops: Wops who had run away when the fighting had become too hot; Wops who had surrendered; Wops who had changed sides when it had suited them; Wops who preferred a life of idleness and ease, reclining in the sun while others worked; Wops who in many ways were little better than the cows or pigs or chickens that so often seemed to occupy the ground floors of their houses. Wops and Wogs, Italians and Arabs, there really wasn't much to choose between them. Who can blame us if this was how we saw them? It was, after all, the picture painted for us by our politicians, and one all too easily acceptable to a victorious army striding across a defeated country.

Understandably, too, we thought of all Italians as a single people, and, first impressions being strongest, judged them by what we saw down in the south. Now I learned for the first time that Italy, so obviously one country on the map, had been a nation for less than a hundred years; that there were very great differences between the Italians of the north and those of the south; and that in Trieste in particular, though all spoke the same language, there was a mixture of races. Hedda herself was partly Austrian. Others were partly Slav. Others again were Italians from elsewhere, who had moved in when the town had been annexed after the First World War. Gradually I began to understand how it was, how it had all happened, how they felt about it; and gradually I began to share their feelings and their aspirations.

I never learned to talk Italian very fluently, because I was still not very fluent even in my own language and found foreign languages a great deal harder to get my tongue around. But I could read. I read about the Risorgimento. Garibaldi became my hero and Abba's *Da Quarto al Volturno* one of my best-loved books. I learned about the Medici, and years later was able to declaim—with an Italian student on a rowboat on Lake Orta, in front of Lesley—Lorenzo's famous poem. I followed the adventures of Don Camillo and *I Promessi Sposi* before either had become known to English readers. And of course I went to opera after opera after opera, enjoying what went on, not only on the stage, but also in the auditorium. There is drama in Verdi, but there is drama too in the queue that forms up outside the opera house—as indeed there is drama everywhere in Italy whenever two or more Italians are present, be it in a railway carriage or the wilds of the Abruzzi.

Thus did my two loves—for Italians in general and for Hedda in particular—grow side by side steadily stronger, until at last the time arrived when the second felt enough self-confidence to make its first public appearance. Hitherto our meetings had been confined to the villa and to her apartment. Now came the next step. Some military purpose—I entirely forget what—took the company for a week to San Dona di Piave. At the same time a need to call on her university took Hedda to Venice. And there we met. There in Venice, where we were both unknown and so unlikely to bump into friends, we first perambulated the streets arm in arm. There in Venice we shyly but proudly proclaimed to the world around us that she was my girl and I her man.

What young man does not feel that his love is unique? What middle-aged man does not look back on his first romance with exquisite pleasure, but at the same time with the realization that every other middle-aged man can do exactly the same? The only thing that was unique about my love for Hedda was that up to then I had never even remotely experienced such sensations. The emotions themselves were ordinary enough: I loved being with her, being close to her, feeling that she was a part of me and I a part of her, proud to feel that someone so lovely was mine. And as the bond between us strengthened, so the future became more certain. Yes, we would marry—one day, when I had established myself in a job and had a home to which I could invite her. Understandably she needed that, and only when I had provided it would I feel that I had proved myself and earned my reward. Yes, I would labor for her; but not for seven years as Jacob had for Rachel, or as I would need to if I were to become an architect. I couldn't exist that long without her. Two years at most was all I could wait.

Cambridge wanted me back. It seemed silly—and here I agreed

with my father—having gotten so far, not to go on and get my degree. But a degree in what? Apparently all I needed, after war service had been taken into account, was a year's residence followed by a single part in any tripos. What tripos? Mathematics was out, and none of the related subjects interested me in the least. So it had to be something I could tackle from scratch and scrape through after a bare eight months of study (for term started in October and exams were in May). There seemed to be only one possibility: English literature. I had not specially enjoyed English at school. But then what had it amounted to? Swatting up Cobbett's *Rural Rides* and *Macbeth* for the School Certificate, reading Shakespeare aloud in class (and praying that I would not be given a part), parsing, précis writing, a weekly essay. Surely this was not English literature. Surely more important was my love of Dickens and Hardy. I hoped so. And since the only purpose of my taking a degree was to be able to call myself a graduate, I also hoped it wouldn't matter too much if all I got was a Third. Then, armed with my Degree, I would find myself some sort of job, perhaps one involving a bit of writing, and then—yes, *then*—she would join me.

And meanwhile? Should we become officially engaged? I, impulsive, was willing. She, wiser, was not.

Was there ever the possibility of anything more deeply rooted and lasting than the pleasure we got from each other's letters, from sitting side by side on a sofa, from a shared love of Beethoven? I doubt it. The one great difference between us, that she was Italian and I English, obscured a host of minor differences. Perhaps this would always be so and the minor differences would never matter. Or perhaps one by one they would emerge and come between us. Already, even in the first flush of love, I was aware of some of them.

It was in Venice. We had agreed on the time. We had agreed on the place. I forget now what the time was, only that I was there a quarter of an hour earlier in case she should be early too. But I could show you the place, at the far end of the Piazza San Marco. There I stood; there I paced up and down with ever-growing anxiety while clock bells chimed out the passage of time. I knew where she was staying, for I had delivered her safely back there the evening before. And Laura was with her; so that if anything disastrous had happened between then and now, surely Laura would have come to tell me. Yet all the same I was anxious. Perhaps she had been taken suddenly ill. Perhaps she had not told Laura where our meeting was to be. . . . Another chime. She was now an hour late, a whole hour. Fear and anger in fierce competition with each other were boiling up inside me. And then I saw her. . . .

Oh, familiar emotions! The flood of relief so quickly drowned by the flood of anger, and then the lingering resentment that she should have done this deliberately. I was good at being resentful; I was well able to remain silently furious for the rest of that wretched day. Of course in the end I relented. Of course in the end our affections were restored and indeed seemed even greater as a result, as if the bond between us had been tested and the very testing had given it added strength. And yet, in the turmoil of my emotions, a tiny seed of doubt had been sown.

Never before in my life had I needed to understand the feelings and emotions that governed the life of another person. If someone behaved in a certain way, they just did, and that was that. If I would have behaved in a different way, it was because I was a different person. That was that and it didn't greatly matter. But with Hedda it did matter. It did matter that she should have deliberately chosen to cause me pain and ruin our afternoon together. I did need to know why. And so I needed to build a kind of working model of our relationship that I could study and make sense of; and in the end the model I made pictured her as a wild pony and me as its trainer. Gradually I was taming the pony, but with its taming came the loss of its freedom, and every now and then it would rebel, and just as I thought it was mine, it would kick up its heels and gallop away. But it would come back and I would try again, and one day it would submit and I would have succeeded, and then it would be mine forever. That was how we were: she the pony, I the trainer; and it raised a question. Was I a pony trainer by nature?

The answer was no. She groped for a word to describe what I lacked and came up with two: *noncuranza* and *disinvoltura.* And I have to grope a little to find the English equivalents of what she meant. Self-confidence, nonchalance, an easy manner but with a slight hint of superiority and superciliousness, the manner that in a restaurant needs only a raised forefinger to bring waiters hurrying across to you, that in a queue automatically finds you at the front without anyone quite knowing how you got there. I knew what she meant. I had met it in Germans.

Perhaps in my smart officer's uniform I had looked more the masterful husband she needed, the husband she and others could admire and respect. Perhaps therefore when I made my promised reappearance in March 1947, but now wearing grey flannel trousers and a tweed jacket, she began to have doubts. We met in Venice. We had made no particular plans. Perhaps we might stay in Venice, perhaps go to Bolzano: we could decide when we met, and the decision was really hers. We met, and her decision was to return to Trieste, where she could introduce me to her various friends and relatives: this she felt was the proper thing to do. And because there wasn't a spare bedroom in her apartment, she had found me a nice hotel. "You don't mind, do you? After all, we will be spending the rest of the day together." I only minded a little bit and tried not to show it.

So we traveled to Trieste by train; and since I was now a civilian and the town was still occupied by Allied troops, I had to acquire an entry permit. She knew where I had to go to get it, and together we went; and it was just as such places always were in those days, a milling crowd of Italians and somewhere out of sight in the distance an official behind a desk taking no notice of them. The perfect situation for testing one's *disinvoltura.* "Say you are English and go up to the front . . . of *course* you can . . . of *course* you must . . . of *course* it's all right . . . you'll never get your pass if you don't. *Please* . . . to make me proud of you." So I had to. "*Permesso . . . Scusi . . . Inglese . . .*" I muttered my passwords and edged my way forward. It worked. As the waters of the Red Sea had fallen back on either side to allow the

Children of Israel to pass through, so did the flood of gesticulating, chattering, *documenti*-clutching Italians give way before the Englishman, and I passed dry-shod to the man at the desk. The Englishman secured his permit, honor was satisfied, praise was awarded, smiles returned; but I suspect that we both knew that the Englishman who had pushed his way to the front of the queue was not I. And so, although my visit was a happy one, and although when I said good-bye to her we were outwardly as confident about the future as we had ever been, I think inwardly we both wondered if we would ever meet again.

We didn't. For another six months we continued to write to each other, and I continued to think of her as my fiancée. Then, without too much heartbreak and with no ill-feeling, it came to an end.

I last heard from her on May 7 the following year. It was one of a number of letters I received around that time from various of my friends. For sentimental reasons I kept them all, and so I kept hers; and the other day, thinking I might find it there still, I looked, and there it was, the last to reach me and so at the bottom of the pile.

A te e a Lesley i sensi della mia più viva simpatia e auguri vivissimi per il vostro fidanzamento avvenuto al 17 aprile.

(To you and to Lesley my warmest affection and best wishes on your engagement announced on April 17.)

To discover what you are, you must also discover what you are not. To learn what sort of husband you might make, you must learn what sort of husband you can never make. Hedda taught me this. She taught me a lot of things: about Italy, about Italians, about women, about love, about myself. She even succeeded in teaching me the two-step. She helped to loosen the bonds that tied me to my father, and she prepared me for new bonds, bonds that have tied me now for nearly thirty years in a happiness that I could never have found with her.

On July 24, 1948, I married Lesley.

* * * * *

TWENTY-TWO

Downward—
The Road to Work

On a May morning in 1947 I made my way to the offices of the Cambridge University Appointments Board to begin my search for a career.

What sort of a job had I in mind? I really had no idea and hoped they would make suggestions. I could list my various qualifications—a good scholarship in mathematics followed by a bad degree in English literature—it was up to them, I hoped, to tell me in what direction they pointed. There was only one direction I would utterly refuse to consider. I would not, could not, become a teacher. Teaching meant talking, and my voice was still not to be trusted.

Just as every seed has somewhere written inside it the most exact details of the plant it will eventually become, so it must be with the human being. We may carry our hopes with us to the grave, but often it will be like hoping that the apple tree will one day produce a crop of plums. No doubt a perspicacious interviewer could have read it all in the young man who sat before him, and no doubt my interviewer did in fact read a lot of it. But would it have helped if he had told me what he saw?

When one is twenty-six and in love, a year is a lifetime, and it was just as well I did not know what lay ahead of me: that it would be four years before I found a career I was going to be happy in, that this career would be in bookselling, and that I would have to wait nearly thirty years before my own first book got into print.

So my interviewer was tactful, and I came away confident that before long something would turn up, something that, in some modest fashion, would blend Newton with Shakespeare. Though there might not be many such jobs, there were surely not many graduates who could rival my particular qualifications. The road to the mountaintop had entered the forest. It was a little hard to be sure exactly where it was leading, but never mind: it was going uphill, and I strode happily along.

A couple of months later I was in London in a bed-sitter. The hunt was now on in earnest. The first application forms had been filled in, and shortly afterward the first letters of regret had been received. And so it was thought (meaning that my father thought and I agreed) that I ought to move to where the prospects were brightest, where interviews would be a bus ride rather than a train journey away. So I said good-bye to Cotchford and left home. And among the few possessions I took with me was my typewriter. I would need it for writing letters, of course, but I would also need it if, in the intervals between interviews, I tried to write other things as well.

"I want to be a writer." I suppose I had said that first at the age of eight or thereabouts, and I had certainly said it again at the age of twenty-five, while I was in Trieste. What is a writer? If I were asked now, I would say that he is half of a partnership, the other half being enough readers to keep the first half in business. In those days I might have answered more naively that a writer was someone who wanted to be a writer. So I sat at my table in my bed-sitter and wondered what to write about.

Another definition of a writer might be that he is someone who transforms experience into words. He can either do this very rapidly, as a reporter does at a soccer match, or he can digest his experience more slowly and more thoroughly, as does a novelist. At the age of twenty-seven I possessed neither a stock of experiences on which to draw nor the ability to go out into the world and seek new ones. I wished to write in the privacy of my room—and I had nothing to write about. So I wrote about nothing. After all, this was what, forty years earlier, my father had done, and done both well and successfully.

I tapped away at airy nothings, sent them off, and got them back. First, study your market: this, of course, is the golden rule, and if I had done so, I would have seen that I was living in the past. In 1947, as far as light articles were concerned, there was no market to study: current tastes and the paper shortage had seen to that.

Then came my first job. It was with the Central Office of Information, the civilian heir to the wartime Ministry of Information. The first Labour government was in power, grappling with the first of the succession of economic crises that have plagued government after government ever since. "The balance of payments," "higher productivity," "fair shares for all," "the nation's housekeeping"; the phrases were fresh in those days, and the problem seemed simple enough, the remedy obvious. All that was necessary (so we thought) was to ensure that everybody knew and understood. So speakers were sent out, and wherever they could find an audience—in factory, canteen, or parish hall—and whenever they could make their voices heard above the clatter of machinery, knives, or knitting needles, they would explain it all in simple, homely terms. The words were theirs; the facts and figures were ours. This was the work of my section and I enjoyed it. And since I was occasionally allowed to attend government press conferences, I had the added bonus of being able to boast of encounters with cabinet ministers, and this made me feel pleasantly important.

So I was happy: happy, that is to say, while I was busy. But gradually the work began to run out. Whether this was because our speakers were themselves the victims of the austerity they urged on others, or because one crisis was so like the next that the same speech served them all, I cannot now remember. All I do remember is increased periods of idleness; and it was then that I learned—if I had not already learned it—how hateful it is to have too little to do.

At first it was pleasant to alternate between work and idleness. Both were welcome, the one providing a relief from the other. But gradually I began to resent the work. The less there was, the more I resented the fact that there was so little, and so resented even the little that came my way. At first the crosswords I did, the papers I read, and the letters I wrote were all done a little guiltily, a little surreptitiously. Later they were done ostentatiously, provocatively, defiantly. And included among those later letters—and giving me particular pleasure in that they were written during office hours—were answers to advertisements, applications for other jobs.

I joined the John Lewis Partnership early in 1949. John Spedan Lewis, the chairman, had great faith in the product of our universities; so my degree in English literature undoubtedly helped, but my chief qualification—as it had been when I joined the army—was my carpentry. For it was as a trainee furniture buyer (or possibly furniture designer) that I was engaged. Indeed there were several similarities between 1949 and 1941. Another was that my training did not aim to fit me for a specific appointment, but merely to give me all-around experience and competence; and yet another was that I started in the ranks.

So on the appointed day I reported to Mr. Jackson, manager of the Lampshade Department at Peter Jones, and thus found myself doing— for the first time perhaps, but not, as will be seen, for the last—the one thing I had vowed that I would *never* do. A year or two previously I had gone into the electrical department of a big store to buy a lightbulb, and while waiting to be served by a young man elegantly dressed in black jacket and striped trousers, I had myself been mistaken for a shop assistant by an old lady wanting a vacuum cleaner. That was when I made my vow.

Was it just his clothes? Certainly the clothes we wear have a powerful effect on our personalities, and so on our relationship with one another. The army realizes this when it dresses its troops in uniform and then allows its officers a rather smarter uniform. Dictators realize it when they give jackboots to their supporters and remove the suspenders of their enemies. The king is more kingly under his crown, the fool more foolish in his ill-fitting trousers. How great a transformation can one achieve in this way? Can any fool, suitably dressed, become a king? Could I, in black and grey, have walked the soft-carpeted floors of Harrods with confidence and poise? Probably not. Clothes can accentuate: I doubt if they can change. The seed, the potential, must be there in the first place.

So, as the elegantly dressed young man handed me my lightbulb, I was conscious of a vast gulf between us, a gulf that could, of course, have been summed up by that single, haunting, Italian word, *disinvoltura*. I felt it then acutely. What is odd is that I didn't feel it at all during my first day at Peter Jones. Instead I felt only my feet.

I enjoyed selling lampshades. I enjoyed the companionship of my fellow assistants: they were a cheerful, friendly lot. And I enjoyed serving customers. Altogether it was a good and happy start to my new career.

There is no need to retrudge every step I took from department to department during my year and a half with John Lewis. I can list about fifteen of them, which would seem to indicate that I spent about a month with each. I can't think it was anywhere near as long, so perhaps there are some I have forgotten. I learned a lot, most of it at one time or another to come in useful. I learned many practical things—though not, alas, by practicing them, for I was never allowed to do, only to watch. Watching the expert throw a handful of tacks into his mouth and then bring them forward one at a time between his lips, I learned how to upholster a sofa. I learned how to make slipcovers—and later put theory into practice on our own armchair at home. I learned how to French-polish, how to make curtains, how to paint straight lines—and the lines that still decorate the chest of drawers in our bedroom today are testimony to that particular lesson and to my enthusiasm at the time.

I learned how curtains were hung and valences fixed, and accompanied the hangers and fixers as they went from house to house, and occasionally ("Here's something for the boy") picked up a tip when the job was done. And I learned—though I've yet to find a use for these particular skills—how to apply gold leaf, and how, with a feather dipped in paint, one can imitate the effect of marble. In a different field, I learned how secondhand furniture was bought, and I accompanied buyers on their visits both to private houses and to auction rooms. I helped myself to books from the partnership library and learned about Chippendale, Hepplewhite, and Regency. I visited two factories near High Wycombe and watched machine tools in action: to excellent effect at one, to appalling effect at the other. I read *Partnership for All* and was as favorably impressed by what Spedan Lewis was trying to do as I was unfavorably impressed by the way he wrote. But of all the things I did and saw, the most important of them all came when I was told to design a dining room suite.

I wonder if the departmental manager who gave me this particular task realized at the time how totally unequipped I was to tackle it. At home I had made small pieces of furniture—stools, shelves, and so on—and I had altered and repaired larger pieces. But I had never *designed* anything in my life; that is to say, I had never taken pencil and paper first and made a drawing. My furniture making started with a plank of wood and a saw. Consequently, not only did I not know how to make a scale drawing; I had no idea of the sort of shapes, proportions, and dimensions that were appropriate to chairs and tables. Though I might have been able to measure and copy, without a pattern to follow I was helpless.

This must have been all too obvious to him as soon as he saw my efforts. He made little comment. What was there to say? Instead he lent me a book to read, a large and beautiful picture book of modern furniture; and from the moment I opened it I began to have a feeling for furniture that I had never possessed before, a feeling that could perhaps be summed up by the word *love*.

Up to then I had "liked" the furniture my parents had in London. It was mostly old, Italianate, and painted with gay floral themes (for my mother hated what she called "brown wood"); and I had liked the rather more rustic furniture we had at Cotchford. I didn't specially like, but I was beginning to know something about, the various secondhand pieces we sold at John Lewis, and I knew that I disliked most of what we sold in our new-furniture departments. Then I opened my book and for the first time met Gimson, Waal, and Barnsley. For the first time I saw beauty—not just prettiness—in proportion, in shape, and in the very nature of the wood itself, and I saw this flowing from something that had its source in a rural past where beauty lay not in ornament but in simplicity. I saw twentieth-century inspiration coming not from the nineteenth but from the sixteenth century. But in 1949, this newfound love was virtually confined to illustrations in books. Outside books, in shops generally and in John Lewis in particular, "secondhand" meant eighteenth and very early nineteenth century, and "new" meant either "repro," with its stained wood and cabriole legs, or "contemporary," splay-legged and pale. Furniture design was at its lowest ebb. Only in the Craft Centre near Piccadilly could I see on exhibition individual pieces of furniture: handmade, beautifully designed, and following in the tradition of those early twentieth-century masters.

It was at the age of eight that I first learned the pleasure of handling tools, finding in wood something satisfying to cut and shape. It was at John Lewis that I discovered the added pleasure that could come from good design. There was pleasure in the making: this I knew. There was beauty in the shape and in the material: this I now discovered. I won't pretend that I went home and set to work on my own dining room suite: I've yet to do that. It was just that where before there was a single seedling growing, now there were two.

These were the things I learned about the world around me. But I also learned something about myself. I learned that, much as I might enjoy myself with a chisel and a plane, even with a hammer and a mouthful of tacks, I would never be at home in John Lewis. It was as it had been at the Officer Cadet Training Unit during the war: I impressed my various departmental managers as little as I had impressed my officer instructors, and for almost exactly the same reasons. Like Hedda, they too had a word for it. It caught my eye as I glanced at one of their reports: a French word this time. *Gauche.* Just as I had felt ill at ease in Service Dress, so would I have felt ill at ease in a Business Suit. Service Dress was obligatory, the Business Suit optional. They urged me to buy one, but I never did: and this in itself probably told them all they needed to know—that I was unable to become one of them, that I would always remain an outsider. The shop assistant—poised, polished, and self-assured—from whom, years before, I had bought my lightbulb, did in fact typify what I would never be. I imagine that this was blindingly obvious; and I don't suppose that Spedan Lewis, when he sat down to dictate his letter to me, had a moment's hesitation. It was not a letter that I welcomed at the time: nobody likes to be given the sack. Gratitude came later, when I had found what I was looking for and realized what a stony path I had escaped from.

His letter was waiting on the mat when Lesley and I arrived home after a holiday spent in France. In spite of the fact that this holiday had been punctuated (or rather I had been punctuated) by a succession of boils under my left arm, it was, and remained, one of our happiest and most memorable. And this was fortunate, not only because the memory lingered on to warm the bleak days that were to follow. There was another reason. I had gotten the sack. I was out of work. I was beginning to feel that nobody wanted me. I was beginning to lose confidence in myself. There was now no doubt about it: the road was going downhill fast.

From time to time Lesley's parents used to come to London and stay with us in our flat in Chancery Lane. It wasn't just for the pleasure of seeing their daughter that they made the long journey from the Isle of Wight. It was to perform on the BBC. They wrote stories and talks, and from time to time came to London to broadcast them. And so, when the moment arrived, Lesley and I would put one or other of them into a taxi and then, an hour later, switch on the wireless. And as I listened to the familiar voice, so I knew that of all the things I could never summon the courage to do, giving a talk on the BBC headed the list. Reading aloud—whether from Shakespeare in class, from the Bible in chapel, or from a list of names at roll call—was the one thing I had always, determinedly, unashamedly, and usually with very great success, done my utmost to avoid. Reading aloud into a microphone, with the thought that there were thousands listening to me at the other end, would have been the ultimate refinement to the torture.

But this was not to stop me from *writing* a talk. Probably it wouldn't be accepted; and even if it were, no doubt they could arrange for one of their professionals to read it.

During our holiday we had had a small adventure. Setting off on a walk one morning, we had been caught in a violent storm and, seeing a small solitary stone hut ahead of us on the hillside, had hurried toward it. Inside we had found two men and all the apparatus for making and storing cheese. So I wrote a little piece called "The Story of a Cheese" and sent it off to a BBC friend. To my delight it was accepted; to my horror I was invited to read it. "But I can't possibly. I can't read. Couldn't you get someone else to?" His answer was a very firm "No." I looked at Lesley in despair . . . and surely one of the bravest things she has ever done was to offer to read it for me. This she did: she not only read it and read it beautifully, but during the rehearsal they discovered that the script was a couple of minutes too short. So, with the clocks ticking away toward the fatal hour, she wrote an extra paragraph, spliced it in, and polished around the edges so that the join didn't show. The BBC gave us fifteen pounds, and I reckon that her share was about thirteen pounds ten. But we didn't divide it up. Instead we went round to the Craft Centre and had a coffee table designed and made for us by Robin Nance.

If that was Lesley's bravest moment, mine came shortly afterward. Buoyed up by hope, humbled by shame, I wrote another talk—this time about painting a food cupboard. It too was accepted—and I read it myself on "Woman's Hour." I stammered during the rehearsal, but not during the performance. I then wrote—and gave—two more talks.

Such was the sunlit glade in the middle of a very black forest. For when not writing, I was answering advertisements and being interviewed—with total lack of success. Indeed my search at one point took me—unwittingly—to the very brink of that path that so many once-proud ex–army officers had followed on its sad journey from hope to despair: at one point I found myself in the office of the sales manager of a firm of encyclopedia publishers. Kind man: he knew, and he knew that I didn't know, and he sent me away.

Finally, in desperation, I grew a moustache and, after nursing it in private for a day or two, took it out and showed it to the world. It was scarcely visible, being gingery in color, so I darkened it up with some of Lesley's mascara. The moustache marked the nadir in my fortunes; and I find myself now wondering how many moustaches owe their origins to some period of depression in the lives of their owners, and were grown initially more as a gesture of defiance than anything else. Mine lasted a fortnight. It was totally out of character, totally idiotic, but it served its purpose. For with its removal I was able to make a fresh start. I cannot recall exactly the succession of events that led to the decision. "Two roads diverged. . . ." Does the wise man standing at the junction attempt to draw up a balance sheet? I never have. Indeed I dislike making conscious decisions at all. I prefer to wait until either the matter decides itself or instinct prompts me. Just as the right key slips easily into the lock and turns the wards smoothly and sweetly, so, without effort and without forcing, should one know what to do.

On this occasion the two roads were very unequal. I was in my glade. It was either back to the stony track I had left or on through the trees, with scarcely the ghost of a footpath to reassure me that here was a way forward that led anywhere at all. Would I have ventured that way if I had been on my own? I think not. Happily, Lesley was with me. It was a shared conviction that this was the right course that made the decision so easy, so inevitable.

On August 1, 1951, I shook the dust of London off my feet and, clutching our bowl of goldfish, caught the train from Paddington to Kingswear where Lesley, who had gone on ahead, was waiting for me.

TWENTY-THREE

◆ ◆ ◆ ◆ ◆

Lesley de Selincourt

To be socially graceful one must not only say the right thing, but say it at the right time; and this is what I am bad at. The right time comes, but the conversation flows on without the hoped-for lull, and the right thing remains unsaid. It is so often like this with me, and it was like this in the last chapter. Lesley slipped quietly into its pages, and I never properly introduced her. So I must do so now.

In the early days of our marriage, people would ask us: "How did you two first meet?" And I would say: "I invited her to supper. We had dried-egg omelette and chips. I made the omelette. She made the chips." In those days this was an adequate explanation—adequate as far as it went, I mean. Dried-egg powder was to be found on every pantry shelf—and little else. Today I would perhaps need to explain that in 1948 eggs were so scarce that they were known as "shell eggs," and the ration was one a week. No guest would have expected her host to feast her on a fortnight's supply.

Of course I would then go on to add that she was my cousin. This was how I knew of her existence. I knew her address, too; and having nothing better to do at that particular time, I thought it might be interesting to discover what she looked like. So I wrote her a letter.

She was a cousin on my mother's side, a de Selincourt; and de

Selincourts were not always on speaking terms with each other. In particular my mother hadn't spoken to her brother Aubrey for about thirty years. That was why we had never met before. It was my Grandfather's second wife, Nancy, who, in an attempt to bring us together, had given me my cousin Lesley's address.

I was in London, living alone in a flat in Chancery Lane. She was in London, living with a friend in Claverton Street, working in the showroom at the Cambridge University Press. At seven o'clock on Thursday, February 5, 1948, she knocked on my door.

Well, she could certainly fry potatoes: a useful accomplishment. And no doubt, lying in bed that night, she pondered over the fact that I could certainly make dried-egg omelettes. But as she didn't like omelettes, even shell-egg ones, I doubt if this made me immediately more desirable than any of her other young men. Come to that, I wasn't particularly keen on chips. But I had recently taken my farewell of Hedda, and my heart was vacant.

You can use a diary in one of two different ways. You can use it as a journal to record events that have happened; or you can use it as an engagement book to remind you of events that are still to come. I use my diary in the second way. In fact I can think of only one single entry in the past thirty years in which I recorded an event that had already occurred. Nevertheless, dull though they are to reread, limited almost wholly to dentist's appointments, with day after day left blank, I do not like to throw them away at the end of the year, but add them to the growing pile that I keep in my chest of drawers. And it was here that I have just found my diary for 1948, the oldest of them all and unique in that, being a present from Hedda, it is an Italian one.

So I can report that on Thursday, February 12, I had supper with Lesley at Claverton Street; on Sunday, February 15, we went to Kew Gardens; on Monday the sixteenth we went to a play; and on Thursday the nineteenth we met for lunch. Nevertheless it was not really, as this might seem to suggest, love at first sight, but rather the discovery that we liked doing things together. Particularly we liked doing nothing much together.

Although Lesley had an older sister, a four-year gap and a great difference in temperament lay between them. So, like me, she had led the life of a solitary child, and like me she had enjoyed it. We had both of us been brought up in the country, both of us had spent long, happy hours wandering alone through fields and woods, sitting alone under trees, lying alone in the grass. Like me, she preferred animals to humans. Our discovery was that though we were both solitaries, we liked being solitary in each other's company. We enjoyed walking together along a country footpath, we enjoyed sitting together on a sofa, we enjoyed lying together beneath a hedge. Together we were yet separate; touching, yet silent; she and I each engaged with our own thoughts—yet lost and lonely now without the presence of the other.

"Lesley lunch" says my diary. I was working in Baker Street, she in the Euston Road, two stops away on the Tube. If it was sunny, we could take sandwiches into Gordon Square or Regents Park. If it was not so sunny, we could go to a pub near Warren Street Station, where we could get a good meal at a modest price. "Lesley 6.30." This would be at Chancery Lane, of course, so that we could be on our own; and then I would escort her back to Claverton Street on the bus.

On Sunday, March 14, there is a complicated timetable indicating a trip on the Green Line to West Wycombe. On Friday, March 19, there is the entry "W'loo Platform 7, 6.15," indicating my first visit to the Isle of Wight to meet her parents; my first meeting with my Uncle Aubrey. On Saturday, April 10, are the words "Sir Charles Napier Hotel, Spriggs Holly."

Of all the things I enjoyed doing in the country, a longish walk was what I enjoyed most, for not only could I then be a naturalist looking out for interesting birds, I was at the same time an explorer, finding my way. I shared my father's passion for maps and map reading, for planning a route and then following it. The best route was a circular one—

out one way, back another—and as far as possible following footpaths rather than roads. Lesley and I had already discovered the Chilterns on our visit to West Wycombe in March, but the walk had been a short and simple one. It was time to try something more ambitious. If it turned out a success, I might even look upon it as a sort of omen for the future.

The Green Line Bus took us to High Wycombe, and a local bus took us on through West Wycombe to Stokenchurch. From there a footpath led across country to the tiny hamlet of Spriggs Holly. (The Ordnance Survey today spells it "Sprigs Holly." I rather think that in 1948 it was spelt "Sprigs Alley." However, I prefer the spelling I recorded in my diary.) And here—no more than a modest country inn, despite its grand name—was the Sir Charles Napier Hotel. A friend of Lesley's had recommended it. He had recommended well.

The following day, in perfect spring weather, we set out on our walk. I had planned it the evening before, planned it on my own, as I liked to do. I understood maps. Lesley didn't. We set out toward Chinnor Hill in Bledlow Great Wood and made our way to where the ground falls steeply to the valley of the Thames. From there we took a track diagonally down the slope to the village of Bledlow and then by footpaths came to Saunderton. This was the limit of our walk. Of our return journey I am less sure. I know that at one point we came to a wood where the path was indistinct and I was in fear that we might lose our way. And I know that, almost at the end, the path ran up beside another wood toward a gate in a hedge. Beyond the hedge was the road. Once on the road, it was half a mile back to our pub. So we had done it. We were practically home. I looked again at my map to be quite sure and found that the wood we had been walking beside was called Venus Wood. Beyond the gate on the other side of the road was a little corrugated-iron chapel.

Here undoubtedly was the right place and the right time for saying the right thing; and for once I was not going to miss it. I had navigated her through the Chilterns. We had done the entire homeward journey with arms around each other's waists and her head on my shoulder. If I could navigate her so successfully and we could walk like this so happily through the spring countryside, surely we could go on together a little farther.

I stopped just short of the gate and we turned to face each other.

"Will you marry me?" I said.

"Of course I will, darling," she answered.

In my diary on April 11 occurs that retrospective entry, the only one I have ever made. In ink are the words "Got engaged!"

TWENTY-FOUR

✦ ✦ ✦ ✦ ✦

Westward

On March 3, 1951, the following advertisement had appeared in *The Bookseller:*

> PARTNER WANTED: Young man, well educated, with initiative, offered one-third share in West Country bookshop. Ability to drive essential for developing traveling bookshop to remote parts. Home given with some social life. Capital required, minimum £350.

At the end of my long, stony, downward road, here was the signpost, its message the famous and familiar one that had first appeared in the columns of an Indiana newspaper exactly a hundred years earlier: "Go west, young man."

A fortnight later we were in a train heading for the Cotswold Bookroom in Wotton-under-Edge near Gloucester. Dr. Paxton had apologized for the fact that he would not be there to greet us, as he had a christening that afternoon, but his wife would be in the shop and would look after us until his return. *Dr.* Paxton? D.D., presumably. The local vicar? We pictured an elderly clergyman and wondered what sort of books he would want me to drive to remote parts with. . . . So it was a delightful surprise and a great relief to find that the Paxtons were about our age and that he was a prep school master. Not D.D. but

Ph.D. Not christening anybody: being christened himself ("and a great mistake," as he confessed many years later).

Though we never went into partnership with them, John and Joan Paxton were exactly the people we needed to find. The jump that we were eventually to make, from London to Dartmouth, from the security of being employed to the insecurity of being self-employed, was greater than we could have managed on our own. We needed an intermediate stepping-stone and a helping hand. For this the Cotswold Bookroom was ideally placed, almost exactly midway, geographically and metaphorically, between the world we were leaving and the world we were going to. And as for the Paxtons, two kinder and more helpful people, both then and still, we have yet to meet. Though we briefly contemplated the idea of opening a companion shop in the nearby town of Chipping Sodbury, John, who was an economist, knew that there wasn't really enough money in it to support the two of us with no other source of income.

But if the idea came to nothing, it pointed the way ahead. Inspired and encouraged by the Paxtons' enthusiasm, by their evident enjoyment of what they were doing, by what they had already achieved, by their faith in what it was possible for a small-town bookseller to achieve—and indeed by their whole attitude toward life generally—and bearing with us their promises of help and advice whenever we should need it, we returned to London convinced that this was the life for us, that we would snap our fingers at London, and at all those employers who had refused to employ me, and open our own bookshop in a town of our own choosing.

Today the road westward is lined with young people, their belongings on their back, their worldly wealth in their pocket, boldly thumbing their way toward new hope and a fresh start. Where are they bound for? What will they do when they get there? Anywhere! Anything! Were we more timid twenty-five years ago? Had my generation less self-confidence, less optimism? Possibly this is true generally. Certainly it was true of Lesley and myself, and the reason lies partly in our nature and partly in social attitudes. Yes, we were timid and we did lack self-confidence. But at the same time, in those days and even at our level, *noblesse oblige:* which meant that I had to earn a living and earn it in a way that was considered appropriate for someone with a university education. Failure to do this mattered very much. Failure in London was bad enough. To leave London and then to fail would have meant an ignominious return—and that would have been very much worse. An employee can always blame his employer: the self-employed has only himself to blame.

"Really," said my mother some two months later, when I announced our plans, "it does seem a very odd decision." And of course in many ways she was quite right.

In 1945, when my father had suggested to me a career in publishing, I had said what I thought of the business world. Five years later, the business world—in the form of J. Spedan Lewis—had said what it thought of me. The antipathy appeared to be mutual, and it was indeed odd that I should be trying again to do something I both despised and was bad at. But that was not all. There was something even odder in my choice. There were two things that were then overshadowing my life and that I needed to escape from: my father's fame and "Christopher Robin." Yet, here I was apparently deliberately seeking out his shadow so as to work beneath it, choosing a trade that would put me on public exhibition as Christopher Robin, wrapping up the books he had written. Was it that I was deliberately turning to face the dragon that had been pursuing me? I must be honest and confess no such courageous intention. I was running away, all right. I was running away from London.

London was the scene of my father's successes. London was the scene of my failures. Neither Lesley nor I had any love for the place, and every weekend we used to escape into the country. What was there to keep us here? Why should we not make our escape permanent?

"But what made you choose *Dartmouth?*" So often we have been asked this question. Our London friends wondered why we had chosen a place they had never even heard of. Our Dartmouth friends wondered—in our early days, at any rate—why we had chosen a place where the prospects of making a fortune seemed so remote.

Looking back, I still think we chose as intelligently and as carefully as we could. Certainly, as it turned out, we chose extremely well, but equally certainly a large amount of luck came into it. I doubt if any modern "feasibility study" could have offered us a town in which both bookselling and living have been such a pleasure for so many years.

This was how we went about it.

First, an atlas. The whole of England lay before us, but instinctively our eyes turned to the southern half. We were southerners. Cambridge was my northern limit; Oxford, where she had been born, was Lesley's. North of that, despite our Scottish blood, lay foreign country. Anywhere south of London we could feel at home. South of London, yet at the same time well away from London. This sent our eyes westward. Lesley had been brought up in Dorset and the Isle of Wight. Her father had a boat, and from sailing holidays she knew the Dorset and Devon coast. I too had holidayed in Dorset and Devon. Lesley had a special fondness for the sea, and I was very happy to share it with her. A coastal town, therefore, somewhere between Weymouth and Plymouth. Large or small? Small, for choice, to be as different from London as possible, and because there was inevitably going to be a sort of amateurishness, a sort of tweediness, about our shop, that would be out of place in a big town where smart suits were worn. A small seaside town then, a holiday town that would give us a bit of extra business during the summer. A town that didn't already have a good private bookshop. . . .

So first, the atlas to list the towns. Then a gazetteer to tell us their populations. Then a guidebook to describe their appearance. And lastly a classified telephone directory to locate existing bookshops. This gave us about half a dozen possibles. Back to the telephone directory for local estate agents; and finally a dozen letters.

This, when I am asked, is my story. But there is another story I would now like to tell. It is a detective story, and I wrote it during

Christopher Milne and his mother, Daphne, in 1926

Christopher and A. A. Milne in 1926

Christopher and his nanny, Olive Rand, with Pooh.
Piglet in the foreground is a reproduction, larger in size than the original.

Christopher and Pooh in the hollow tree

The original Eeyore, Pooh, Kanga, Piglet, and Tigger, which reside at the Donnell Branch of the New York City Public Library. Owl and Rabbit were entirely fictional; Roo was lost in the Hundred Acre Wood when Christopher Milne was a boy.

The original Winnie-the-Pooh

Poohsticks Bridge in Ashdown Forest, Sussex, England

Christopher Milne in 1971

those bleak days when I was still searching for a London job. The *Evening Standard* was at that time running a series and was welcoming contributions from their readers. They didn't welcome mine, and I resurrect it now, not for its intrinsic merit, which I am prepared to accept is slight, but for a reason which will emerge.

The story was built round an idea, and the idea was this: A murder is to be committed. It is planned to look like an accident. Fate, watching from the wings, decides to lend a hand. Unknown to the villain, his victim meets with exactly the accident that was being prepared for him. The victim dies. The villain of course is innocent. But alas, the ingenious scheme that was designed to make murder look like an accident now makes an accident look like murder. And so the villain is arrested. Ironic—or so I hoped. . . .

I need not fill in the details, except to say three things. First, the victim was to be pushed over a cliff. Second, I wanted a wildflower. And third, I wanted a name.

The flower had to be a rare one, such as one might hope to find growing on cliff tops by the sea. It also had to be an attractive one, such as a keen gardener might wish to dig up to plant in his own garden. So I went to a public library to search through books on wildflowers: and in the end I found just what I wanted: the white rockrose.

The name was the villain's name. I wanted a collection of letters that sounded possible but in fact was not a name at all. And for this I went to the London telephone directory to check that it wasn't there. And the name I failed to find was "Prout."

Soon after our arrival in Dartmouth, I made two discoveries. The rare white rockrose grows on the cliffs at Berry Head. And there were Prouts all round us.

It was almost as if Dartmouth had known all along that we were coming.

TWENTY-FIVE

✦ ✦ ✦ ✦ ✦

Bookselling—
Setting Up Shop

It was of course a big event in our lives, opening a bookshop in the West Country, and one that we might in later years like to look back on, reminding ourselves exactly how we set about it. So I bought myself an exercise book and began keeping a journal.

The exercise book still survives, and in this chapter I record some of my entries.

1951 May 9th
Among all the unlikely premises that we have been offered—the cafés, the fishmonger's shops, the butchers (complete with marble slab), and the guest houses—are three possibles. Two of them are in Brixham and one in Dartmouth. And since Brixham and Dartmouth are neighboring towns, we felt they might be worth a visit. So, leaving Lesley behind—for she is still working—I catch a train from Paddington, arrive at Brixham, and meet Mr. Webster, estate agent. He is short, fat, bow-tied, and exuberant. He takes me to a boardinghouse that is off the road and miles from shops. But never mind. "Brixham is expanding," and there would soon be shops all round me. Sorry! Can't wait—and anyway it's too expensive. Next he offers to show me another boardinghouse "belonging to a lady in the theatrical profession who has been told by her husband to sell out at any price so that they can go touring." However, she is out. So he takes me on a guided tour of

the town, nudging me in the ribs to draw my attention to Brixham's fleet of twenty-seven taxis, to the best grocer's shop in England, to the new car park, etc. "Brixham," he assures me, "is fast coming to the fore!" I mention that I am going on to Dartmouth tomorrow. "Dartmouth!" he cries in horror. "Dartmouth is *dead!*" He takes me to my hotel and we part. After supper I call on the actress. Nice house—but it is a shop I'm wanting.

May 10th

I meet Thomas John, estate agent. He shows me a place but advises against it. "Position is everything for your business," he says; and I'm sure he's right. Then he tells me that a baby-linen shop in a better position might be closing down. He goes to find out, while I walk along the cliffs in the sun. On my return he tells me it is indeed closing, "but the owner won't be hustled." I leave Brixham, catching a bus an hour later than I had intended.

The bus takes me to Kingswear, and I stand on the ferry slip looking across the river to my first view of Dartmouth sparkling in the sunshine on the other side. A dead town? From here it could hardly look more inviting. I cross on the car ferry, walk along a narrow street—and there on the corner facing me is the very place I have come to see. What a position! I call on Victor Newton, estate agent, and he tells me that the owner waited until eleven o'clock but has now gone out and won't be back until seven-thirty. We go to inspect. It is called Fairfax Sports and is as crammed with goods as a stall on market day, so that what you don't trip over on the floor you bump your head against hanging from the ceiling; all of which makes it seem smaller and darker than it probably really is. We arrange to meet again at seven-thirty, and I go exploring. There are one or two stationers that sell a few books but, as we had guessed, W. H. Smith is the only genuine bookshop: so that's all right. I wander through the narrow streets and then down to the sea and feel very happy. I like it all: town, river, sea, hills, woods, position of shop, and its price. Strolling along a narrow lane, I notice a blackbird's nest and then a hedge sparrow's: a good omen?

Supper, booked for seven o'clock, doesn't arrive until seven-fifteen. I bolt it but even so am ten minutes late for my appointment; and in those ten minutes another prospective buyer has slipped in before me. So Newton and I have to stand outside in the road; I in an agony of suspense and cursing myself that this is the second appointment I have made and missed. At last the door opens and a man comes out. We hurry in. What is the position? He likes it, we are told, and he is prepared to buy freehold, goodwill, and stock for £5,000 . . . but . . . And it is this "but" that makes my firm offer of £3,500 for freehold alone acceptable. No time to consult my solicitor. No time to arrange a survey. No time even to bring Lesley down to see it. I must decide *now*—or risk losing it. Help! So I ring her up. "I've got to give an answer straight away." And two hundred miles away a faint voice answers: "I leave it to you. If you like it, we'd better have it." Half an hour later Montague has summoned his solicitor and the three of us are in the kitchen signing documents, while Mrs. Montague is at the sink and younger Montagues come and go with a great shouting and banging of doors. . . . What a way to buy a bookshop! I go to bed with my head in a whirl.

May 18th

A hectic day, beginning at 9:45 with my BBC talk, "My Ascent of Mont Blanc" (a Petit Mont Blanc in the Haute Savoie, one that we had discovered on our honeymoon), and followed at twelve o'clock by our journey to Dartmouth. This time we both go. The train takes us to Kingswear, and then we cross the river by boat to Dartmouth station on the other side. It is not quite Lesley's first visit. She came once in her father's boat on a sailing holiday many years ago. All the same, I am nervous she might not approve of the shop. Luckily she does. We call on the Montagues, look around, and ask a hundred questions. At the back of the shop is a dark and curious room which we can use as an office. Next door, and belonging to us, is a separate shop rented to an electrician. On the first floor and reached by a *very* narrow staircase are two rooms. On the right a dining room/kitchen, a pleasant room with a glimpse of the river at the end of the road from one window, and from another a view up a hill toward distant woods. This is really their living room. Next door to it, on the left, is what I suppose would be called their front parlor, respectably furnished with a three-piece suite but clearly never used—not even for the signing of contracts! Upstairs are two bedrooms and a bathroom; and, at a bend on the stairs, no bigger than a cupboard and obviously put in as an afterthought, is the lavatory. Decoration is dreadful: dark-green paint, dadoes, and jazzy wallpaper. Altogether there's masses to be done, and we decide to get builders to tackle the outside. I'll do the inside. Shop first, of course: the awful wallpaper and paint upstairs will have to wait their turn. I call on Michelmores, the builder I had been recommended, and arrange for them to send us an estimate.

May 24th

Visit Longhurst's bookshop in High Holborn and ask them if they would like an unpaid assistant for a few days. They wouldn't, and suggest I try the great Mr. Wilson of Bumpus. So I call there a little nervously, but he is nice and allows me to look around and take notes—provided I don't tell anybody who I am or what I'm doing.

May 25th

List-making at Bumpus's.

May 31st

In reply to our letters, several publishers have now sent us catalogues; one or two have written; Blackie has refused to open an account with us; Customs and Excise have given helpful advice about Purchase Tax. A letter from Richard Bell says: "I think it is very brave of you at the present time, . . . " and I suppose that by "brave" he really means "rash" or possibly even "foolish." The other day I called on Alan White of Methuen. He was pleasant and friendly, of course, but he too talked about "these difficult times." On the whole, however, people are enthusiastic, almost envious. And certainly the idea of a little shop by the sea does sound very attractive. It will be hard work—but who cares?

We have now examined many bookshops both for their stock and for the way they display it. I have made what I think is a good list of basic stock; and I have designed some display stands and have ideas about shelving. Today I made a model of our window fixtures, which was useful as it showed up one or two faults.

June 15th

We have continued our listing. Going round bookshops and trying not to look too suspicious, we have completed our subject lists. These we have now rearranged, under publishers, giving us a fair idea of what we will be wanting to buy from each. I have also planned our shelves, calculated total length, and thus reached an approximate figure for the total value of books we can stock. Lesley and I then independently divided this up into the money to be allocated to each subject—and reached almost exactly the same answers. The actual shelves are a problem. I went to a timber merchant in the Euston Road and learned that for most wood you need to have a permit. Would I be able to get one in Dartmouth? I decided not to take the risk and bought 230 feet of off-permit French poplar. Add it to the existing shelving I'm buying off Montague, and we'll have enough.

It seems to be generally agreed that one can't survive on books alone. So we have decided to sell a few "fancy goods" (awful expression) as well—some of which I hope to make myself. Bookends, for instance. Today I made a cigarette box. It took about six hours but should eventually take much less—say four.

Lesley stops work today—I mean resigns from her job—and we celebrate with a bottle of wine.

✦ ✦ ✦ ✦ ✦

July 15th

We have now finished our tour of publishers. From some we just collected catalogues; at others we talked to sales managers. All were kind and helpful. One or two gave advice, urging us not just to sit in our shop waiting for customers to come to us, but to go out and find them. Terms vary. Most publishers only give you 33⅓ percent discount if you order two copies of a book; a few, like Collins, allow 33⅓ percent on single copies; while a few want you to order three or even *six* copies. Some asked for references, others didn't bother. Some had showrooms, others not.

After two rather exhausting weeks of this, we visited the Paxtons again for a few days, learning a bit more about all the paperwork we are going to have to grapple with; learning also something about secondhand books, which we might decide to sell. Then we went to France for a quick holiday: probably our last for many years.

July 30th

Lesley has departed for Dartmouth and I am alone with our packing. Our stock orders have now all been sent off. Mysteriously we left out Churchill's *The Hinge of Fate* and—of all books—one published by Batsford called *Dartmouth*. However, this has now been put right. Michelmores, for all their friendliness, never sent us our estimate, so we have written to another builder called Watts. We have at last been officially "recognized" by the book trade. (Without recognition we couldn't have gotten trade terms.) We have met the secretary of the Booksellers Association, who happened to be a friend of our neighbor Felix Barker. And with John Wilson of Bumpus and Christina Foyle agreeing to be our sponsors, we found ourselves members of the Booksellers Association by return of post.

(If it is wondered how we were able to enlist as sponsors two of the most eminent booksellers in the country, the explanation is that my father wrote to them. These were the last two letters he was to write on my behalf. For the past twelve years he had been watching, helping where help was wanted, occasionally very gently urging, and on the whole, I think, approving. And I was conscious of his presence in the background, not always willing to take him into my confidence, but grateful for his help when it came. When we left for Devon the last frail tie that bound me to him was broken. My pilot had turned back and I was on my own.)

August 15th
We have now been here two weeks—though it doesn't seem like it. The move was successful though exhausting. Lesley left two days ahead of me and found poor Mrs. Montague waist-deep in chaos. The chaos at Chancery Lane was only ankle-deep; and I threw away a lot of it to the accompaniment of comments from Mrs. Roberts, our caretaker. The moving men were very good. The foreman's brother-in-law kept tropical fish, and this established an immediate bond between us. At three-thirty, I and our own fish caught the Paddington train.

The furniture arrived the following day, and virtually none of it could get up our staircase. So after some discussion it was decided to remove the dining room window, park the van beneath it, haul the stuff up onto the roof of the van, and then pass it through the window. This, the foreman explained to me, would be *very heavy work*, and it would have been much easier if they had gone to get a block and tackle. But this would have cost me *a lot extra*. I got the message.

The shop has vast windows, and, working inside, one feels terribly naked and exposed. So my first task was to whitewash them over. "What are they doing that for?" a small child asks its mother; and two boys pressed their faces to the glass while I painted smaller and smaller circles around their noses. Privacy at last! My second task was to get rid of all Montague's thumbtacks and crepe paper. Never was a shop so full of both, so that in a little while what had seemed emptiness was knee-deep in the stuff, and the soles of our shoes were studded all over. After that, soap and water. Then grey distemper. The grey goes quite nicely with the existing not-too-bad yellow ceiling. Then shelves and stands. Lesley and I slave away inside. Watts has sent an estimate for the outside but has not yet started work.

August 24th

Today Lesley removes our protective whitewash and, though still closed, we are visible to the outside world in all our glory. Faces peer in. Mostly children and old ladies. Two boys ask, "Is this going to be a library?" "No," says Lesley, "a bookshop." And she almost adds, "I'm afraid." "We can buy books?" "Yes." "Oo—oo—oo!" and they hug each other and dance a jig. An old man enquires of the world, "Is this a free lending library?" and gets no reply. We put on our window lights after dark and go out to inspect ourselves. What a nice-looking shop! Pity it is still nameless, however. Watts has managed to finish our painting in time but has not yet produced our store sign.

The other day came a letter from Enid Blyton, saying she had heard we were opening a bookshop, and enclosing her catalogue. It lists over two hundred of her books, coming from twenty different publishers. What a woman!

I wrote back to remind her that very many years ago she had presented me with a copy of *The Enid Blyton Book of Bunnies,* which in the end I almost knew by heart; and I asked if she would care to send a photograph of herself to go in our window. In reply I received three photographs, the latest version of her *Book of Bunnies,* two letters, and a postcard.

Across the street is a newsagent, stationer, and—yes—bookseller! with a small stock of children's books and paperbacks to prove it. Inside it is dark and gloomy, and behind a counter, scarcely visible in the twilight, stand two elderly, gloomy men. They never smile at me. They never even speak. Just hand me my *News Chronicle* and take my money. Oh, dear! Are they bitter about our arrival here? Are we going to be *enemies?* Will there be war between us? Thus were we imagining it; and then yesterday one of them came up to me and said: "I want to wish you the best of luck." And he really meant it. How easy it is to misjudge people.

How easy too to misjudge buildings. Ours, because it looked so smooth and square, I imagined to have been built between the wars, built of brick and plastered over. Inside, Montague's decorations somehow reinforced this impression. How wrong I was I discovered when attempting to peel off some of his wallpaper. Underneath was more wallpaper, and underneath yet more, layer under layer going back through the decades. I peeled away, expecting eventually to reach solid brick—and instead came to the outside world. Help! I hurriedly replaced it all and resolved never again to probe too deeply. We are in fact a very old building. Our front wall is "half-timbered," wooden frame with lath and plaster on either side. Where the plaster is soft and crumbling, you can put a knife right through.

Percy Russell brought us a letter today. He is the author of *Dartmouth*, the Batsford book we so nearly didn't buy. He wrote to wish us luck, implying that we would need it, for Dartmouth, he said, was not an easy town to make money in. This letter, coupled with a long article in our local paper about the town's declining population and prosperity, left us momentarily depressed. But soon we cheered up, for now we can imagine ourselves as Dartmouth's saviors. The worse things are, the greater is the challenge, the greater the scope for improvement. Can the Milnes bring new life to a decaying town? No harm in dreaming so.

August 25th

At nine o'clock, without ceremony though with trousers newly pressed, the Harbour Bookshop opens its doors. We had sent letters to several of Dartmouth's leading citizens (though not necessarily their most enthusiastic book buyers); we had put an advertisement in the local paper (and their reporter had come around for an interview); and that was about it. At nine-fifteen we have our first customer, who buys a couple of "Thrift" books. Then nothing until around ten-thirty, when there is a sudden influx of shoppers, mostly locals, and business is brisk. "How nice to see a really good bookshop," they say. "What a wonderful collection of books." And the children say "Oo Mummy, aren't they lovely!" Two little girls spend hours looking at everything, occasionally glancing at us and then telling each other "not to spoil the nice books"—to show how well-behaved they are being. Several people introduce themselves. Will we remember their names when next we see them? They are all complimentary and kind and make us feel welcome to their town. Our sales include three copies of *The River Dart*, two Mazo de la Roches, several Zodiac Books, and lots of Swiss flower cards. At five-thirty. tired but happy, we close our doors and count our takings. Twelve guineas. Not bad for a start!

✦ ✦ ✦ ✦ ✦

TWENTY-SIX

Not Just Books

Secondhand Books

In the early 1950s you could walk around almost any small town, and if you kept your eyes above shopwindow level, you would have no difficulty in finding a bookseller. Lower your eyes and you would most probably discover that he was selling not books but stationery or toys or tobacco or fancy goods. No doubt he had started off with books on his shelves and good intentions in his heart; but over the years the "other goods" had crept in, proved more popular, proved more profitable, and gradually elbowed their way along, until in the end all that remained of the bookshop was a revolving stand of paperback thrillers and romances or (at Christmastime) a pile of children's annuals: that—and a store sign which for one reason or another ignored the changing scene within.

We knew that we too would have to sell "other goods," but we were determined that—when eventually Mr. Watts produced it—*our* store sign would announce not only what we were but what we would always be: booksellers. So if this chapter is about all the other things that from time to time we sold or did, it is just to get them out of the way, so that bookselling can then have an uninterrupted chapter all to itself.

The obvious accompaniments to new books were of course secondhand books. Indeed many people, hearing that we were to become booksellers, assumed that by this we meant secondhand booksellers. Also it gave our parents a chance to help us on our way with various unwanted volumes from their own shelves. These gleanings—our opening stock—traveled down with us in the furniture van. However, it was not until the end of September that we made our first and most important purchase and felt justified in adding the words "and Secondhand Booksellers" to our visiting card. At a local auction we acquired three sackloads of books, bore them home, tipped them out onto the dining room floor, and crouched down to inspect them.

They were all old. To our inexperienced eye most of them seemed to have little but their age to recommend them. Among them were some Bibles, very large and heavy, and these were our first problem; for it seemed as wrong to price them at a few pennies each—which we thought was all we were likely to get for them—as it was to put them out with the trash; and so in the end we offered them to the vicar. Then there were half a dozen rather more attractive-looking volumes published between 1750 and 1850; and finally there was an atlas of the world published in 1815 and a book of Victorian fashion plates. It was Lesley who recognized this last as our winner. And here we met our second problem: how could we discover its value? Was it worth five pounds or twenty? We sought in vain for advice. In the end we just made a guess, advertised it in the appropriate trade paper, and from the number of booksellers who wrote to us (one of them even sending a cable from America), realized that we had guessed too low.

Nevertheless our small investment had shown us a very good profit, and with such beginner's luck we were encouraged to continue. So we went to auctions and we were invited to private houses, and it was exciting, because you never knew what you might find. But always there remained this problem that with the better books we had no means of knowing how much we ought to offer or how much hope to get. Another difficulty was that, as we had no car, we had to rely on bus and muscle to get our purchases home. So a complete set of Waverley novels from a house at the top of the town or a miscellaneous

collection of rather battered and smelly children's books from an iso-
lated cottage on the other side of the river really did earn the modest
price we sold them for when the effort of transport had been taken into
account. However, in those days we were young and strong, and the
buses ran more frequently than they do today. And in fact it was the
people who brought books to us that were the greater trial: the frail old
ladies who had struggled across the ferry bearing treasures that were
surely worth a fortune, for they had been in the family so long and the
ss's were like *ff*'s. Could I bring myself to say that they were worth
practically nothing? Did they really have to cart them all the way
home again—with the day's shopping too, *and* in the rain? So in the
end I usually paid a price which, though very much less than had
been hoped for, was also very much more than I reckoned they were
worth.

But what finally turned us against secondhand books was not the
buying but the selling. It was the discovery—totally unexpected
—that those who came into our shop to look at them bore no resemblance at all to those who came in to look at our new books.
Our new-book customers, from the very first, surprised and delighted us by their obvious enthusiasm for the shop and its wares. They
enjoyed coming in, they enjoyed looking around, they enjoyed
making their purchases, and they were clearly going home to enjoy
reading whatever it was they had bought. And naturally their pleasure was our pleasure, too. How very different was the attitude
of those who came in to look at our secondhand books. In fairness
I must admit that in one sense of the word this attitude was not
their fault. For it was we who had chosen to keep these books in the
narrow passageway that separated the rest of the shop from our
office and till. This meant that every time we served a customer with
a card or a new book we had to squeeze our way past the secondhand browsers, and do so twice, with two sets of apologies, one
on the inward journey, once again on the outward. The fault was
ours, yet, because we so disliked their attitude in the other sense,
we found ourselves most unjustly disliking it in this sense as well;

and more and more did we resent their crouched, unyielding forms, less and less apologetic did we become as we pushed our way by.

I recorded an early encounter with a typical secondhand book customer in my journal:

> The man came in with a brisk, businesslike air and carrying a briefcase. He positioned himself in the gangway, ran his eye quickly over our shelves, picked out three books, flipped through them, put them on one side, picked them up, glanced at them again, handed them to me and said: "Three-and-six?" I did the addition and got the answer to five shillings. "Four shillings, then?" said the man. I said, "Sorry, five." He said that wasn't the way to do business, and if I wanted his continued custom, I must be more accommodating. He then looked at the books again, rejected one, tried to get the other two for three shillings, and finally, grudgingly, paid the full three and six. No doubt if I had priced the books up to seven-and-six in the first place and then allowed him to beat me down to five, he would have left the shop delighted with his bargain. But I hate doing business in that way.

It was customers such as this—collectors, I suppose, or possibly dealers, whose measure of a book lay in how much they had paid for it and what they thought it was worth, rather than in the pleasure it might give anybody to read it—that made it such a happy day for us when we finally stopped being secondhand booksellers.

By that time, however, we were already well established in another line of business: we were selling greeting cards.

Cards

I have already mentioned the Swiss flower cards that we sold so briskly on our opening day. This was how it started, and they came to us out of the blue, a bundle of specimens sent to us by an enterprising

Miss Channing who looked after the sales of a small firm of importers. Up to then cards had entered little into the lives of either of us. We knew about Christmas cards, of course, and sent them to our friends. We knew about picture postcards, occasionally bought them on holiday, and inherited hundreds of extremely drab Dartmouth ones from Montague. But that was all. Birthday cards, "Best wishes" cards, "Get well" cards, "New Home" cards, "Congratulations" cards: all these were quite unknown to us. And so our delight at seeing these Swiss flower cards arose not only from their beauty but also from their novelty. We fell in love with them at once, ordered them, and decorated our window with them. And at once they caught the eye of passersby and brought them into our shop. "I just want that card . . ." they would begin, then see that we had others, and hunt through them, and start making a collection . . . then go on to look at the books. . . . And when they had assembled all their purchases and were handing them over to us, they would say, almost apologetically: "You know, I really only came in to buy that one card."

Thus very early on we learned that cards were worth much more to us than the profit from their sales. They gave people an excuse to come in and browse. Holding their card, they could then go on to look at the books—and it didn't matter in the least if they couldn't find one they wanted to buy.

We started with Swiss flowers, and they remained our favorites and the favorites of our customers for many years. Indeed you could say that they were the foundation stone on which our card reputation was established. And of course they pointed the way forward. But in what direction? We needed a guide; we needed advice; and very luckily for us there entered Mr. and Mrs. Worth, able and willing to help. Our luck was not just that they had themselves run a card business in another town before coming to Dartmouth, it was that their taste was the same as ours. The suppliers they introduced us to had just the cards we wanted.

The cards we wanted? I might almost say the cards we loved. For another discovery we made was that there were two distinct categories:

those we loved and those we hated. Our reactions really were as strong and as different as this, and there was very little in between. But it was many years before we hit on a definition of those in the second category that did not seem to be an insult either to the customer who preferred them or to the salesman who was offering them; and at first much time was wasted, to our growing misery and the growing exasperation of the salesman, as he turned the pages of his album of samples and we shook our heads. The phrase that saved us in the end was "stationer's cards." And all that then became necessary was a quick glance at the album while his opening questions were being rehearsed ("How's trade?" and "Been on holiday yet?"), and then we could interrupt with "Sorry, but these are stationer's cards," and direct him across the road.

By confining ourselves firmly to those in the first category—we never bothered to find a generic name for them: they didn't need one—we very quickly established a reputation that was, in one respect at least, quite undeserved. "I've never seen such lovely cards anywhere else before," customers would say. But of course they had. It was just that they had seen them mixed in with all the others, and in such company—flamboyant, tinselly, ostentatious—they appeared small and drab. Only when they were among their fellows did they shine. It is the same with people.

As we chose our books, so we chose our cards: slowly, thoughtfully, pleasurably, one by one; never if we could help it accepting a "mixed assortment," always preferring to make our own selection: a dozen of this, a dozen of that, and then perhaps, greatly daring, four dozen of something that specially took our fancy; influenced very much by our own tastes, but realizing, naturally, that we were buying for others. I used to love these buying sessions, eager to see what was new, eager to discover a publisher or importer who could offer us something entirely original. Each season brought fresh delights. Each card gave us a double pleasure: the pleasure of finding it and buying it, and then the pleasure of displaying it and selling it. "What *lovely* cards you do have!"

Were they extra attractive in those days, I wonder, or were they like the first spring flowers after the long winter of War and Austerity? As I look at our cards today and remember those cards of twenty years ago, it is like looking at a hedge bank in high summer heavy with vegetation and remembering the starry-eyed celandines that first pricked it into color. It is like remembering spring gentians on a hillside in Italy.

Framing

A single incident, happening out of the blue, starts one off on a new course. It was Miss Channing and her Swiss flowers who had introduced us to greeting cards. It was Harold Finlinson who now introduced us to old prints and thence to picture framing. If Miss Channing had never written her letter; if Finlinson, visiting Dartmouth, had called elsewhere; or if in either case I had said "No" instead of "Yes," would the fortunes of the Harbour Bookshop have been very different?

They were small steel engravings, and they had come from topographical books published in the early nineteenth century. In their original state they had been black-and-white, and perhaps over the years they had become blotched with brown. But this didn't matter. They were torn out, bleached, washed, sized (to make the paper nonabsorbent), tinted with watercolors, and then mounted. This was how Finlinson offered them to us, and since they were all of South Devon scenes and many of them were of Dartmouth itself, and since they were modestly priced, I was able to assure him very quickly that he had come to the right place.

Dartmouth in the 1830s was not so very different from Dartmouth in the 1950s. The Butterwalk, Bayard's Cove, Dartmouth Castle, the views up and down the river: these had changed little in those hundred-odd years. This gave the prints an added charm: they showed not just what had been but what very recognizably still was. We put them on display and were delighted to find that our customers shared our enthusiasm. And at once the question arose: what about frames? I asked Finlinson, and he recommended a black-and-gold Hogarth molding and suggested that I arrange this with a local framer. So I went to Skinner.

I had discovered Skinner the previous year, for I was already thinking of framed pictures as a possible addition to our books. One or two of our greeting card suppliers also sold prints, and it seemed natural that we should, too. There was a framer in Dartmouth but he was unwilling to help us; so I had to go farther afield. Skinner was in Torquay, and this meant catching first a boat, then a train, then a bus. But the bus landed me almost at his door, and then came half an hour with just the sort of man whose company I so specially enjoyed—that of an elderly, Devonian craftsman—and after I had shown him my prints (they were mostly pictures of sailing ships and coastal scenes) and discussed mounts and moldings, I could listen to his stories and laugh at his jokes and store them up for passing on to Lesley when I got home.

So now I took him my old engravings. But, alas, he could offer me only narrow oak or plain black; he didn't have Hogarth. It was too expensive, he said.

In the end, therefore—for there seemed no alternative—I became my own picture framer. I started in a very modest way with a hundred feet of half-inch Hogarth, some sheets of cardboard, glass from old pictures picked up for next to nothing at auctions, and a table in our dimly lit office behind the shop—which made it difficult, when I was working, for Lesley to get to the till. Then, as our business expanded and my skill grew, I acquired a larger, lighter workshop, added more and ever more moldings to my range, and tackled larger and larger pictures in an increasing variety of ways. "I expect you need lots of special tools," people would say; but in fact I didn't. I think the only tool I had to buy straightaway to add to my existing collection was a very fine nail punch. The devices I needed for cutting the angles at the corners I designed and made for myself. Today there are books telling you how to do it, but I don't think there were then; at any rate I never found—or needed—one. I was a self-taught frame maker. Only when it came to mount cutting did I need Skinner's advice. He showed me how he did it, using a chisel and a homemade ruler, and I copied him: I don't think I would have discovered so simple and effective a way on my own. The only luxury I ever allowed myself was a machine for shooting metal tacks into the backs of frames to hold everything in place. This was so much quicker than hammering in panel pins that I felt the expense was justified. When you make things for yourself, it doesn't matter how long you take over it, but when you make for resale, speed is important.

One might be excused for thinking that framing picture after picture is dull, monotonous work; but this was rarely so, even if I were putting six more Finlinson prints into Hogarth frames or six more Redouté roses into pink mounts and white box frames. It depended on what I was framing, and how: very much it depended on this.

What and how: the picture in the middle and the mount and frame that surround it—these are the two components of the completed whole; and both were able to arouse in me the strongest feelings. If I liked what I was framing and if I could frame it the way I wanted to, then the work gave me intense pleasure. I never got tired of old engravings, nor did my customers; and fortunately—Dartmouth being a more famous town at the beginning of last century than it was when Mr. Webster gave me his opinion of it—many artists (including Turner) had come here, and a great variety of steel engravings, copper engravings, mezzotints, aquatints, and lithographs had survived to record their industry. Finlinson was able to keep me supplied with a very considerable number, but not enough, and I had to go hunting elsewhere. I searched in Dartmouth, I searched in London, and on the way I came upon other delights: old maps of Devon, old road maps, old charts, prints of old ships, flower prints. . . . Sometimes, too, my prints would come in their original state, dirty and uncolored, and so I had to learn how to smarten them up. I had to find out how to bleach and clean them, and I have memories (and Lesley has too) of prints in the kitchen sink, prints in bowls on the kitchen table, prints floating in the bath, and throughout the house the smell of chlorine.

Parallel with this we were building up our stock of modern reproductions, becoming members of the Fine Arts Trade Guild and so being allowed to buy the larger, more expensive color prints. Here was almost my first encounter with Art, for it had never entered much into my life before. Now, handling these luscious collotypes, I learned something of the artists who painted them, something of what they were trying to express, and felt the first prickles of the thrill that Art can give its devotees.

Much depended, then, on what I was framing. And much, too, depended on how. One might be tempted to think that, of the two components, the frame was of relatively minor importance. "I just want a very simple frame," customers would say to me, and sometimes even: "It really hardly needs a frame at all, just something to hold the glass." So, to restore the balance, may I mention those many customers who, seeing one of our completed pictures, fell in love with it and bought it scarcely even noticing the print in the middle, choosing it *solely* for its frame.

Buying moldings was like buying cards. Once again I discovered that it could be as painful to look through the range offered by one supplier as it could be a pleasure to look through that of another. I bought from two suppliers, and their salesmen called once a year to show me their latest patterns. You could say that they were just sticks of colored wood, but, oh, how I loved them and how I loved choosing them! How hard they were to resist, and (in consequence) how hard it became to squeeze our way through the ever-growing forest of them that—because of their length—I used to keep on the stairs!

Moldings and mounting boards; wood and paper and canvas; their color, pattern, and shape; their look and their feel: what materials these were to work with! You start with the print. How will it be treated? You choose the ingredients, decide the proportions, blend them together, admire the result, put it on display. . . . I never made book-ends. I never made another cigarette box. But I framed many hundred pictures, and, oh, what pleasure it gave.

Yet within the bud there lurked the worm; and just as it was one of our happiest days when we closed down our secondhand book depart-ment, so it was with our picture gallery. There were, in fact, two rea-sons—two worms, you might say—one attacking our prints, the other our framing.

I have already said that I never got tired of framing our old engravings, even though the treatment was always the same. Nor did our customers ever get tired of buying them, even though they grew progressively more expensive. The trouble came with our modern prints. Here the range was very considerable, stretching from the sort of pictures you might find in the National Gallery to the sort you might find at the Royal Academy. My own preference was for the for-mer, but I was prepared to accept the public's preference for the lat-ter. What I wasn't prepared for was their addiction to a tiny range of best-sellers. I could frame ten Peter Scotts with some degree of plea-sure, but not fifty. And it was the same with Tretchikoff and David Shepherd, with moonlit seas and galloping horses, with sunny Spain and clipper ships. A best-selling print is so very different from a best-selling book. How nice it is if we like the book, for then each sale gives added pleasure; but if we don't, it doesn't greatly matter, for books do not press their attention on those who do not wish it. They keep themselves to themselves within their covers, and the cus-tomer who chooses and the bookseller who wraps need exchange no more than a "Please" and a "Thank you." But it is not like that with pictures. Pictures do not lurk in shelves; they hang on walls for all to see, staring you in the face, hiding nothing. And there is another dif-ference too. A book becomes a best-seller because it is talked about and its name becomes known: people buy it *because* it is a best-seller; *knowingly* they follow the herd. Prints are not bought in this way: they are seldom asked for by name, rarely chosen because everyone else is choosing them. Yet the best-sellers emerge, for all that; and unconsciously the public is drawn toward them; *unknowingly* they follow the herd.

So what happened was this.

I would look through publishers' samples, seeing them all: liking some, disliking others, buying those I liked and hoped might be saleable, buying also those I knew would be saleable but liked rather less. From this selection of loose prints I then, later, picked out those I wanted to frame for stock. Framed prints always sold better than unframed: they looked better, you could display them better, and there they were, all ready for hanging on the wall. Which ones did I choose? How could I not include some of my favorites? After all, they were going to decorate our showroom before they decorated some private living room: *we* were going to have to live with them first. And how could I not, when customers came in to look around, point them out with special affection, put in a friendly word on their behalf, and hope that my feelings might be shared? Alas, they weren't. In the end I could bear it no longer. We took our unsold pictures home and hung them on our own walls. The rest of the stuff we sold off cheap to be rid of it.

Such was the fate of our modern reproductions. Now for the picture framing.

If you set up as a picture framer, a thing you must quickly decide is whether or not you will accept customers' own pictures. It is what might be called a wedge-shaped decision. For if at first you say "Yes, choose one of our prints and we will frame it for you," you are led on to accept similar prints that had been acquired elsewhere, to accept awful prints that *could* only have been acquired elsewhere, to accept family photographs and amateur oils. And the curious thing I found was that my own distaste was so often matched by that of my customers. They didn't like the picture any more than I did; and so they would want me to frame it as cheaply as possible. And then, to save themselves even that expense, they would fail to call back for it. Picture framers are often used as dumping grounds in this way. It eases the conscience of the dumper that he's "done something about it." Understandably he wants to do as little as possible.

From making frames it is a short step to repairing them: to replacing broken glass, refixing corners that are falling apart; remounting and rebacking where the mildew has got in. This was depressing work, and I would spend weeks not doing it, and Lesley would spend weeks apologizing on my behalf: so our dislike of it was shared.

As our business grew, I tried various ways of relieving the pressure; for I was, after all, a bookseller. First I tried sending some of the work to London; later I got someone in to help me here. But in the end the worm triumphed. A friend of mine, an artist who also framed pictures, closed his own business down at about the same time. We compared experiences and found much in common. On his last day he had assembled all the pictures that, over the years, his customers had brought in for framing, brought and never returned to collect—the smirking children, the alderman in his robes, the certificates; I knew them all—and he had carried them out and lined them up at one end of his backyard, and at the other end he had assembled a pile of stones. . . .

Our own uncollecteds met a less violent end: one at a time, and with a decent interval between them, they were slipped into a tea chest and put out with the rubbish.

Reasons

So for a while we were picture framers and print dealers. Then we gave it up. In the same way we ran a lending library, starting when Smiths and Boots closed down, getting our books from a man who supplied a chain of West Country shops, ran it for a while, enjoyed it for a while, then closed it down. Dilettantism? Did we simply flit from one thing to another like a butterfly, unable to do anything properly, giving up as soon as the going became hard and the first flame of enthusiasm had burned itself out? You could say this. You could also say that we only ran a line while it was profitable, dropping it as soon as profits fell. Neither alone is the whole truth.

Whatever one does, whatever one sells, affects a number of different people, and it affects them in different ways. It affects us personally; it affects our staff; it affects our shop, its profitability, its reputation, and its prospects; it affects the local population; and it affects or may affect our suppliers and other traders. All this should be taken into account when deciding what or what not to sell. One may say, "To hell with Mr. So-and-So up the road," but at least one says it: the decision to compete against him is a conscious one, and his possible reactions are anticipated. One may consider net profit more important than customer satisfaction: that is a personal matter. But both have to be considered.

In describing some of the "other goods" that we sold and then stopped selling, I have made no attempt to justify our decisions, no attempt to draw up a balance sheet of arguments in favor and against. For this is not a manual on retailing; it is the self-portrait of an individual. All the same, I feel I ought to add that there were reasons other than my own personal taste in Art that turned us against pictures. Nor did we altogether abandon our customers when we closed down our library and our framing. We handed them on, together with our books and our moldings, to those who took over when we left off.

And now to turn to a question that is surely pressing for an answer: where, in a shop that I have described as small, did we find room for all these varied activities?

Room Upstairs

With cards, with pictures, and with our library, the choice was a simple one: do we or don't we? But in 1956 an event occurred that called for a much harder decision. In 1956, Clare was born.

So now we had not just an extra mouth to feed, but for a time at least only one of us at work to feed it. There was thus an immediate need to increase our earnings, to expand our business. The question was how, and the answer clearly lay upstairs. We were living over the shop, and this was fine while there were only two of us. Indeed we would not have wished to live anywhere else. How nice that Lesley could go upstairs and get something ready for lunch while I was still serving down below. How nice that we could linger together over our meal, with the bell on the shop door (it was a homemade device, of course) set to ring when anybody came in.

What fun it was, sitting at our table by the window, to be able to look down on Dartmouth life going about its everyday business. Dartmouth was that sort of town: we were all by turns either actors or spectators; and so probably ours were not the only eyes to watch the young man from the yacht courting Sylvia from the ironmonger's. Nor did it matter that we hadn't got a garden—or even a backyard for drying the washing. We had a clothesline in the attic, and the country was so close that we didn't need a garden—not yet, at any rate. On a sunny day we could take our lunch and eat it sitting on a grassy hillside looking down over the rooftops to the river. In the evenings we could stroll down to Sugary Cove or find a pleasant spot among the rocks below the footpath that leads to Compass Cove, or cross the river by the Lower Ferry and walk along the railway line to the Higher Ferry, so getting the last of the evening sun. It was a new experience for us to live, to work, and to find our recreation all in the same place; and for five years we enjoyed it.

With Clare's impending arrival, however, we had to think again; and there could be no doubt that the time had now come to look for a separate house, one moreover with the garden that we were both now beginning to long for. If we moved out from the shop, this would leave us with four vacant rooms. Here, clearly—though in a way yet to be decided—was the source of our extra income.

I seem to remember that our first thought was to let the rooms as offices, but the problem would then have been to provide separate access. In the end we decided to turn the first floor—our old dining room, kitchen, and sitting room—into a showroom. Selling what? Not books or cards or Dartmouth prints. For the extra sales we might hope to make would not be in proportion to the considerable amount of extra space we would have available. It would have to be something quite different.

The answer can be given in a single word. It was a word we disliked, but we searched in vain for another, and in the end we had to accept it. It was "gifts"; and so the Harbour Bookshop became the Harbour Bookshop and Gift Gallery. Having decided on our new name, we then had to decide exactly what it would encompass. Things made of wood, obviously; perhaps also things made of pottery. What else?

The advantage of being a gift shop is that you can sell almost anything as the fancy takes you—and as the fancy seems to be taking your customers. You can sell it one year and you can stop selling it the next: you are not committed. You can sell china, and it won't make you a china shop. You can sell tables and chairs, and it won't make you a furniture shop. You can sell bedspreads and tea cloths without becoming a draper, fire irons and frying pans without becoming an ironmonger, jewelry without becoming a jeweler, dried herbs and dried flowers without becoming a grocer or a florist. Indeed over the years we have sold all these things. Moreover (and not surprisingly) what we had found with cards and pictures we now found with gifts: there were those we liked very much and those we liked very little. Once again we chose only what we liked; and in order to avoid being influenced by overpersuasive salesmen, for our first few years we did almost all our choosing through the Design Centre in London.

Gradually we established our contacts and built up our stock. Gradually our bookshop customers discovered that we now had an upstairs department. "But we've had it for *years!*" The holidaymakers knew all about it, of course; it was our regulars who failed to notice, seeing only what they had always seen. Odd how familiarity blunts observation.

Today Lesley does all the buying, and I don't envy her. She does most of it at the annual Gift Trade Fair in Torquay, placing enormous orders in January for what she hopes to sell in July and August. How can she know? What instinct tells her that the pottery cruets that were so popular one year will not sell at all the next? Pokers with colored knobs, teak mice, gaily decorated tin trays and egg prickers: each in turn had its year and was then forgotten, abandoned by the public in their search for the latest novelty. What will it be this year? Spoon rests? Today half our showroom—the old sitting-room half—sells kitchenware. The other half sells pottery and glass and table mats and . . . and . . . Yes, Lesley is quite right: I really do hardly know. How soon one loses touch. Once I did all the buying. Now I'm scarcely even aware of what is bought.

TWENTY-SEVEN

✦ ✦ ✦ ✦ ✦

Books and Selling Books

Choosing

For twenty-one years Lesley and I lived on the profits of our shop, and the bulk of this came from bookselling. We had no other source of income. I say this loudly and proudly. Loudly, because a number of people seem to have suspected that all the while Pooh's earnings were keeping my pockets comfortably lined. Proudly, because it is not easy to survive as a bookseller—in fact as well as in name—in a town whose population is under seven thousand.

I have already described how we started, going round other book-shops, studying their stock, going around to publishers to see what they had to offer, then making our choice and sending in our orders. And at once there will be seen a similarity to gift buying—and a difference. The similarity is that booksellers do in fact choose what they wish to stock. No book arrives uninvited. "Don't they send them down to you automatically?" we are asked. Indeed they don't. Nor can we automatically send them back to their publishers if we fail to sell them; and so there may well be books on our shelves whose continued presence we are beginning to regret. But at least we have no one to blame but ourselves. That is the similarity.

The difference is that our choice is made from the *entire* range of books published. In theory (if not quite in practice) the books that we stock on, for instance, wildflowers, have been chosen as being the most suitable for our needs of *all* that are available: the others for one reason or another we have rejected. This is not so with gifts. With gifts we stock what takes our fancy, and it does not bother us that there might be something a little better that we don't know about. With gifts our customers choose from what they see: if they like what they see, they buy it; if not, they walk out. With books this is only partly what happens. For in addition there are those customers who come in asking for a particular book. And our stock must aim to satisfy them as well.

So the question that everybody asks us is: "How do you know what books people are going to want? How do you know what to buy?"

First let me say that, although we are influenced by reviews, we do not wait until they appear before deciding; for this would be leaving it far too late. Every book has a publication date. On this date—but not before—it may be reviewed. On this date—but not before—it should be available in bookshops. It is launched with a fanfare of trumpets, a fanfare that would be incomplete without the bookseller's participation. Sometimes customers say to us: "I've seen it in London, but probably it hasn't got down here yet." This infuriates us. If we haven't got the book in stock when it is in stock in London, it is because we have decided against stocking it, not because Dartmouth is a small provincial town two hundred miles away and we have to wait our turn.

So most of our choosing is done before the book is published. We may do it from a publisher's catalogue, or we may do it as a result of advance publicity, but most often and most satisfactorily we do it with the help and advice of the publisher's representative. Books come flooding in on two great annual tides, the spring tide and the autumn tide, and so ideally a representative will call twice a year, showing us spring books in March and autumn books in September.

What does he carry with him? Sometimes the book itself and this can be helpful; but it is not always either necessary or possible. We may not need to see it to know whether or not we want it; or it may not be possible to see it because completed copies are not yet available, or because the representative's bag is not big enough or his arm is not strong enough to carry all the seasonal offerings of his firm. If we are shown the book, it is not so that we can sit down and read it before deciding whether or not we want it. Only if it is very short—a book of cartoons or a children's picture book—might we have time for that. In any case, reading a book does not always make it easier to arrive at a wise decision. We are not, after all, buying for ourselves. We are buying for our customers, trying to anticipate their reactions, their demand. Is this a book they will hear about and come in and ask for? Is it a book that will catch their eye and arouse their interest? These are the questions we must ask ourselves; not: "Did I myself enjoy it?" One book in a hundred we may be able to sell by communicating our own personal enthusiasm—and doing this is one of the supreme pleasures of bookselling—but the other ninety-nine must be able to sell themselves.

So we must know our customers, know their book-buying tastes (not their book-reading tastes, for this is quite another matter), and be able to put ourselves in their position as they watch a television interview with the author, or read a review, or see the book in our shop. What are the factors that influence their choice? The subject? The author's name? The price? The book's appearance? Its jacket design? The general excitement or controversy that will surround its publication? Sometimes the one, sometimes the other. I have met books whose success depended almost wholly on choice of title, and I have met others whose title alone condemned them to failure. These are all things the representative can tell us about. "Macramé? What on earth is that?" I asked—as everybody must have asked, meeting the word for the first time. So he told me about this little-known craft and advised me that it might soon become very popular. He was right—and I was ready with my copies when the demand came.

A book to us, then, is very much more than a piece of writing. It is the joint product of author, typographer, papermaker, printer, binder, jacket designer, and publisher's publicity department. It is a rectangular object possessing certain qualities; and one of its most important qualities is that alone, all by itself, it is quite useless. To achieve fulfillment it must find a buyer. So if we keep only one eye on our stock, it is so that we can keep our other eye on our customers. In fact, of the two, the eye that studies the customer is almost the more important.

Lesley and I are conscious of this when engaging a new assistant. A person who likes people—who is friendly and helpful and makes them feel welcome—is far more use to us than one who likes books. Books don't need to be liked: people do. Books don't mind if you are rude to them or offhand in your manner: people do. A bookshop is like a marriage bureau: it arranges meetings between likely partners—likely book and likely buyer. The introduction may be a formal one. "Mr. Smith, I would like you to meet this book: I think you might enjoy it." Or it might be more casual—so placing the book that Mr. Smith's eye will fall on it and his hand will reach out toward it. . . . This is the art of book buying and bookselling: knowing your customers, knowing their tastes, realizing that their tastes are constantly changing, anticipating what they will be next season, choosing your stock accordingly, and then so displaying it that you achieve the maximum number of introductions leading to the maximum number of happy marriages.

Consequently, when people say to us: "What lovely, lovely books. If I had a bookshop, I would just read and read all day: I'd never want to sell a thing," we smile politely—and change the subject. There is immense pleasure in book reading, but it has nothing to do with bookselling.

So what sort of books do we sell? This question is usually accompanied by an amazement that we sell anything at all. "*Do* people buy books these days? They are so expensive, aren't they?" Yes, luckily for us they do; and perhaps it would be helpful if I first tried to show why.

I was once—a very long time ago—invited to give a talk entitled "Why Buy Books?" I remember it vividly because the clergyman who introduced me thought I was going to talk about the ten books I would take with me to a desert island, and he began his introduction by telling the audience which ten books *he* would take to *his* desert island. So when my turn came, I had to start by apologizing that this wasn't what I had been asked to talk about at all. . . . As I have already said, one mustn't confuse a desire to buy books with a desire to read them. Booksellers are not in competition with librarians: the two serve different needs.

People buy books for one of several possible reasons. They may buy them to give away as presents; they may buy them because they need them to refer to; they may buy them because they are collecting books on a particular subject; they may buy a book because, having enjoyed reading it, they now wish to possess it; they may buy it for its decorative qualities; or they may simply buy it because everyone else is buying it. These (with one more to follow) are the main reasons; and there will be a host of minor reasons—because the copy borrowed from a friend has just been eaten by the dog, and so on. . . . In all these cases the book is intended to last, and it may very well physically outlast the purpose for which it was originally bought. This is a pity, for it then merely clutters up its owner's shelves, providing a bad excuse for not buying any more books.

People will go to all sorts of extremes to avoid putting their dead books on the bonfire or out with the rubbish, and—astonishingly—they are proudly convinced that this shows them to be true book lovers. On the contrary, they are the enemies of literature! For it is this attitude that discourages the buying of books solely for the pleasure of reading them. In particular it discourages the buying of novels.

Fortunately it is an attitude that does not seem to extend to paperbacks. Paperbacks are in the magazine class: expendable; read, then thrown away (or more usually left for someone else to throw away). So this gives us our final category: people buy books to read *provided they are in paperback*.

Having seen why, we can now consider what.

If we had chosen a larger town we could, perhaps, have afforded to specialize. We could have stocked only those books that we liked or books on those subjects that interested us. But in a town the size of Dartmouth, though our stock may betray certain prejudices, we must be general booksellers, aiming to satisfy all tastes, not just our own, selling all—or virtually all—that we find saleable, and consequently selling a great many books on subjects about which we know very little.

Thus we sell hardcover books on yachting and fishing, on Devon, on natural history, on cookery and gardening, on a great variety of crafts, on old things (boats, trains, antiques, etc.), on the instruments of destruction (tanks, airplanes, warships, etc.). We sell the obvious reference books and the sort of safe classics that get chosen as school prizes. We sell "best-sellers" (the more popular novels and biographies). We sell paperbacks on all subjects. And lastly—and I'll have more to say about this later—we sell children's books. Add it all up and—to the surprise of those who equate books with culture—you will find that we sell relatively little that can be said to possess literary merit. Poetry, novels, biographies, belles letters, history: these in hardcover do badly, and their authors, with few exceptions, must survive on their sales to public libraries—and then hope to get into paperback.

"Lovely, lovely books," says our customer, looking around her and trying again. "If I had a fortune, I would buy them *all.*" A very catholic book buyer she must be, with a remarkably wide range of interests. For our part we might perhaps contemplate inviting one book in a hundred into our house. I doubt if it would be more than that. Yet this doesn't mean that we dislike the other ninety-nine. Very far from it.

Books are like people. You may like a person without necessarily wanting to ask him home for supper. You may like a book without necessarily wanting either to read or to possess it. So it is with the books in our shop. We know them all, we like them all, we enjoy their companionship, because to a bookseller a book is not something to read; it is something to handle, something to sell. To a bookseller a good book is one that is well designed and well made, and the handling of it—holding it, feeling it, opening it, turning the pages, letting the eye fall upon the printed word—gives him immense pleasure. I know little and care nothing about—for instance—armored fighting vehicles, yet I know that in Dartmouth there are many people with a passion for tanks. I can recognize a well-designed, well-produced tank book when

I am shown one, and it gives me great pleasure to order it, stock it, display it, and even introduce it to a customer with my personal recommendation. Does it seem wrong that I am prepared to say, "Here is a good book," when I have done no more than glance at it? How can I judge a book I have never read on a subject about which I know nothing? The answer is that I can because I enlist the help of others—the publisher, reviewers, other customers. My personal judgment is confined to the book's production, its look and feel. I leave it to the expert to judge its contents.

I have said that though we are a general bookshop our stock may display prejudices; and of course it does. It displays the prejudices of Dartmouth—so many books on sailing, so few on cricket; novels about the sea rather than sex; biographies of Tories rather than Socialists. It also displays our own. To a large extent we must follow the tastes and interests of our customers. To some small extent, however, we can attempt to lead them; and one of the most fascinating and exciting sides to bookselling is to see how far ahead we can go, and how many of our customers we can carry with us. It may be a single book, one that we feel to have some special merit, not an obvious best-seller but one surely deserving our support, deserving to be read. All right, let us take a chance. Let us buy not just our usual cautious one or two copies; let us take a dozen and then really try to sell it. Or it may be a particular subject or attitude for which we have an especial sympathy or feel the stirrings of a crusading zeal. The vicar might have made it the theme of a sermon; or the editor of the local paper might have devoted an editorial to it. We, when the representative comes to it, say, "Yes. That's one I'd like." And we add it to our order. Or perhaps we may be not for it but against it, and then we say, "No. Not that book." And the representative is surprised, perhaps even a little indignant, struggling to hide his anger or his scorn, trying to remain polite. "But it is selling fantastically well. You're the first shop to refuse it." Can anybody be so perverse, turning away good money like this? "I'm sorry, but this is my shop and you must allow me to run it my way."

So we choose our books, influenced by the likes and dislikes of our customers and also of ourselves, seeing each book (or rather trying to visualize each book) as a rectangular object to be handled and looked at as well as read. How many copies? One? Two? Four? Ten? We tend to play safe. Better too few than too many. We can always reorder. It is not so easy to return unsold copies.

And then the books arrive and we have to sell them. Yes, it's one thing to picture a bookseller as a person who lives and moves in a world of books—even if it is not quite such a cultured, "Eng. Lit." sort of world as one had perhaps imagined. But it is quite another thing to put the accent on the second half of his name; for isn't there something not quite nice about selling? Isn't it all a bit *commercial?* And the librarian, sitting at his desk in the Public Library, feels smugly superior. *He* is not involved with money in this rather sordid way. *His* success is measured in "issues," not "net profit." This is the difference between us: the one is a member of a learned profession; the other is engaged in trade.

Anybody with this sort of attitude toward selling should not become—and in any case would not long remain—a bookseller. For bookselling most emphatically involves both books and selling; and so, having said something about the one, I must now turn to the other.

Selling

The man who, encouraged perhaps by a remark of Emerson's, made a mousetrap and then waited for the world to beat a path through the woods to his door, would have waited in vain unless he had first done something, however hesitantly, however reluctantly, to inform the world of his existence. Every one of us who earns a living is earning it by selling something he has—a product, a skill—to someone who wants it. Everyone with something to sell must first promote it, advertise it, look for likely buyers.

He may find that this does not take up much of his time, so that having once nailed up his signboard or found his employer, he can then get on with his trade. Or he may find that it takes up a lot of his time; and he may well enjoy it.

Thus you have two extremes of attitude toward selling. At the one extreme are the makers who, if they are also their own salesmen, see their job as *finding* people who want what they have to offer; and at the other extreme are the salesmen who see it as *persuading* people to want what they have to offer. To the maker, what matters most is what he has to sell; to the salesman, what matters is success. What he is selling is almost irrelevant.

Where between these extremes does the bookseller stand? The answer is that he can stand where he likes. He can see himself as a professional salesman, his job simply to get books moving out of his shop as fast as possible in exchange for money moving in. Such a bookseller once horrified the book trade by suggesting, loudly and publicly, that books could and should be sold like soap. Or he can see himself as a sort of maker, not making the books, of course, but making his shop and then, as it were, making marriages between book and customer. So for him books matter, and the final wrapping up, handing over, taking of money, and giving of change is only a very small part of his work.

Where did we stand? Does the question need to be asked? For you have only to start listing the qualities required in a professional salesman to see at once how few of them I possess. Hedda saw this well enough. They saw it at John Lewis. Probably the sales manager of the encyclopedia publisher saw it when I presented myself for interview. And certainly I see it myself in the bookshop when I meet the professional on his rounds. In he comes, instantly recognizable, smartly dressed, highly polished all over, radiating self-confidence and after-shave, all set to make his killing. Poor shabby, shambling, provincial bookseller! He seizes him by the hand and wishes him a very good morning, flicks open his briefcase, and starts doing conjuring tricks with its contents. Does it make any difference what he is selling? Advertising space, insurance, it's all the same. "Just sign here, sir. They'll invoice you from the office."

But if I recoil from the professional, it is because I cannot buy from this sort of person in this sort of way, not because I dislike buying things. And if I cannot myself adopt his techniques, it is because I am not myself a salesman by nature, not because I dislike or disapprove of selling or feel it in some way undignified.

In fact I enjoy both buying and selling, particularly when what is being bought or sold is books. Books—new books, that is—have two things in their favor. In the first place, they are introduced to us not by a "salesman," thank goodness, but by a "representative"—a word which implies, usually correctly, someone who shares my attitude toward doing business. So we meet as equals and sit down together and discuss his books. We do not maneuver for position in order to do battle with each other. The books are allowed to sell themselves; there is no pushing. That is the first thing; and there is no further problem with buying. You have only to announce that you have become a bookseller and representatives will soon be queuing up to see you, undaunted in our case by the fact that they first have to queue up to cross the river on our ferry. The second thing in favor of new books is that they all have fixed selling prices. So at least we are spared the arguing and the haggling that so blighted our venture into secondhand bookselling.

However, books have one great disadvantage compared with gifts. With gifts we usually hope to establish what are called "sole agencies," which ensure that the manufacturers who supply us do not also supply our nearby competitors. With books this cannot happen, since every bookshop is free to buy from every publisher. So although to some extent individual shops will show individual characteristics, the universally popular books—the best-sellers—will usually be stocked by them all. Why then, since the book will be the same and cost the same in each, should a customer favor one shop rather than another? It can only be because one shop in some way gives better service. So although we could promote our books, saying: "These are good books," at the same time we had to promote our shop—and indeed (like it or not) ourselves—saying: "Ours is a good shop and we are good booksellers." And this we found less easy.

First we chose a town in which there was no other private bookseller. Naturally, had there been one and had he been a good bookseller, this would have made the task of establishing ourselves very much harder, and our excuse for trying to do so very much smaller. But whether he had been good or not, it would have meant our setting up in opposition to someone else, trying to persuade the public to come to us rather than go to him; and this we would not have enjoyed. Admittedly there was in Dartmouth a branch of W. H. Smith: we could hardly expect to have the field entirely to ourselves. But the difference between a private bookshop and the branch of a well-established chain was, we felt, great enough for there to be no animosity between us. Then we chose a name that we could shelter behind. Not Milne & Milne, but the Harbour Bookshop—which allowed us to boast about the shop without giving the impression that we were boasting about ourselves. And initially our self-promotion amounted to little more than saying "Here we are." Fortunately this was fairly obvious, since our site was a good one. (Our attempts to say *who* we were were less successful; our store sign didn't appear until three weeks after we had opened and was then virtually illegible.) After that we could turn our attention to promoting our books.

The simplest way to promote books is to put them on display, and the best place to display them is the shop window. And it was when arranging our window that we became conscious of another characteristic that books possess: they have voices; and our job as window dresser was to see that they were saying the right thing to the right people in the most effective way.

So we were like the puppeteer who, standing unseen, pulls unseen strings; or like the conductor of the orchestra who, silent himself, gets the best from each instrumentalist. Each book has its own individual voice, saying "I am me: buy me!" Some books say this very loudly, clearly, and persuasively. You put them in the window and people at once know all about them and come hurrying in for them. These are our soloists, and probably our best soloist when we opened was *The*

Cruel Sea. Other books are better in chorus. "We are cookbooks. We are gardening books. There are lots more of us inside." Some books speak for themselves. Books with titles like *Devon* or *Sea Fishing for Beginners* need no help from us: they say exactly what they are. But *Jim Davis* needs a little notice pointing out that it is an exciting smuggling story with a Dartmouth setting. Only those with the best voices qualify for the window or for display face forward inside the shop, and each must be carefully chosen—not just for what it has to say, but to whom we want it said. For this is important, too. Who are the people we are addressing? Who are the people walking along the pavement outside? Are they holidaymakers visiting the town for the first time, and so needing to be told what a wide range of books we stock? Or are they our residents who (we trust) know this already and so can be told something else?

Thus gradually we began to understand what it is that makes books saleable and learned how to make the most of their saleability. And parallel with this we began to understand what makes people come in and buy them.

Before you can get someone to come into your shop—assuming he hadn't all along intended to do so—indeed before you can get him to look at your window, you have to attract his attention. You have to say "Stop!" In our early days, when we lived over the shop, we had a cat who lived with us, and every now and then, because it was warm and sunny there, he climbed into our shop window. He sat very still. He made no noise. But he was saying "Stop!" and he was saying it very well. We have to use other devices now, but I doubt if any can do it better.

Having stopped the passerby, you then have to hold his attention. We found that the best way to do this was to give him something to read. People seem to like reading things, and they particularly like reading things aloud to each other. I learned this when a notice was nailed to the wall below my office window. The notice gave information about a nearby building. I never read it myself, but I heard it read aloud so many times that I almost knew it by heart.

First "Stop," then "Look," and finally "Come in," and this is best said by the books themselves—with perhaps a helping word or two from us. The difficulty is that you never know how well they are doing it. It is obvious enough if someone, handing over a pile of purchases, says: "And I only came in for that card I saw in your window." But much more often you have no idea what brings people in; and more important than that, you don't know what has kept the others out.

People don't always find it easy to walk into a strange shop. They are frightened: frightened perhaps that they will find themselves buying something they don't really want, frightened they might make a fool of themselves. It is very easy to make a fool of yourself. I once went into a bank I found inside Victoria Station. I was on my way home from school and wanted to let my parents know which train I was catching. I suppose I should really have been looking for a telephone booth, but I was, if anything, even more frightened of telephones. So I found this bank instead and went in and said to the man behind the counter, "I want to send a telegram." And he looked startled and said, "But this is a *bank*." Well, I knew it was. What I didn't know was the difference between a bank and a post office. It is the fear of making this sort of mistake that keeps so many people out of bookshops: they are frightened of being told by a superior person in a superior voice: "Oh, *no*. We don't sell *that* sort of book *here*, madam!"

This is why it is helpful if you can sell something else other than books—newspapers, for instance. It gets the nervous outsider into your shop. We used greeting cards for this purpose. We now use a revolving stand of paperbacks. We hated this stand when we were first given it, and complained bitterly to the representative of the paperback publisher who provided it. "We like to keep your books in a proper order so that customers can see exactly what we've got, and so that if we are asked for a title we can quickly find it. In this stand nearly half the books are invisible." He said that this didn't matter in the least. Customers mostly just wanted a good book, not a particular book. Grudgingly we accepted it, and as soon as we could we replaced it, and since he didn't want it back, we were on the point of throwing it away. But suddenly Lesley had a bright idea. "Let's put it just inside the doorway and fill it with all our most popular books." So we did, and it provides a sort of stepping-stone for those who are too timid to come straight in.

Once someone is properly inside, it is reasonable to assume that, if he has not just come in to escape the rain or to while away half an hour, he does genuinely want to buy a book and will be disappointed if he has to go out empty-handed. It is also reasonable to assume that somewhere in the shop is a book that will suit him. It is therefore up to us to bring the two together. And gradually we learned the best way to do it, how best to approach each type of customer, how best to arrange our books in their shelves (though there is always room for improvement, always room for argument here), how best to introduce book and customer, giving the customer a choice but not too baffling a choice, helping him to make up his mind, and finally how best to ensure that he is happy with what he has bought and so will come back another day.

So we are indeed professional salesmen after all, with an armory of techniques every bit as subtle and elaborate and carefully perfected as those taught to smooth young men in smart grey suits; and bookselling to us is not just *book*selling but also book*selling*, the one every bit as fascinating as the other. It is, I suspect, a little like the fascination of angling. The angler must learn his river and his equipment, his fish and their habits. He may well ask his wife to cook what he has caught, because after all fish is food and man must eat; but the pleasure he finds by the river lies not so much in thoughts of supper but rather in the exercise of his knowledge and of his skill. And with us there is a further bonus. Our fish, we like to think, are the happier for being caught.

Joyce

Joyce Green joined us in 1963. We had known the Greens in a vague sort of way ever since we had arrived. He was a biology teacher at the grammar school, and she could often be seen standing in the street with a sheaf of papers in her hand, interviewing passersby on behalf of the BBC. I knew that she was wanting a more exacting job than that, and it seemed ideal that what we needed—help with our expanding school business—was term-time work that would leave her free to share school holidays with her husband. So initially a "job description" would have been simple: to deal with school and library orders and to answer the telephone.

Thus she became the bookshop's voice, and a most admirable voice it was, too, leaving you in no doubt that you had dialed the right number, no fear that you were getting a little deaf. "Good morning. Harbour Bookshop. Can I help you?" And it became her pride that she could, that if she were asked a question, she knew the answer, whether it was a school asking about the availability of a textbook or a private customer wanting something whose title was uncertain and whose author was forgotten. "Yes, we have a copy in stock. Shall we send it or will you call?" Or sometimes, in answer to a stranger who had been telephoning shop after shop in vain: "I'm sorry, we haven't. It's been out of print for several years, you know. Didn't they tell you? But there's a new edition coming in the autumn. . . ."

She knew better than anybody how rare and how welcome it is, when you ring up with a problem, to be able to speak at once to someone who knows what you are talking about. For frequently she would have to ring up publishers. "Oh!" she would say crossly afterward. "I spoke to a wetty!" And she would imitate the wetty's voice. But sometimes: "I got on to *such* a nice man and he called me 'dear' and he was *so* helpful. . . ." And this would make her day. What a pity that more publishers don't invest in nice men who take a pride in knowing the answers, rather than wetties who don't.

Of course it would be an exaggeration to pretend that, even after doing a little spadework (as she called it), Joyce could answer every question; for there were some that offered no clue at all, and these she would deal with in her own peculiar way. She would leave them and wait until she was looking for something quite different. Then, apparently quite by chance, she would happen on the answer. This technique worked so often that we used to rely on it. Serendipity, like water divining, is one of those mysterious gifts that you can't quite believe in but which some people undoubtedly seem to possess. Another gift she had, useful to us if perhaps a little exhausting to her, was the habit of waking up at three o'clock in the morning to remember things. No job description would have included night work of this type; and in fact Joyce very quickly found herself doing a great deal that it would have been hard to define—and doing it all so well that when term came to an end, we were extremely reluctant to let her go on holiday.

Twenty-one Years

In 1972 we celebrated our twenty-first birthday. We did it in style, for it was not just an important landmark in our bookselling lives. In one sense it was the finishing post. The Harbour Bookshop would continue, but my life as a bookseller was coming to an end. In our Christmas catalogue that year we looked back and gave thanks, as was proper, to all those books we had sold with such pleasure—and, yes, with such profit—over those years.

> First: three books that helped us right from the start. Two of them of local interest, just out, and which we continued to sell happily for a number of years, first at full price, later reduced: Ruth Manning-Sanders' *The River Dart* and Percy Russell's *Dartmouth*. The third, a national best-seller whose birthday virtually coincided with our own: Nicholas Monsarrat's *The Cruel Sea*.
>
> Then two more national best-sellers of our youth, two books that gave us immense pleasure in the reading and so a double pleasure in the selling: Laurens van der Post's *Venture to the Interior* and John Hunt's *Ascent of Everest*.

Next, two more books of exploration, but spiritual rather than geographical. They may seem odd partners at first sight, but we have always felt they had much in common: John Robinson's *Honest to God* and D. H. Lawrence's *Lady Chatterley's Lover*—both deeply serious, both tilting against the establishment, both (for better or for worse) opening the floodgates of pent-up feeling.

Then a miscellaneous collection of books with this in common: that their authors kindly helped us make a success of them by putting in a personal appearance—and in most cases, too, a personal word—on their behalf for our benefit. Stanley Smith's *The Wind Calls the Tune*, Peter Churchill's *Of Their Own Choice*, Brian Fawcett's *Exploration Fawcett*, Elephant Bill's *Bandoola*, Gerald Durrell's *Bafut Beagles*, Robin Knox Johnson's *A World of My Own*, and Nicolette Milnes-Walker's *When I Put Out to Sea*. How many of our customers can boast signed copies of all seven?

Then *The New English Bible*. And would you have been wiser than we were in the months before publication and guessed that the version with the Apocrypha would outsell the version without—by somewhere around ten to one?

Then W. Keble Martin's *The Concise British Flora*, the book that so many publishers turned down before Michael Joseph made it the best-seller of best-sellers. Readily identifiable by us, even if described as "that book by the clergyman," or "that book that the Duke of Edinburgh . . ."—even, on occasion, merely as "that book."

Then two books that television (not always our rival) turned into winners: John Galsworthy's *Forsyte Saga* and Kenneth Clark's *Civilisation*.

Finally, a book that sold well everywhere, but especially here: Nevil Shute's *Most Secret*. Six shillings in hardcover in 1955. Six shillings in paperback today. Of special interest, of course, not only because the story has a local setting, but because we can proudly claim Nevil Shute Norway (to give him his real name) as a Dartmouth author.

Where does one stop? There are still a dozen more titles we have listed, and dozens and dozens we could well add. Most of them fairly obvious and unexciting—books about Devon, about the sea, certain children's classics. . . . So let us end by thanking that vast army of books, tens of thousands of them, of which we have sold only one solitary copy. Add them together and it is they, rather than their more popular companions, that have kept us in business selling books here in Dartmouth.

There are two sorts of bookseller (this is my theory): the male and the female. The male bookseller is concerned with the territory over which he operates, defending it, enlarging it. It is the male bookseller who wants to expand his business, the male bookseller who opens new branches. The female bookseller, on the other hand, is concerned with her shop, furnishing it, making it attractive, making it not the biggest but the best shop in the area.

I am a female bookseller. Once, for about a week, I did contemplate the idea of a branch in Torquay, then wisely abandoned it.

The Harbour Bookshop is very much our home—not just a machine for making money. It is old and rambling, awkward in many ways, especially when heavy parcels have to be carried. But it has a friendly feel, a personality of its own. I like it. I wouldn't want it different. I wouldn't want a modern shop with modern fixtures and an electronic till. I like just being in it, especially in the evening when we are closed and it is empty. I like making things for it. All this is part of the pleasure of being a bookseller. Other shops may have grown bigger, but I don't envy them. I don't feel jealous. I would only feel jealous if I were told they were also better.

To be a good bookseller you need three things: you need a goal (or a succession of goals) to aim for; you need the spur of necessity; and you need all your working hours. After twenty-one years I was about to lose all three.

It seemed that I had done as a bookseller all the things I had aimed to do, all the things I could find to do. There was no other goal in sight.

For twenty-one years the Harbour Bookshop had been our sole source of income. We had proved to ourselves that we could do it: that we could survive as booksellers here in Dartmouth. In 1971 my mother died. From now on a part of my father's royalties would be coming to me. So the spur had gone.

For seventeen years my daughter, Clare, had been at school. They had taught her a lot of things in that time, though not as much as some children learn. But they had not taught her how to walk. School was now finished. Clare would be living at home, and I would be helping to look after her. So I could no longer be a full-time bookseller.

So it was time to leave my grassy plain. I had found what I had wanted to find. I had done what I had wanted to do. The cloud hung its curtain across the mountains. It was time to go.

TWENTY-EIGHT

✦ ✦ ✦ ✦ ✦

Clare

The one question we always used to dread—the obvious question to ask of someone in their thirties to whom you have only just been introduced—was, "And do you have any children?" And I became adept at steering the conversation onto safer ground. Today, older, less sensitive, I find it better to make the matter quite plain from the start: it saves later embarrassment. "Yes, a daughter. She has cerebral palsy." There follows, of course, a momentary pause; then "Oh . . . I'm sorry to hear that." And then, after a few more words, we move to another subject.

Hope is like a life belt: it buoys you up and may keep you afloat until you are rescued; but if it fails you and you are forced to abandon it, you sink. So it is better if you are able to swim without it. In other words, it is better if you can accept things as they are, rather than live in hope that they will improve.

Once we had accepted Clare's disability and its effect on us all, there were plenty of other things we could be happy about, plenty to enjoy, plenty to be grateful for. And at the top of the list was her own very evident zest for life, her high spirits, her sense of fun, her cheerful acceptance of all she couldn't do, her delight in what little she could. She set us an example and taught us a philosophy that parents don't usually expect to learn from their children.

We tend to think that, if someone is deprived of a blessing that we ourselves possess, their life is the sadder. This is particularly so in today's Age of Equality, when we are made to feel almost guilty at having what others do not have. But in fact the man who has less than his neighbor is only unhappy if he had been hoping for more and chooses to feel jealous.

Is it sad that there is so little that Clare can do? Not necessarily. There are plenty of things that even the most agile person cannot do. Happiness is not measured by agility. Most of what the average person does in his daily life—housework, office work, factory work, commuting—is fairly dull and may well seem almost unbearably dull to others. "How can you go on, day after day?" Yet we can. Much of our pleasure comes not from doing, but from watching. Only twenty-two men actually play soccer, but thousands watch with almost equal enjoyment. So it is with Clare. She doesn't do any gardening in the accepted sense, but if Lesley is digging among her vegetables and she is watching, then she is "helping with the gardening." "Helping?" Of course. It is, after all, the word the French use. *Assister* includes being a spectator.

I suppose that if Lesley or I had been ambitious, pursuing our chosen career with single-minded determination, we might have felt that we didn't want to be burdened with the various domestic tasks that needed to be done. We might have preferred others to do them for us. This, after all, was the way our parents and grandparents had ordered their lives. The master worked, the mistress supervised, and a team of retainers scrubbed and cooked and mowed and stoked the boilers. And although it is not like this today, something of the tradition still lingers here and there. But Lesley and I have never wanted it this way. It is not that she likes housework, but rather that she dislikes even more the idea of someone coming in and doing it for her. So most of what has needed to be done we have done ourselves, and only reluctantly have we asked for help. We have needed help in the bookshop, and Lesley had a little help with Clare when she was a baby. And if a fairly large building job has been necessary, we have called in builders to do it. But it is really much pleasanter, much more satisfying, if you can manage on your own. In our parents' day it was, in any case, economically sensible for the specialist to specialize. Today it is not even that.

So when the question arose: "Who is going to look after Clare now that she is growing up and cannot look after herself?" the answer was obvious: "We are." And if this meant there were other things that in consequence we couldn't do, then we didn't do them.

All children limit the freedom of their parents to some extent. And in fact Clare limited ours less than most. For at the age of five she went to school, and since this had to be a special school, it had also to be a boarding school. Very luckily there was one conveniently close, the Dame Hannah Rogers School at Ivybridge, twenty miles away on the edge of Dartmoor. So our lives fell into that pattern that Lesley and I both knew so well from our own school days, the alternation between term time and holidays; with all the misery that attends the approach of the one, and all the bliss that heralds the other. For Clare, the depths and the heights were probably no less and no more than they had been for us.

With Clare at school, Lesley and I were once more free to work together in the shop. And it was a happy chance that the beginning of her school days coincided almost exactly with the beginning of our school library business. Lesley was thus able to accompany me on all my more exciting expeditions and make them twice as enjoyable.

During the holidays, however, one of us had to be at home, and we took turns: Lesley in the mornings, I in the afternoons. August was our most difficult month, the town and the bookshop crowded with holidaymakers, and even with extra help it was a struggle to do all that had to be done. For in addition to the problem of keeping our shelves adequately stocked, we had to handle the books—hundreds and hundreds of them—that our schools had ordered for delivery at the beginning of September. Checking them, sorting them, finding somewhere to put them, carrying back-breaking parcels up and down our narrow stairs, and loading them onto our van—when all this had been done, and the holidays were at an end, and Clare was back at school—well, at last we could relax.

So, term by term, the years went by; and I have no doubt that our friends, looking at us, now and again shook their heads sadly and said to each other: "What a pity that . . ." and "If only . . ." It is always easy to see and solve the problems of others. "If I were you . . ." But of course I am not you, and this makes all the difference. Could we have done more? Should we have done differently? But we do only what by our nature we are able to do.

As a child I was shy and self-conscious, awkward in company and embarrassed both by my name and by my appearance. At school I would often wish I were a John or a Peter and could join all the other lucky Johns and Peters. At school one lives the life of the herd, and in the herd there is no place for the individual who is different. It is the same in the world at large. The black man in the white community, the Catholic in the Protestant community, the Jew among Gentiles: each has known what it is to be an outsider. Each has longed to be accepted as an equal, treated as a fellow human.

> *Hath not a Jew eyes? Hath not a Jew hands, organs, dimensions, senses, affections, passions?*

Shylock's famous words have been echoed down the ages—and sadly they are sometimes still echoed by the disabled today.

Of course we are not deliberately cruel to the disabled as we have at times been deliberately cruel to Jews. It is just that we are sometimes thoughtless. Or perhaps instead, and with the best of intentions, we try too hard. The blind man waiting at the curb does not need to be seized by the arm as if he were also lame. The deaf are not better able to hear the kind of language normally reserved for small children. Walking down the street, we do not wave or smile at strangers; or accost them and inquire solicitously after their health, and then pat them affectionately on the head. Yet complete strangers will do this to Clare.

The disabled person may need special attention, but he doesn't welcome it. He wants to be treated, as far as possible, as if he were ordinary—his differences, as far as possible, ignored. Those who travel in wheelchairs ask only that they can go where the rest of us go, without too much fuss, without too much loss of dignity.

Happily it is not Clare who minds, who is sensitive to how others behave and to what they say. It is I. And how tempting I find it to take the easy way out: to stay at home. It is always pleasant at home and there is plenty to do. There is no need to go out, to push a wheelchair through the streets of Dartmouth and into public places. But luckily Lesley is braver—or more determined or wiser or kinder, or probably all four. It is she who plans the outing, and who then insists that I not be merely the chauffeur but come too. I go reluctantly, making an obvious effort, making my effort all too obvious. But when it is over and we are home again, I can admit that I too enjoyed it; and I can feel suitably shamed by two brave girls. Lucky Clare to have such a mother!

But to compensate for what I am bad at—and have, after all, been bad at all my life—I have a skill which, small and unimportant in the normal way, has with Clare come into its own.

Anyone who was taking door locks to bits at the age of seven to find out how they worked, who at the age of eleven was inventing burglar alarms for a Secret Passage, and who was happily defusing German mines at the age of twenty-three, was obviously the right sort of father to have when Clare, sleeping alone in her bedroom, waking in the morning and unable to get out of bed, needed a word with her parents. An electric bell that she could work and then—to make a voice pipe—a plastic funnel and a length of garden hose . . . The amateur inventor, gadget maker, and general handyman was in his element.

The chair we sit on, the table we sit at, the knife and fork and plate that we use when we have a meal, all these are designed to fit the average human body and make use of the things that the human body—and in particular the human hand—can do. Thus the hand can grip and move to and fro, and a knife converts this into the cutting up of meat. So if there are certain movements we cannot manage, then certain tools become useless to us and must be redesigned to make use of different movements.

There were very many things that Clare couldn't do. In fact there were very few things she *could* do. When she was young, she could scarcely even sit in a chair. She could certainly not have sat at a table and fed herself with a conventional spoon from a conventional plate. But she could grip and she could manage a sort of circular sweep with her arm. Could the right sort of tool convert this into an ability to collect food from the right sort of plate, and then carry it to her mouth? I thought it could, and sat and watched her and then went away to work it out.

The chair, the tray, the plate, and the fork that I made for her were all a little unusual. Thus the plate was made from an aluminum saucepan sawn off to leave a rim that was one inch high over three-quarters of its circumference and two inches high over the remaining quarter. It fitted into a well in the tray that was one inch deep. Thus there was no fear that the approaching fork might get entangled with the near edge of the plate before it reached the food and pressed it against the far edge. The fork had a wooden head set at an angle into a wooden handle; and fortunately the angle that was best for collecting the food was also the best for delivering it.

It was all a little unusual, but it worked. For the first time in her life Clare was able to feed herself, and this was a very great triumph for her and a very great excitement for us all.

On another occasion, some years later, her school allowed me to take home an old and battered tricycle that no one specially wanted. Could I do something with it? It would need a different seat, one that gave much greater support; it would need different handlebars to give a much simpler method of steering; and it would need different pedals, since the only movement Clare could manage was a straightening of both legs at once.

It was enough. And in triumph, when the new term started, she propelled herself down the long corridor and into the school hall to prove it.

But designing something that worked was only half the problem. The other half was to make it look presentable.

It is a sad fact that much of the equipment designed for the disabled is inefficient, and nearly all of it is ugly. To some extent the one follows from the other. An efficient design has a natural elegance which needs little embellishment to make it attractive. Whereas the wheelchair issued to Clare was such a mechanical disaster that nothing could have redeemed it. How unfair it is that a person who most needs a chair should so often have just the one—and one so very far from beautiful—while the rest of us, who need chairs only now and again, possess so many.

Why should Clare not have as many chairs as we have? Why should she not take the pride and pleasure in them that we take in ours? Why should they not be every bit as decorative and pleasing to look at? No reason at all. They couldn't be bought, of course; but they could be made. And so I set to work to make them.

When I first started carpentry lessons at school, the pleasure I got was the pleasure of cutting and shaping the wood. The lines were ruled for me, and I sawed along them and chiseled between them. At John Lewis I began to look at furniture rather more critically. Some I liked; some I disliked. But it was not until I was puzzling over Clare's needs that I discovered another pleasure as great as the pleasure of making: the pleasure of designing.

It is in fact two pleasures, and they are quite distinct. The first lies in solving the mechanical problem. This is what gives to the things I make for Clare their special fascination: they are all unique. There is no standard pattern to follow as there is if you are making, say, a kitchen table. For example, Lesley might want a device that will hold a mixing bowl and an egg whisk so that Clare can turn the handle and make a cake. Working out the best way to do this is very like working out those mathematical problems that so intrigued me at school. Merely to solve them is not enough: the satisfaction lies in finding the simplest, neatest, most *elegant* solution. The second pleasure lies in taking this, the theoretical design, and giving it a bit of style, giving it shape and proportions that are pleasing to look at.

But of course the greatest pleasure of all was to see Clare sitting comfortably where before she had been uncomfortable, doing something she had not previously been able to do. And it was a pleasant thought that this was, in a sense, a legacy from her grandparents whom she had never known—a product of the fusion of my father's fondness for mathematics with my mother's competent hands. If she had inherited neither, she could at least benefit from the fact that I had inherited both.

The wise man lives in the present. Where the future is certain he may make preparations; where it is uncertain he may take precautions. But beyond that he had best forget it. While Clare was at school, our lives settled into their pattern. She was at school for twelve years, and for those twelve years there was no virtue in bothering ourselves with the question of what we were all going to do when she left. The question could wait. And its answer must wait now.

Lesley and I were booksellers, but though bookselling dominated, it never monopolized our lives—nor should it monopolize these pages. When people come to see me—people who have not been here before—we usually arrange to meet at the shop. It is an easy place to find and I am usually there, and so it seems the logical starting point for whatever is to follow. They come in and look around, and then after a moment or two we go upstairs and find a room where we can sit and talk without being disturbed. Then, if they are not in a hurry to be on their way, I like it if we can spend a few minutes looking at Dartmouth. Lesley and I are proud of the bookshop because we made it ourselves. In a rather different way we are also proud of Dartmouth, proud to feel that we belong here, and so we like showing it off to those who do not know it.

✦ ✦ ✦ ✦ ✦

TWENTY-NINE

From Town Life
to Country Life

There are four ways into Dartmouth. On my first visit, in 1951, I had come from the east. This is the usual direction for visitors from up-country; and whether they travel by car or bus or train, their first view of the town will be from the other side of the Dart, the final lap of their journey will be made on the ferry. Lesley, on her first visit, before the war, had come in her father's boat, and her approach had been from the south, by sea, through the narrow river mouth guarded by its two castles and then up the river to look for an anchorage. Or you can approach from the north, coming down the river from Totnes. Your first view of the town may be less dramatic, but this you can forgive after so magical a voyage. Lastly—in one sense the least and in another the most important of the four—you can come by road from the west.

Here you will have a choice. You will have been traveling along a ridge five hundred feet above sea level. Half a mile from the river the ridge comes to an end, the town lies beneath you, and six roads lead down to it. And in these six roads much of our history can be read.

The approach to Dartmouth from overland with its final precipitous dive has always been a problem. For what was good enough for foot and hoof was not good enough for pneumatic tire, and what was good enough for our grandfathers was not good enough for us. And so, as our means of locomotion demanded it and as our engineering techniques allowed it, new routes were found, new roads built. Thus you can date the six roads into Dartmouth by their steepness and their width.

Having made your choice, what will you find when you reach the bottom? First and most important, you will find that you have arrived. This is not by any means true of towns generally. Most towns are not for arriving at but for passing through on the way to somewhere else; but Dartmouth is not on anybody's way to anywhere. So, having arrived, you will be ready with your first question. "Which is the main street?" The answer is: "The river."

One may hesitate to call it a street, but it is certainly the town's main thoroughfare: the means of communication with the rest of the world which decided the earliest settlers that here was the place to build. Take away the river and no town would ever have sprung up for so little a reason on so inaccessible a site. So the town was built on the river and the roads were added afterward. The river remains what it has always been, Dartmouth's High Street, the only way into the town from the north and from the south, wide enough and deep enough for its purpose in medieval times, still wide enough and deep enough today. Its purposes may have changed over the years; today it carries holidaymakers rather than trade, and in some ways it is more of a barrier than a thoroughfare, discouraging communication with Torbay. But for all that it is still both our High Street and the center of our activity, the stage where the drama of the town is performed. And what more perfect stage could there be than this deep and wide anchorage right in front of the town, its narrow entrance, guarded by Dartmouth Castle, less than a mile away. And what more perfect seating arrangements for the spectators than a steep hillside allowing each row of houses to peer over the rooftops of those below, so that all can see and each has its own most prized and cherished view. What do you do when you arrive in Dartmouth? You go down to the river to see what's happening. Then, having spent an hour or so in contemplation, you are ready with your next question. "Where is the shopping center?"

There isn't one.

For five years Lesley and I lived over the shop and stared at the river. Now and again destroyers would come in and moor just opposite us, wedging themselves in the gap at the end of our road. Once a school of porpoises came surging up the river. Once, very late at night, we saw a family of otters. Then, when Clare came to join us, we moved to a house on the edge of the town.

On the edge of the town? Here again Dartmouth is not quite like other towns. It hasn't really got an edge—at least not the usual sort. Most towns grow outward from the center, adding a succession of annual rings rather as a tree does. But though Dartmouth eventually got the better of its mud, it has never gotten the better of its hills, and so when it had taken possession of all it could at the bottom, it jumped to the top where the ground was once again level enough, and built there. And in between, still grazed by cows, the grassy hillside remained. So when I say that our house was on the edge of the town, what I mean is that below us were houses and above us the cows leaned over our wall and nibbled the tops of our pear trees. But if you climbed the wall and threaded your way past the cows, you came to Townstal—and then you were back in the town again.

We lived here for ten years, and though we eventually bought a van, we always walked to work—down and up twice a day, for we liked having lunch at home. It was not a long walk. Measured horizontally it was only half a mile. Measured vertically it was 250 feet. And the route we took, from edge to center, must surely have been one of the most beautiful walks from edge to center of any town. I knew this at once, but it took me four years to discover exactly why.

You look at a town and you say, "Isn't it pretty!" You say this as soon as you see it. Lesley and I said it when first we came to Dartmouth. Almost every first-time visitor says it. But if you come to stay, then, after a while, when the first fierce flames of passion have died, you find that you marvel each day a little less—until suddenly something happens to jerk you awake. . . .

With us it was the wall at Warfleet. We had not been that way for some time, and so it came as a complete surprise: the widened road, the new retaining wall, twenty feet high, with its smooth, grey, cement-rendered finish, topped with huge rectangular castellations. It could have been a prison wall, it looked so stern and forbidding. Dartmouth is a town of walls, it is true, but they are warm and friendly, built—and most beautifully built—of natural stone. And there had been a natural stone wall here at Warfleet before they pulled it down and replaced it with this. We felt a surge of anger. What could we do? What powers have ordinary citizens to prevent their local council from mutilating their town? There must be an answer. Who would know it? At that time Ian Nairn was editing a column in *The Observer* called "Outrage." Well, here was an outrage, and I wrote to tell him so.

Our reply came not from him but from an organization then unknown to us called the Civic Trust, and it urged us to form an Amenity Society—an obvious enough answer today, of course, but less obvious in 1961. This we did, and we called it the Dartmouth and Kingswear Society, and at various times I have been its chairman and Lesley its secretary. I like to think that in our first sixteen years we have done a lot for the town. I like to think that in the first six years (when Lesley and I were most active) we did particularly well, though perhaps there may be town councillors who would have reservations about this. One thing, however, is certain: the Society did an enormous lot for me. It gave me a whole new field to explore.

You look at a town and you say, "Isn't it pretty!" This is your first and, if you are just driving through, maybe your only impression. What a pretty little town that was! But if you live here you will discover that prettiness may be in conflict with other things: with good housing, efficient services, smooth traffic flow, and prosperity generally. What most impresses the newcomer comes low on the council's agenda. Thus you have two opposing points of view, and how easy and tempting it is to ally yourself wholeheartedly and unquestioningly with one side or the other. The banners of each are to hand, ready to be seized and waved aloft. "Progress and Prosperity" on this side, "Our National Heritage" on that. Take your choice! No need for further argument! Into battle!

So the Dartmouth and Kingswear Society, born in a passion of anger, drawing the bulk of its membership from those people—elderly, middle-class, non-Devonian—who had come here to retire, could so easily have assembled its armory of slogans and hurled them at the enemy, could so easily have leapt to the defense of every ancient building and fought every new development. So easily—but, it seemed to me, so fatally.

What was Dartmouth's future? What were we trying to become? That was the question; and as it turned out it was one we had to answer almost at once. The county was on the point of preparing its development plan. If we who lived here were to have any say in the future of our town, it would be as well to get our say in first. I wondered if it ought to be a composite opinion that took into account and tried to reconcile all points of view, but decided that this would be too difficult: it was going to be quite hard enough to build a plan around the views of our two hundred members. And in the end six of us got together, and three of us did the actual writing. In July 1963, our *Plan for Dartmouth* was published. It was, I think, a good plan, and on the whole it was well received. But never mind that. This is not the story of a town or of a society. It is the story of an individual, and a catalogue of activities and achievements is here out of place. The important thing is not what the Society did for Dartmouth but what together they did for me.

For six years I championed the Dartmouth of my dreams, waving my standard aloft, rallying others to the cause, plotting campaigns, battling against the enemy. They were glorious years and I loved them. "Towns," I cried, "are for living in, not for driving through. Towns are for people."

These six years were almost exactly concurrent with the years when our school library activity was at its height, so that I was simultaneously the champion of two causes, preaching at one moment the gospel of the New Education and at the next the gospel of the Civic Trust.

It was, I suppose, just chance that these two movements arrived in Devon at about the same time, but it was a happy chance for me; for I was, I now suspect, looking for a cause to champion, looking for a chance to speak.

"Looking" is perhaps too strong a word; for there was nothing conscious or deliberate about it. And it is only in retrospect that I can guess at the possible subconscious need that steered me in this direction. It was, in fact, two needs.

The first and most obvious one was to fill the vast hole left when Clare went away to school. The second was to find a use for my newly found self-confidence and in particular for my newly found voice.

Whether what had happened within me was just a much-delayed step in the slow process of growing up, or whether it was caused by some event in my life—Clare's birth or my father's death, for instance—I don't know. But the effect was as if a gate had been opened and all Grandfather Milne's pent-up love of teaching was surging through it onto a tongue free at last of its shackles and now able to cope with it. I might still not have achieved that *disinvoltura* that Hedda had wished to cultivate, but at least I could speak in public without stammering.

So for six years I harangued at my two pulpits; then at both fell silent. Why was this? With the New Education the reason was clear: the cause was failing. But the Amenity Society movement was not failing. Indeed it was gathering strength. Why then did I not redouble my efforts, having only the one battle to fight?

If I attempt an answer to this question, it is not only to explain what happened in the late sixties but to point the way to what—of far greater importance—was going to happen in the middle seventies.

A handful of words stick in my memory. They are from the prayer

238 · THE PATH THROUGH THE TREES

attributed to Sir Francis Drake before his attack on Cádiz in 1587, and I heard them in the chapel at the Royal Naval College when they were the text for a sermon.

> It is not the beginning {of an enterprise} but the continuing of the same until it be thoroughly finished which yieldeth the true glory. . . .

Yes, this is true and I have always held it so. Well begun is nowhere near half done. Anyone can be an enthusiast for half an hour. Real enthusiasm is like a well-constructed bonfire, not flaring up and dying out and then having to be coaxed back to life, but burning strong and steady until all is consumed.

Yet, all the same, one can perhaps draw a distinction between the enterprise itself and an individual's contribution to it: the two need not run concurrently. We have our entrances and our exits, and if it is wrong to go too soon, it can sometimes be worse to stay too long.

It was like this in Italy. When we landed in 1943, I was an enthusiastic sapper officer eager for a front seat in the coming battles. My enthusiasm lasted until I was wounded just over a year later, then it burned out. This was partly loss of nerve, I admit, but not wholly. When I returned to my company, the battle was still on, but things were different—different faces, different atmosphere. I didn't want to go back to my platoon, much as I had loved it. I had finished with being a platoon commander. I had finished with the company, too. I had done what I had set out to do. I had proved what I had wanted to prove. It was time to go, and I was glad to accept a more peaceful and less arduous role in another company.

It was like this now: The best of our battles, so it seemed to me, had been fought and the greatest of our victories won. Perhaps I didn't want to go on saying the same thing over and over again. Perhaps I didn't want to listen to others saying the same thing over and over again. Whatever it was, my particular task, I felt, was finished. Once more it was time to go.

I am still a member of the Society I founded, but I am now only a spectator. It was no bloody head that took me out of the battle. It was simply that we moved from our house on the edge of Dartmouth to another, four miles away. And when we stopped being town dwellers to become country dwellers, it was perhaps natural that I should transfer my affections from townscape to landscape.

For ten years we lived in a house on the edge of the town. Then, quite suddenly, one evening, we decided to go. But before I say why we left, I must say why we came.

The house had everything we were looking for. It was within pleasant walking distance of the bookshop (for in those days we had no car), yet at the same time it was virtually in open country. It was away from the main road, approached by a narrow, rural lane, and it faced the sun. It was, however, a house that had come down in the world. Its roof had gone, its floors were rotting away, and it was inhabited only by chickens. All it had to offer now were four thick stone walls. But this was all we needed, for it gave us the added pleasure of doing our own restoration. It had been built as the coach house for the big house below it. The coach and horse had lived on the ground floor; the coachman and his family had occupied the floor above. But the last coachman and the last horse had long since departed, and all they had left behind them to record their existence were the horse's manger and the house's name. We kept the one—though it served no particular purpose—but we changed the other. Swinnerton Lodge Coach House: after all, it was not so much a name as a description, and one that was bound to lead to confusion with Swinnerton Lodge itself. So we changed it to Spriggs Holly, after the little hamlet in the Chilterns where we had gotten engaged.

I still pay an annual visit to Spriggs Holly. Each year on Christmas Eve, Clare and I call on a friend who lives nearby. And I take the opportunity to open the garden gate (still fastened with the wooden latch I made for it) and climb the steps (still unfinished) and stand on the lawn (with its great hollow tree stump that we found washed ashore on a distant beach and towed home behind our dinghy). It is quite dark, of course, and I cannot see the details, but I know that it is much the same as when we left it, and I can see why we loved it so, and I can see, even in the darkness, why in the end we went.

The truth came slowly. First it was no more than the distant hum of a bulldozer at work. . . . Then its appearance over the brow of the hill . . . Then the first row of houses, still comfortingly far away. Then the bulldozer at work again below the houses, its grinding and straining louder now as it wrenched at the hillside, and as penetrating as a dentist's drill on an exposed nerve. . . . Then another row of houses. And still the bulldozer getting nearer. . . .

One day a man came and cut the brambles at the back of our wall, tearing away the fragile screen we had been hiding behind. Then at last we could see. We could no longer pretend. We knew.

Once it had been cows, and we had loved them. Now it was people, and we hated them. No one who has not had such an experience will know the strength of our feelings; anyone who has will understand. Shortly before we left I stood at the bedroom window, a thing I had not done for many months, and I took a photograph. It showed a wall, a screen, and four houses. Because our garden was long and narrow, four plots came down to our wall, four houses surveyed us from above, four families sitting on their balconies had a bird's-eye view. The very steepness of our hillside, which once we had relied upon to halt the advancing estate, now added to its horror. For each house, as if to see the better, was perched on a brick base: a white bungalow on a brown pedestal, a tooth from which the gum had shriveled to expose its root. A row of witch's teeth . . . Or was it perhaps a battery of television cameras? . . .

Suddenly, unable to bear it any longer, we fled.

Embridge Forge, like Spriggs Holly, had been built to serve the needs of the horse, and with the horse's departure its fortunes too had declined. However, since the cart horse had survived the coach horse by some twenty to thirty years, this decline had here come much more recently. The last blacksmith was still very much alive, and Lesley and I might well have seen him at work. By 1966, however, though the house where we had lived was still habitable, the forge itself was dead and decaying, and an air of sadness hung over the place.

Embridge was like Spriggs Holly in other ways. It was built into the hillside—built properly, of course, not perched uneasily on a pedestal—built as if it belonged. And as at Spriggs Holly, there was much altering, adding, and repairing to be done, and it wasn't until some six months after we had bought it that we were at last able to move in.

Oh, the solitariness of it! Once again there was a great hill rising above us. Once again we were overlooked only by cows. Once again in the early morning I could stand at our bedroom window and enjoy it all. Late evening, just as it was getting dark, was another of my favorite times, and I would go outside and watch the darkness come. I suppose it was because in the past, if we had spent a day in the country, the approach of darkness marked the time when we had to think about going home. Now it was others who would be going home. We would be staying. A blackbird, disturbed, flew along the hedge uttering its evening cry. A wren gave a last defiant trill, then slipped from the pear tree to its roost under the eaves. Only those of us who lived here were here now . . . the blackbird and the wren. . . . It was our valley.

Embridge is three miles from Dartmouth as the crow flies. Surprisingly—for there are scarcely fifty yards of road without a bend—you find on looking at the map that it is very little more as the human walks. Even so, this was too far for working booksellers with much to be done in the shop after the doors were shut and much waiting to be done at home. So mostly we drove, and this was four miles, but for good measure it included a view of the sea and of Start Point. It is only now that I am no longer a bookseller that more and more often I find myself doing the journey home on foot. If it takes a little longer and means starting perhaps a little earlier, I can reassure myself that it is not only a great deal cheaper but that while I am walking I am indeed working.

Dartmouth, as I have said, is backed by a steep hill. On the other side of this hill is our valley; so my route is up one side, down the other, and then along the valley bottom for about a mile. It starts with a long flight of steps. Then comes a road flanked by a terrace of houses. It is steep—one in three—and narrow—eight feet: one of the oldest roads out of the town. At a certain point the houses stop and the hedges start. In an instant you have left the town and are in the country. But the road takes no notice of this: it carries on up the hill as if nothing had happened, and thus provides a perfect transition from town to country, as perfect as is the transition from river to town at the Lower Ferry. I wish I could say it was as invulnerable.

Walking home this way not long ago, I found myself wondering what were the essential differences between the urban I had just left and the rural I was just entering. I could think of only two: the country was greener and contained fewer people. The difference that perhaps springs to mind, that towns are man-made while country is natural, is of course mistaken. Certain tracts of Devon—much of our coastline and much of Dartmoor—are entirely wild; but what lies in between is no more wild than our garden. For it was man who cleared the primeval forests, man who laid out the fields, surrounding them by hedges and deciding what each was to grow, man who planted copses, windbreaks, and woodlands, man who tramped out the tracks he needed and later widened them into roads. The beech avenue that I walk beneath is there because someone put it there. The giant oak by the gate is there because someone allowed it to grow. So if we bless our long-dead builders for their instinct for good townscape, we must also bless our long-dead farmers for their instinct for good landscape. Townscape and landscape: the two have a great deal in common; and it is odd that though we in this country have consciously enjoyed, consciously studied, and consciously practiced the one ever since the eighteenth century, it was not until a few years ago that we even acknowledged the existence of the other. Here in this corner of Devon the two go very much hand in hand, with more than a chance resemblance between them. For they spring from a common parentage: our hills.

These hills have influenced everything that has ever happened here, and they will continue to influence everything that is ever likely to happen, hack at them with bulldozers though we may. They gave us the Dart, and that was countless years ago. They gave us Dartmouth, shaping it the way it is, making it small and compact. They gave us our farmlands—small farms, small fields, woodlands along valley sides where the ground was too steep to plough. They kept both town and country that way, so that Dartmouth is still small, and farms and fields are today little bigger than they were a hundred years ago. They gave us roads that were narrow and winding and that have remained narrow and winding ever since. They and the river have been our rampart against the assault of the holiday trade that has overwhelmed Torbay. Our hills have shaped everything we find around us. Is it surprising that they shape our lives as well? "Stay small and go slow" is their command, and only those who are willing to obey are happy here.

✦ ✦ ✦ ✦ ✦

THIRTY

The New Path

In 1956 my father died. In a sense, however, he was already dead; for the operation that had given him an extra year of life had made him a different person. It had made my mother a different person too. And it had made Cotchford a different place. Yes indeed, if it is sad to go too soon, it is worse to stay too long.

Selfishly I was glad that I lived in Devon and had a bookshop that I could not easily leave. Children drift away from their parents as they grow up, and it is right that they should. I had been very close to mine, especially to my father, for rather longer than is usual, and so the drifting when it came was perhaps a little farther than is usual. I saw my father on two occasions during his illness, my mother and Cotchford on three. On his death I never saw Cotchford again. And although my mother survived him by fifteen years, I saw her only once.

On my father's death my mother had taken over responsibility for his estate. If any decisions were to be made, they were hers to make. I was two hundred miles away and only too relieved to be able to say to enquirers, "I am afraid it is nothing to do with me."

In 1971 my mother died. My reaction was not typically that of a child who has lost a parent. There was little sadness, little sense of bereavement. How could there be? I had last seen her at my father's memorial service, and we had scarcely written to each other since.

When Cotchford was sold, I knew only when her next letter came from a London address. No, my chief concern was that a part of my father's royalties would now be mine—and I didn't want it.

It is easy to give. It is extremely hard to receive. I am bad at receiving, bad at having to be grateful. I like to be able to boast to myself that what I have done I have done without help. Hence my insistence that I was a professional bookseller, and that the bookshop was the sole source of our income. Hence my anger when anyone implied that they thought I was only a dilettante, not really having to make the business pay, happily able to rely on a private income.

But in spite of my determination to earn my own living, I looked upon what I earned more as a measure of my ability to sell books than anything else. I didn't particularly welcome the money for its own sake or for the sake of what it would buy. My ambition was to be a good rather than a rich bookseller: there was something not quite nice about being rich.

Whether or not this attitude is understandable, it does, I hope, explain why a sudden, relatively large, and unearned addition to our income was not at all what I wanted. Many dream of winning the football pools. For me this would be nightmare. To travel hopefully being a better thing than to arrive, I didn't welcome the offer of a lift. No, thank you, I prefer to walk. How often have I said this!

To be offered a lift by *anybody* would therefore have been bad enough, and I would have been tempted to decline it. But to be offered a lift by, of all people, my fictional namesake, to have to travel the rest of my way in *his* company—this was the final insult to my injured pride.

Yet however much I might wish to be independent, standing on my own feet, I was very much aware that this, both figuratively and literally, was something Clare would never be able to do. So here was a dilemma. Fortunately it was not one that called for an immediate decision. It would be a long while before probate had been settled, leaving my emotions plenty of time to sort themselves out inside me. Meanwhile Clare was still at school, Lesley and I were still full-time book-sellers, and things could continue much as before.

And meanwhile I had another series of emotions to battle with. These arose from the discovery that, of my father's personal posses-sions, nothing had survived. All had been destroyed.

Looking back on it now, I can understand why my mother did what she did. Indeed I am utterly convinced that she did the right thing and precisely what my father would have wished.

What did his possessions amount to, anyway? I have already described Cotchford. The house and its furnishings, the garden with its flowers, everything that the visitor was so proudly shown, all these, though bought with my father's money, in every other sense belonged to my mother. The things he needed for himself—a chair to sit on, a table to write at, a bed to sleep in, and a chest of drawers for his clothes and his belongings—were just bits of furniture, not par-ticularly his, not particularly anybody's. His golf clubs, his pipes, and his books: these were more personal, of course, and much loved by him. But they were never particularly loved by my mother; indeed, rather the reverse. For she had never shared with him those things that were closest to his heart. So what were they to her now, when all that she had loved was gone? If you have memories, you don't need mementos.

But of course an author leaves more than his table and his pen. He leaves his unfinished manuscripts. This surely is another matter—of public rather than private concern.

Or is it?

To his many friends my father had been "Alan" or "Blue," the man they had talked to at the Garrick Club, the man they had played golf with at Addington or Ashdown Forest; and as they had known him, so they would remember him. To many others he was known only through what he had written. He was articles in *Punch*. He was plays. He was Pooh. We never give all of ourselves to anybody. Even from those who are nearest to us there is a part of ourselves that we withhold. My father was a private person. He gave sparingly; and to the public at large during his lifetime he gave little more than his published words. Why should we expect more on his death and assume that, because he is no longer there to say no, we may rummage without his permission through all he left behind? His feelings for his unfinished writings were precisely those of a mother for her unborn child. If the mother dies, it may be kinder to let the child die with her.

This is how I feel now. But it was not how I felt at the time.

When I first learned what my mother had done, I felt only a sudden surge of anger and a stab of sorrow. My poor father, that she should have treated him like this! And so started the train of emotions that led in the end to my writing *The Enchanted Places*.

It was, I suppose, a feeling of guilt, a guilt which my mother and I had shared. We had both in our different ways failed him. And I owed it to him to make amends. Yes, if nothing had been left, I would provide something. I would write something and I would write it for his sake. This was my first thought. Later a rather more selfish reason occurred to me. I needed to write something for my own sake, too.

For if I did nothing, then sooner or later someone would come to me and propose himself as my father's biographer. And of course he would hope to see what in fact didn't exist and hear what I didn't wish to tell. Could I refuse to have anything to do with him? Or could I agree to answer certain questions but not others? To say no would be hard enough; but to say anything but no would be in the end to open my private world to a complete stranger and allow him to trample all over it, picking from it what he pleased and interpreting it how he wished. There was only one way out. "Yes, I will write my own account in my own time and in my own words." I had only to say this, first to myself, then to Lesley, to become immediately and utterly safe. For here was my reply, my impregnable defense. And twice in the course of the next two years I was to shelter behind it.

It has been said that the difference between the professional and the amateur writer is that the professional writes even when he is not in the mood. I was an amateur. I knew that duty and self-defense were not enough, and that I was surrounded by excuses for saying "Not today." And I was going to need many todays before I had finished. Day after day I would have to ignore all the other things I ought to be doing. Day after day I would have to sit alone at my typewriter. Only the most intense pleasure could hold me to such a task: and at first contemplation I was filled with nothing but intense repugnance.

What exactly was I going to write? At first I visualized it as no more than an introduction to a new edition of the Pooh books, scarcely even deserving its own covers. I could say something about the real toys and the real places. But there were other questions that people would want to ask. Should I just ignore them? Perhaps I could make my essay take the form of an imaginary interview, in which *all* the questions were asked but only the easy ones were answered, the others being warded off in the manner of the skilled politician. This seemed quite an ingenious idea and I began to contemplate it, letting my mind float back among its memories. I had now stopped saying to myself, "This is something I must do," and had begun to consider how I might do it.

It was at this point that I began to see, not the Christopher Robin I had intended to write about, but another small boy. And as I looked at him he grew clearer, and I saw to my surprise that he was beckoning to me. I took a few hesitant steps toward him, and he came to meet me. He took me by the hand and he led me back. . . .

This was how in the end the book came to be written, and when I had finished it, I added an introduction. "If I have imagined an audience," I said, "it has been a gathering of Pooh's friends and admirers." It seemed the polite thing to say, but of course it wasn't true. Having spent my entire adult life running away from Pooh and his friends, was it likely that I should now want them sitting around my table as I worked? No, I wasn't writing for them at all. I was writing for myself. I was back in the place that I had loved. Hand in hand with my small companion, I was re-exploring the rambling old farmhouse, the garden, the meadows, the woods, the river, the lane, the forest—the enchanted places of my childhood. Day after day I returned, happily writing. And since I couldn't altogether forget my reason for writing, now and again I made myself throw in a bit about Christopher Robin so as not to disappoint the reader.

So it was a book that took me a year to think about and then another year to write. The first half of it was written in the afternoons at Embridge. Clare was at school. Lesley was at the bookshop. I was alone—except for a coming and going of cats. At the halfway point I paused, partly to see if what I had written was publishable, partly because term had ended and Clare was home.

She was home not just for the holidays. She was home for good. She was seventeen and had been at her boarding school since she was six. During that time Lesley and I had both of us been full-time booksellers for three-quarters of the year. For the other quarter, the school holidays, I had worked in the mornings, she in the afternoons. What was going to happen now?

For the time being, at any rate, Clare would be living at home: this was what we all three wanted. She had spent little enough of her life at home, and we had spent little enough of ours with her; and now we would make up for it. In any case, there wasn't any very acceptable alternative.

This meant that Lesley would have to remain a permanent part-time bookseller. As for me, I still had half a book to finish; and if it had been hard enough before—hard on the others, I mean—it was going to be very much harder now. Could I for the next few months abandon the bookshop altogether? Luckily for my conscience, I had no option. For I had now gotten what I now needed, a contract to deliver the completed manuscript by the end of March.

So we would struggle on—but not indefinitely. Eventually we would have to reorganize our lives, and eventually we would have to decide how.

As I said in an earlier chapter, to be a good bookseller you need three things: a goal to aim for, the spur of necessity, and all your working hours. If I had been deprived of any one of these, I might well have questioned whether I wanted to continue. Very happily, I was deprived almost simultaneously of all three. There was no question about it: once again something had come to an end, and it was time to go.

But if my personal decision that I wanted to stop being a bookseller was an inevitable one, it still left two questions unanswered: What should we do with the shop, and what should I then do with myself?

The first question was the easier. Lesley wanted to go on working there. If half of every day was now to be spent at Embridge with Clare, she wanted to spend the other half in Dartmouth—and what pleasanter place than the Harbour Bookshop? So, although we did consider the idea of selling, it was an idea we quickly abandoned. In any case, we wanted the shop to continue as a small private bookshop. We wanted its customers to continue being its customers, finding the sort of books they had been accustomed to find. In other words, we wanted it to remain the *same* shop. Of course there would be changes. In bookselling there are always changes, and this is what gives it its fascination. No two years are alike, and you must be forever on the alert to seize opportunities as they come by. But in spite of change, something remains constant: the shop's identity, its personality. It was this we wanted to continue. And we knew from observation of the book trade, from seeing what had happened to so many small private bookshops when their proprietors had retired and newcomers had taken over, that the chances of this happening were not large.

Ideally, therefore, we wanted someone—or perhaps a married couple—a little like us as we had been when we started; someone who would work with us for a short while and then gradually take over. The proudest and happiest moment in a shopkeeper's life is when he adds the words "& Son" to his signboard. If we could never do this, let us at least aim for the next best thing.

Thus we planned the future of the shop. As for me, I would remain a bookseller until we had found someone to whom I could hand over. I would enjoy this: setting the shop on its course for what I could hope might be the next twenty years of its life, passing on what I had learned. This would make a good and satisfying end to my bookselling life.

But after that, what?

This, as I have said, is the story of someone who at birth was blessed—or was it cursed?—with two talents: his father's head and his mother's hands. To "succeed in life"—if that is what you want to do—you need a single talent to command your undivided energies and steer you, dedicated and determined, to the mountaintop. To have two talents is like trying to ride two horses: you don't get there any quicker. In fact you are lucky to get anywhere at all. On the other hand, you may be a great deal happier, for mountaintops can be cold and lonely.

It was my mother's skill with her hands that had qualified me as a carpenter and joiner in the Royal Engineers, and it was my father's aptitude for mathematics that had subsequently qualified me for a commission. My mother had got me into John Lewis and—assuming one or other of my parents must take the blame—it was my father who had got me the sack. As a bookseller I could be grateful to both of them, since not only did I have to choose books for our shelves, but I first had to make shelves for our books. And all the while at odd moments I had been making things for the house.

I have already mentioned the satisfaction I had found in designing and making furniture and equipment for Clare. And it did seem to me that, financed perhaps by those royalties I was so reluctant to accept for myself, this was something I might do for others. I might almost convince myself that it was something Clare and I might do together. "C. R. Milne & Daughter—Makers of Furniture for the Disabled." The idea appealed to me: a pleasant dream. But it was never more than a dream.

I doubt if I could have turned it into reality. Meanwhile there was my book to be finished.

I had spent a year not writing it, a year writing it, and then eight months helping it into print. It was published in November 1974. And that, I thought, was that. My venture into authorship was at an end. Back for a while to the retail side of the trade; and then perhaps on to the carpenter's bench.

But it didn't happen like that.

The first part of *The Enchanted Places* was concerned mainly with the Sussex countryside. The second part was concerned with my parents and especially with my father. In other words, I was writing about a writer. Many sons follow their fathers; but mine had never wanted this, and I had wanted it only at odd moments in my life. He had feared that, whatever I wrote, comparisons would be made and one of us judged less good than the other. Jealous by nature—as I was too— more than anything he hated rivalry. Yet here I was, not just writing a book but writing one which, whether I liked it or not, was going to be put alongside the Pooh books and tested by its ability to hold its own in such company. Not only that, but one of my purposes was to show the extent to which the son was a product of his parents—thus tacitly inviting the all-too-inevitable comparison.

Clearly, if the general verdict had been that, though doubtless there were many things I had inherited from my father, an ability to write was not one of them, that would have been that. I would have done what I had initially set out to do, but not what I had later privately hoped to do. Sad, but not altogether surprising.

An autobiography is quite unlike any other form of literature. Not only is it a public *apologia pro vita sua,* but during the actual writing of it, each session at one's typewriter is like a session on the analyst's couch. Consequently, its effect on the writer is considerable. In my case the writing and its reception combined to lift me from under the shadow of my father and of Christopher Robin, and to my surprise and pleasure I found myself standing beside them in the sunshine, able to look them both in the eye.

"Why, you're only a sort of thing in his dream!" cried Tweedledee to Alice, seeing the Red King asleep beneath a tree. That—for so long, and for so many people—was what I had been. And now at last I could feel that I was myself. If I had any lingering sorrow over what had happened on my father's death, it was a pleasing thought that, out of the flames of the bonfire that had destroyed what was left of him, had been born something that was in another sense his too. And at that moment, whether he liked it or not—and I hoped that he would have liked it—the words "& Son" had been nailed to *his* signboard.

I have said that a professional bookseller needs all his working hours. Happily, a professional writer does not. If mornings only were all I could now manage, mornings only would be enough. So here was something I could do and here was the moment to start doing it. Here was a challenge and both the encouragement and the opportunity to accept it. The current served. The tide was at the flood. I took it.

I doubt if it leads me on to fortune and luckily it doesn't need to; for I have accepted my namesake's offer of help. I had to accept it for Clare's sake, of course. But perhaps I might need to accept it for my sake and for Lesley's as well. For although one might measure the ability of a bookseller by what he earns, this has never been the measure of a writer.

So each morning I work at the Harbour Bookshop—not on the ground floor among the books, not on the first floor in our Gift Gallery, not (thank goodness) on the second floor where the invoices are sorted and the accounts paid, but up again, up a very narrow flight of stairs, to the attic beneath the roof.

It is still as unlovely as it was when I described it in *The Enchanted Places,* but at least it now has a proper light and an electric fire. Through the little window (which still lets in the rain) I can see the sky, and if it is blue and inviting, then, in the afternoon, I shall be happy to accept its invitation. Up again, up, up, up, carrying Clare this time, to the "Top" that isn't a top, to where the bluebells grow and the longhorn moths fly, to where I have planted my trees and once intended to build a hut.

Of course the hut has not yet been built. In fact I am not even sure now that I want to build it. For it will mean putting a wall between me

and the rocks at my back, and a roof between me and the sky overhead. And who wants that on an afternoon in late autumn when there
is still a bit of heat in the sun and the wind is warm and caressing?

Here we come, Clare and I. It is a tiring climb with one set of muscles having to do the work of two, and I am grateful that she is little
and light. And here we sit and dream, and perhaps I do this and that
among my trees. There is much to be done, but there is no hurry. I can
do a bit more another day. Small and slow is our world, and luckily
this is how we like it.

Just below our terrace the ground drops away steeply. Here there is
a patch of gorse seedlings—over a thousand, I should guess. There
is much around me that I can't explain, but this I can. We had a fire
here the summer before last—that very dry summer of 1976. It had
been our last surviving area of original jungle, a tangle of furze and
bramble and blackthorn. Then one evening it all went up in flames;
and we returned from an afternoon on the river to find a landscape
transformed, to see a boundary wall we had never seen before and
contours we had only been able to guess at, to see black stumps jut-
ting out of black earth.

It is not only the wise bookseller who seizes his opportunities: it is
all nature. Gorse seeds lie dormant in the soil waiting for the intense
heat that is necessary for their germination. And so the flames of the
fire that had destroyed what was left of their parents had brought life,
phoenix-like, to a new generation. This was their moment—and mine,
too. For within hours the fire had done what had daunted me for years;
and I set to work with mattock and spade to cut the path I had always
been meaning to cut, another path to the top.

Up here we are now a little more exposed than we were: the bush-
es that had sheltered us from the southwest are gone; and a chill puff
of wind comes across the valley, warning us that the afternoon is
nearly over. The sun is only a fraction of an inch above the horizon.
Sunset comes early to those who live in a valley, but the higher slopes
remain aglow and sunlight shines on the herring gulls as they fly
overhead.

Lesley will be walking home from the shop. Shall we go and meet her?

If she leaves at half-past five and if the journey takes her fifty minutes (because she may stop to pick blackberries or look for mushrooms on the way), and if we want to meet her somewhere about the end of the beech avenue, what time should we leave? There's a mathematical problem for you! I ought to be able to solve it: I was a mathematician once, or so I boast. But I'm getting rusty: I'd need pencil and paper and no interruptions; and by the time I'd worked it out we'd be too late. So perhaps it would be wise to start now; then we needn't hurry. Which is it to be: tricycle or wheelchair?

I grip Clare around her waist and she puts her arms around my neck and I hoist her up. Comfortable? And away we go, slowly because the path is a little slippery, down through the trees.

PART THREE

From Hill to Open Garden

*To A.A.M. on your hundredth birthday
from C.R.M. with love*

{Dedication from the original 1982 edition of
The Hollow on the Hill—The Search for a Personal Philosophy}

*For Lesley
whose welcome to all who visit our garden is
(with the exception of a few who visit her vegetables)
as warm as my own.*

{Dedication from the original 1988 edition of
The Open Garden—A Story with Four Essays}

THIRTY-ONE

✦ ✦ ✦ ✦ ✦

Emotion

When I was a child I never lost my temper. This, perhaps the most distressing of all childhood emotions, was one that I was mercifully spared. But I suffered from most of the others. I burst into tears on too many occasions for too little reason. I could be jealous and resentful and unbearably shy. And I knew what it was to be afraid. I was afraid of the dark. I was afraid of witches. At school I was afraid of boys who liked hitting other boys on the nose. I was very far from brave.

So, like most of us at that age, I looked upon my emotions as inner, painful, and rather unmanly things that I must do my best to conceal.

I was little more than a schoolboy when war came. I no longer cried, but I could still feel afraid. Would I feel afraid? In peacetime this is not a question that need bother a young man. If he feels the urge to test his courage, he can look for a mountain and climb it, look for an ocean and sail it, or buy a fast car and drive it to the terror of other road users. But he has no need to do such things. At school I had happily left it to others to be heroic on the rugby field. If the war had not come, I have no doubt that I would have been just as happy to leave mountains, oceans, and fast cars to others. No one would have pointed a finger at me and cried, "Coward!"

But the war left me no option. Here was a challenge, a test of my physical courage that I must not avoid; for I knew that if I did, I could never forgive myself.

In 1941 my battles still lay ahead of me: battles with Germans, maybe; battles almost certainly with fear. It was the latter that I had to win, and I was pleased with myself that, at least in prospect, I was not afraid. I was pleased that, on the whole, I seemed able, for the first time in my life, to keep my emotions under control.

Yes, emotions had to be controlled. It was childish to give way to anger. It was girlish to give way to tears. And soldiers did not give way to fear. I was grown up now; no longer childish, no longer girlish. I was a soldier and in command of myself. And so when in the summer of 1941 I came upon Karl Pearson's *The Grammar of Science*—in which he argued that reason should be our sole guide in every field of human experience, and that we should not be "led by mere appeal to the passions or by blind emotional excitement"— I agreed with him, not only as a fellow mathematician but also as a man.

As I lay on my bunk with *The Grammar* I saw at once how right Pearson was. Be content to discover *what*. Don't try to guess *why*. Here was an attitude that combined both pride and humility: pride in the power of the human intellect; humility in admitting its limitations. I knew now how far reason could take me, and I would go no farther. Better than any set of ready-made answers, what Pearson had given me was the apparatus for testing such answers as might be offered to me. Did they depend upon evidence that no scientist would accept, did they speculate more deeply than science would allow? Then I would reject them. Were the arguments dressed up in scientific language? Then I was at once on my guard. I was not going to be deceived by the pseudoscience of the unscientific.

For it is not only the rationalist who likes to think himself a rational human being. We all do—especially men. We are (rightly) proud of our ability to reason, to think logically. We are (excusably) a little ashamed if inadvertently we display our emotions rather too publicly. "Mere" emotion. "Unrestrained" emotion. Those childhood memories still haunt us. If we hold a belief, it is, we firmly claim, a rational belief. No, no. It is absurd to suggest that it might be a "mere" emotional belief; and so we do our best to scratch together rational arguments in support of it.

It was when, in 1964, I came up upon John Macmurray's *Reason and Emotion* that I began to see how our emotions were being underrated. We had two guides, not one; two voices whispering in our ear and prompting our actions. Nor was reason necessarily the senior partner. There were of course many occasions when the voice of reason was to be preferred. But there were other occasions when reason was unable to advise us and we must listen instead to the voice of emotion. Reason depended upon experience—which was why in our childhood, lacking experience of the world, we had to rely so much on emotion. Experiences, to be of any value to us, had to possess something in common. It was this common factor that enabled us to make our predictions. Reason therefore worked best in the mechanical world, where things ran true to expectation. But much of the world was not mechanical. The moon's behavior was mechanical; man's behavior was not. Man's behavior was often emotional, unpredictable, following no known laws. But here, where reason gives us least assistance, emotion comes to our rescue. It is emotion that determines our relations with our fellow men, and our closest personal relationships are almost wholly emotional. Emotion guides us elsewhere, too. The astronomer may tell us something about the moon, but so too does the poet. The astronomer's moon is everybody's moon; the poet's is very much his own, and not everyone can share it with him.

I was up at the campsite contemplating the primroses that were then just coming into flower. I could look at them with the eye of reason, the botanist's eye, or I could look at them with the eye of emotion, the artist's eye. I thought I understood how the brain rationalized on what the eye saw. I had made a model of the brain based on an office filing system. But as yet I had not tried to understand the workings of emotion. I had kept the two quite separate, so as not to confuse them. I had—as most people do—located reason in the head and emotion in the heart, an elementary model that served its very limited purpose. Perhaps the time had come to attempt something more complicated. Perhaps the primroses might suggest something.

Devon is famous for the profusion of its primroses. They grow not just in woods and along hedgebanks as in other counties. They grow also in open fields and can turn a grassy hillside as yellow as daisies can turn it white. Not surprisingly, during our first years in Devon when spring came around and the hills became yellow, I felt the familiar thrill that I had first experienced when I was a child at Cotchford. I had experienced it very strongly then. I was experiencing it almost as strongly now. And so it continued to be, year after year, until one year, well into the month of May, I suddenly realized that the primrose season was almost over— and I had scarcely noticed it.

Shortly after that I began to write *The Enchanted Places,* and this meant making a deliberate effort to unearth childhood memories in order to describe them; and it was then that I found myself thinking of Wordsworth's "Immortality" ode. How very true! The vision that one saw as a child with such piercing clarity does indeed fade as one grows older.

At the time I merely recorded in my book that this was so. It was not until quite recently that I asked myself where this vision came from and why it faded. I searched around for a moment or two, then came up with an answer.

The first thing I realized is that there is nothing in a blob of yellow to tell the eye anything. The eye is simply the postman that carries the message to the brain. Nor is there anything in the message itself for the brain to get excited about. The excitement comes when the folders are produced and the previous correspondence is studied. It is like the letter that merely says "I agree": it is meaningless until one refers back to discover what is agreed. Thus the primrose I contemplate at any time is not only that particular flower, but all the others I have ever seen; and I am thus reminded also of the various occasions on which I saw them. Since primroses meant a lot to me as a child, I am reminded of my childhood. Thus the thrill I feel today—such as it is— is in part the stirrings of memory, the echo of an older thrill. But what about the thrill I felt as a child? What memories were there then? The six-year-old could perhaps look back a year or two. What about the four-year-old? At some point in time came the first primrose. Then what? The files were empty. No memory could be evoked. It was simply a pattern of color to the eye, a soft feel between finger and thumb, and a very slight sensation to the nose.

It is true that in retrospect those early primroses seem set in idyllic surroundings. But this has nothing to do with it. For if we can find nothing intrinsically thrilling in our first primrose, how can there be anything intrinsically thrilling in the circumstances of that first meeting? If the primrose could stir no emotion, then neither could the wood where it grew.

So at what point *did* emotion enter the experience? As it is undoubtedly strong in childhood and appears to diminish as we grow older, I could only conclude that it was there from the start, that the primrose file was *not* empty at my birth. Something was already in it, something which, as the years went by and more and more correspondence was added, became increasingly hard to unearth. Memory is like a chain. We reach back into the past by a succession of links. I cannot necessarily remember a thing, but I remember remembering it. I am in contact with the intervening memory. Thus it is I have kept alive little pictures of my childhood, by repeatedly recalling them. I can get back so far but no farther. It is like those ancient manuscripts that come down to us through copies of copies. I have an early copy; but the original, the document that was at the bottom of the file, is lost.

I had never bothered to think about such things before, and now that I did so the explanation, as I have said, came quite suddenly. It was this:

The brain at birth is not, as I had supposed, an empty filing cabinet. It already contains a store of memories acquired and accumulated by preceding generations. In animals this is known as instinct. In humans, although certain animal instincts survive more or less unchanged, others have been refined, and these have become our emotions. The emotion I felt on seeing my first primrose came from the inherited memory of primroses seen by my ancestors.

It was at this point that I abandoned my projected natural history of Embridge.

Let me first consider instinct.

A dog growls and the child, encountering a dog for the first time in its life, instinctively recoils. Another dog growls and a different child, remembering the time a growling dog once bit it, recoils for good reason. In both cases the brain receives messages from eyes and ears, and in consequence sends out instructions to the body. The second set of instructions is clearly the result of memory; and so it was easy to persuade myself that the first set, apparently so similar, was the result of some sort of "memory," too. In this case it could only be a "memory" that was present at birth. I therefore called it "inherited memory."

Instinct, I argued, is inherited memory. Without it, the brain would be a filing system with no files. The senses would send in their messages and the messages would have no meaning. All knowledge would have to come gradually by trial and error, and any error would be instantly fatal. No species could survive its earliest days without the closest attention from its parents, attention a great deal closer than is given by the mother fish to its fry or by the butterfly to its caterpillar children. Hence the immediate need for an instinct that will advise on food, on shelter, and on avoiding enemies.

How is this instinct acquired? It is obviously acquired by previous generations and handed on to their offspring. But this doesn't quite answer the question. For it could still be acquired in two different ways. It could be the result of "natural selection," the "survival of the fittest." This is the way (so I was taught) in which protective coloring is acquired. Those without it are eaten. Those with it stand a better chance of bringing up a family. Protective instinct could be acquired in the same way. Those who froze best lived longest. Thus the instinct to freeze could grow over the centuries in a series of jerks, each generation being a little better than the preceding one. Alternatively—and this is the theory I prefer—it could grow more gradually, day by day, hour by hour, minute by minute, as a steady stream of experience flows into the brain, is collected, and is then—in some form—handed on.

To say this is not to suggest that I am protected against potentially fierce dogs by the memory of the dog that bit my father when he was a boy—any more than I would suggest that I could inherit from him the scar on his finger caused by that bite. But it is to suggest that there might be, at the very beginning of my "Dog" file, some sort of précis of inherited experience that says, "Beware of dogs that growl."

Once I had persuaded myself of this, I could see that instincts need not necessarily have any survival value at all. Consider kittens, for example.

Among our collection of cats we like to have at least one productive female, and the consequence of this is a couple of litters every year. As this has been going on for over twenty years, I can write about kittens with some authority.

One thing I have noticed is this: As soon as a kitten can open its eyes, it will stare at me. As soon as it can crawl, it will drag itself toward me. As soon as it can run, it will run to me; and as soon as it can climb, it will haul itself up my trouser leg. Why? You might have thought that a vast moving object would be something to hide from, not run toward. Yet instinct tells the infant kitten that this is not so; and this is an instinct that has nothing to do with survival. Later on in its life, cat may come to depend on man; but the newborn kitten depends solely on its mother. However, if man is no protector, he is, almost immediately, tremendous entertainment value; and the trousered leg soon becomes a wonderful adventure playground. For generation after generation—ever since cats first became domesticated—kitten and man have given each other endless pleasure. Is it fanciful to believe that memory of this lies at the back of every kitten's brain and is stirred the very moment man's dim shadow first looms into view? Fanciful or not, I was prepared to believe it.

The next thing I had to consider was the connection between instinct and emotion. There were obviously certain points where they touched. The instinct for self-preservation becomes the emotion of fear. The baby's instinctive cry for help becomes the crying of the child when it is upset. The miniature explosion that occurs when a kitten encounters an inquisitive dog becomes the explosion of temper we meet in children. Equally obviously, both instinct and emotion, though they could be modified by experience, seemed to originate in some source that was outside experience. A seed of some sort was there at birth. The parallel seemed close enough, and I now felt able to adapt my model of the human brain to describe the workings of both reason and emotion.

All human actions apart from reflex actions (I argued) originated in the brain and were of two kinds—and only two kinds—rational and emotional. Under "emotional" I included "instinctive," since there was no essential difference between the two. The brain records all experience, that is to say all the sense impressions it receives, and it files these away in what I pictured as a series of folders. Whenever a new message is received, the brain instantly brings forward the appropriate folder and examines its contents to see what conclusions, if any, can be deduced and what actions, if any, are called for. At the bottom of each folder is an item that is different from all the others that lie on top of it. It is a précis, inherited at birth, of the two similar folders possessed by its parents. This précis will therefore have been conditioned by experiences going right back into our ancestral past.

Acquired memories can be examined one by one in the detached way of a scientist examining the results of his experiments. Inherited memory cannot be examined in this way. Instead it has a potency all its own. We *feel*. If the conclusions that can be drawn from an examination of acquired memories agree with the conclusion urged by inherited memory, all is well. But if the conclusions differ, then we have to decide between following "our head" or "our heart."

That was my model. The next step was to see what could be deduced from it.

Because it is the custom for a woman on marriage to assume her husband's surname—because of this bias in favor of the male—we tend to think of our family tree as consisting of a single root linking a succession of fathers. Although it is usual for the family name, titles, and estates to be passed along this male line only, family features and characteristics come equally from father and mother, and if we trace *these* backward, we find the number of our ancestors doubling at every generation. Thus, if there had been no intermarriage at all, we could claim a thousand million ancestors alive at the time of the Norman Conquest. Obviously this is an impossibility: the population of Europe at the time would not have allowed it. Obviously a lot of intermarriage between more or less distant cousins must have occurred. But at least this gives us an indication of the very widespread nature of our origins. We are like a tree whose roots, buried underground, divide and subdivide again and again as they spread outward. And of course our neighbors are the same. Their roots too spread out and out and interlace with ours. We are like trees in a wood, our trunks quite separate one from another, but beneath the soil an inextricably tangled network of fibers. The farther away we get from the trunk, the finer and more numerous the fibers become and the more they intermesh. If one individual can claim up to a thousand million ancestors alive in 1066, then one Norman soldier can likewise claim a thousand million descendants alive today. And nine hundred years is the merest flicker of an eyelid in the history of mankind.

From this we can see how vast and how widespread is the source of our emotions. They come to us from as far south as the Mediterranean and from as far north as Scandinavia. The Phoenicians, the Romans, and the Norsemen did not leave only their bones here, they left us their memories, and among them, no doubt, memories of snow and ice, of mountains, of the sea, and of the desert sands.

The next thing to appreciate is simply that we are the survivors. Millions upon millions perished—died at birth, died soon after, failed to reach maturity, failed to mate and have children. But every single one of our millions upon millions of ancestors *all* succeeded, *all* lived to bring into the world at least one tough and healthy child. What a triumphant heritage is ours! What an amazing success story is our life!

Did we fight battles? Then we won. Others may have been slain. Not us. Did pestilence or famine strike down our community? We survived it. Did we hazard our lives in some great enterprise? The risk paid off. Others may have been wrecked. We came safely ashore. Memories of childhood are ours, memories of youth, memories of gathering strength and growing toward maturity, memories of love. And there we stop. For at the moment of our conception the flow ceases. We know nothing of what follows, the gradual decline that leads in the end to death. We may see it in others. We do not know it in ourselves.

Is it then surprising that we love the world? The world was good to us. Through the woods and the fields, across the hills and the valleys, over the mountains and the moors and the sea we made our way in triumph. It is only in the last two hundred years that man has enclosed himself in towns. Is it likely that the preceding thousands will have been quite forgotten?

> There was a time when meadow, grove and stream,
> The earth and every common sight,
> To me did seem
> Apparelled in celestial light,
> The glory and the freshness of a dream.

This is our inheritance, the treasure of a hundred thousand years, collected by our ancestors and handed on to us at birth. What we do with it afterward is another matter.

First memories are always the clearest. First day at school, first day of married life, first day in a new job, first view of Dartmouth. Later memories usually make less impression. They come flooding in and piling up, one on top of the other, so that the Dartmouth I glance at today is the Dartmouth I glanced at yesterday and the day before and the day before. . . . Only if I make a conscious effort, or if the sun is just right, does it become the Dartmouth I first saw on that May morning thirty years ago. Later memories can obscure; but they can also keep alive. It depends how we use them.

When I was writing *The Enchanted Places* I remembered how much as a child I had loved daisies. Yet I had scarcely given them a glance since. Or rather I had glanced at them too often and with too little thought. Fortunately I had also glanced at them from too great a height—from a distance of five feet or more. A child is nearer to the ground and peers more closely. So I picked a daisy and looked at it as I had not looked at a daisy for over fifty years; and in the deep crimson tips to its petals I saw at once the daisies of my childhood. It was a sudden, dazzling revelation, a moment of vision and as near as I could ever deliberately get to that first daisy I had inherited at birth.

Thus by making this conscious effort did I re-establish a link with a childhood memory, and thence to an emotion so deeply buried that I had forgotten its presence. It was as if I had opened up a long overgrown path. Today, no longer snared and distracted by the tangle of intervening memories, I can travel that way with greater ease. It still needs an effort but the effort is so much less. I know where the path lies and I know how to find its entrance.

> I was utterly alone with the sun and the earth. Lying down on the grass I spoke in my soul to the earth, the air, and the distant sea far beyond sight. . . .

In this way at Liddington Castle did the naturalist Richard Jefferies find the entrance to his path, stretching himself out physically on the ground so that every part of him could feel the ground beneath bearing him up; stretching himself out spiritually until in imagination he touched the far horizon and could feel the great earth speaking to him.

I won't for one moment pretend that this is what I do at my campsite. I think I might feel a little embarrassed with myself if I did. But I know exactly how Jefferies felt; and I think I am now a little nearer to understanding why I feel that way too. Today we may look elsewhere for our shelter from the elements, for protection from marauders, for a place where we can worship our gods. But we have long memories. We have not forgotten!

THIRTY-TWO

* * * * *

Efficiency
and the Oil Beetle

WWhen we first came to Embridge there were three things we found living here that were until then quite unknown to us—and which I have yet to find anywhere else.

The first (to give its more formal name) was lungwort. There was any amount of it sharing a little flower bed at the back of the house with some marigolds.

Lungwort is in fact a wildflower, native to Europe though not to Britain. At some distant time it was introduced into Britain and at some more recent time it was introduced into our garden. But, though a wildflower, it is, like the primrose or the violet or the foxglove, perfectly at home in the flower garden. No one would dream of treating it as a weed. Indeed, so happy does it look, edging the bed that now surrounds our terrace, that I cannot picture it growing in the wild.

Lungwort is its formal name. Even more formal is pulmonaria. But the name we preferred was soldiers-and-sailors. It is also known as soldier-and-his-wife, or Josephs-and-Marys, or Adam-and-Eve, or thunder-and-lightning, because the flowers when they first open are pink and later turn blue, giving pink flowers and blue flowers the same stem. Yet another name is Jerusalem cowslip, which suggests its general appearance. The first buds open early in January on very short stems—far too short to pick. But gradually, as the days lengthen, so too do the stems, until by March they are five or six inches long and hold themselves more elegantly. And the flowering continues into June, thus allowing us six months to enjoy them.

The terrace is a pleasant place for sitting, sunny and sheltered. It is particularly pleasant, therefore, in the early part of the year when the wind is still keen and the soldiers-and-sailors are newly on parade. In February and March on milder days we may prefer to sit elsewhere to enjoy the celandines and primroses and wild daffodils. But a sunny day, whatever the wind, will often find us on the terrace; and to the terrace to visit the soldiers-and-sailors come the first of the bees. In February they come in ones and twos, and we greet their return as one of the many eagerly awaited signs of approaching spring. By March and April there is continuous bee activity among the flowers, and watching it in an idle way gives us added pleasure. A town dweller finds the same sort of pleasure sitting at his window looking down on to the to-ing and fro-ing in the street outside.

To the casual eye, bees fall into two categories: "honey" bees and "bumbles"—the one smooth and small and slender, the other large and round and furry. Both sorts come to the terrace, and as we watched them and got to know them rather better, we noticed one of each sort behaving toward the other in a strange way. The "bumble" was small and black. It moved unhurriedly from flower to flower, the flower heads nodding to mark its progress as its weight pulled them down. The "honey" bee flew at immense speed. It swooped down on the soldiers-and-sailors, raced two or three times up and down the line of flowers (like a visiting general in a great hurry), and was off. But if during its lightning tour of inspection it came upon a black bumble, it would instantly stop and remain hovering in midair, motionless. Then, as the bumble moved unconcernedly among the blossoms, the other would stalk it, darting and stopping, all in midair, keeping out of sight about four inches behind its victim. This would continue while perhaps four or five flowers were visited. The suddenly came the pounce. The hovering bee would shoot in and grab the unsuspecting bumble, and together they would fall to the ground. Bee murder? No, for after a moment both would reappear; the attacker would fly off and the attacked, apparently unhurt, would continue her shopping.

Again and again we watched this happen, day after day throughout the spring and then year after year. What was the explanation? We asked a naturalist friend, a great authority. But alas his authority extended only to birds, and he could not tell us. This is the trouble with naturalists these days. They know so much about so little. They specialize too narrowly and outside their chosen field know less than I do. In the end I found the answer quite by chance—in a book I was reading. The two bees, so different in appearance and behavior, were in fact male and female of the same species. They were "flower bees," and he was not attacking her. He was making love.

My book mentioned in particular their passion for lungwort. It mentioned also a liking for polyanthus and aubretia, but though we have both, it is only among the soldiers-and-sailors that we have seen them. Nor have we noticed them at any other time of year but the spring when they are courting.

Though we prefer the name we first knew them by, they have another which describes a less visible activity of theirs. They are called "potter bees": not on account of the way the female wanders from flower to flower, but because of the way she makes her nest. She burrows a hole into the ground and furnishes it with several small clay pots. These she fills with a mixture of honey and pollen, then she lays a single egg on top of each and covers it with a lid.

I said there were three things we found living here that we had never met before. Lungwort and flower bee were two of them. The third was the oil beetle. The link between the first two was obvious, for I never saw a flower bee except around the lungwort. The link between the bee and beetle is far from obvious. Indeed it is quite invisible to the casual eye, and I must rely on the testimony of that greatest of entomologists, J. H. Fabre.

Oil beetles are not common. They are described as "local," meaning that they have their small settlements here and there, but in between are vast tracts of country where there are none. One of their settlements is in our garden. And I have never found another. Here I meet them frequently on sunny days in the spring, crawling over the grass. They move slowly. They are easy to see and once seen will never be forgotten, for they are like no other creature. Fabre makes no attempt at politeness. He describes their appearance as "uncouth," "clumsy," and ugly," and their behavior as "disgusting." But just as one may recoil at first sight from an ugly face but later, as one gets to know the owner better, feel toward him an affection made all the stronger for his very ugliness, so I have developed a special fondness for my oil beetles. The "disgusting" behavior that filled Fabre with "repugnance" has no such effect on me. If you pick up an oil beetle and allow it to explore your finger, it will probably in self-defense exude little drops of yellowish liquid from all its joints. It is this oily liquid that gives the beetle its name. It is supposed to be evil-smelling, like the milky liquid you get on your fingers when you pick up a grass snake, and this is intended to discourage would-be assailants. But though Fabre says it makes your fingers "stink," I have not noticed it; and I have even tried tasting it without ill effects. But I will agree that at first sight there does seem to be something wrong with the beetle's shape. It is as if the Creator had assembled it out of the bits and pieces left over after the other beetles had been made, so that nothing quite matches or is quite the right size. Meeting a female for the first time, you think she is carrying something on her back. I am reminded of peasant women in southern Europe weighed down beneath huge bundles of sticks, or of the caddis fly larva that crawls around dragging its homemade stick-house with it. But the burden that the oil beetle carries is not fuel for the fire or a home to retreat into. It is itself: its own vast stomach. All other beetles have elegant wing cases, smartly styled, smoothly tailored, gleaming in the sunshine, black, brown, green, red, often iridescent and with spots or stripes. But the oil beetle, so it seems, has to make do with the cast-off and rather bent wing cases originally made for a beetle a quarter its size. And even these are not stitched on properly, but overlap in the middle. Finally, its antennae have an odd kink, as if they had been broken and rather badly glued together.

The life of the young oil beetle begins when its mother lays her eggs in a hole in the ground. It is not often that I can claim to have seen something that Fabre has missed, and so I will here proudly state that I have watched an oil beetle laying its eggs. Fabre was not so lucky, and he had to rely on the British naturalist, Newport. Newport went rather farther than I did: he counted them and made the total at the bottom of the hole 4,218. I would certainly agree that there were quite a lot. The eggs are laid in April or May and hatch about a month later. The creature that emerges is so unlike the larva of any other beetle that for a long time it was thought to be a louse. It is long-legged and slender, agile and active, and as the eggs hatch so these tiny yellow creatures race all over the grass. On one occasion they raced all over Fabre. They are searching for flowers, and when they find one they clamber up the stem and settle down quietly among the petals waiting for a visitor. When someone arrives (and it may well be a fly or the wrong sort of bee), they scramble aboard and ride away. Most, therefore, are unlucky, going to unsuitable homes. But some find the right host, the flower bee, and are borne off to the bee's hole where the honey pots are waiting. And if one of the riders is even luckier and has come on the right day, it will be able to watch an egg being placed on top of the honey. It can then dismount and climb on top of the egg and wait for the bee to put the lid on her pot. Then comes the small creature's first meal. It tears open the skin of the egg and eats the contents. After that it settles down on top of the now flattened egg case that is floating like a raft on the honey and goes to sleep. It wakes up to find it has become a white and very torpid slug-like creature with (fortunately) an appetite for honey. When it has eaten its way to the bottom of the pot—by which time it is about half an inch long—it pupates and emerges in a larval form that is still somewhat slug-like. It pupates again and finally, the following spring, makes its way up into the fresh air a fully developed beetle, hungry now for buttercups.

The obvious lesson to be learned from this is that one species can depend upon another in ways that are not at first sight apparent. Who, coming to Embridge and seeing, as we had, the lungwort that grew close beside the house and the oil beetles that wandered through the grass on the hillside, would have imagined any connection between them? Yet I guess that if we dug up all our soldiers-and-sailors, we would lose our beetles too.

So when I am assured by a "spokesman" or an "authority" or even an "expert" that no link has been established between something that they are in favor of and something that the rest of us dislike, I am skeptical. Such links may be quite hard to discover. And they are, of course, even harder if one is not a very enthusiastic searcher.

That, as I say, is the obvious moral—that there is much less independence in this world than we commonly like to suppose. But there is another, which occurs to me as I remember the beetle I watched one April afternoon about ten years ago.

I was sitting on a patch of earth that I had recently leveled and was planning to turf when she appeared, making her slow and stumbling way through the surrounding grass to join me. She crawled across the bare earth and, finding a suitable place, stopped and began to dig. She dug awkwardly, as one might expect from such a creature. Her front legs seemed ill-adapted for excavating, her back legs ill-adapted for pushing the earth out behind her. Frequently the earth she had pushed fell back on top of her. It was as if her legs, too, had come from the oddments box when she was being put together. However, the hole was at last deep enough: her whole body was now inside it. So she backed out and then lowered herself in the other way around. Finally she emerged, dragging fragments of earth down into the hole as she pulled herself out.

What impressed me most about this little incident was the beetle's almost unbelievable clumsiness. She and her ancestors had been digging holes like this for maybe millions of years. For millions of years they had been slowly, slowly developing their skill, perfecting their technique, and adapting their bodies. And indeed their legs had become the most complicated of mechanisms, reminding me of those multipurpose pocketknives favored by Boy Scouts. All beetles' legs are a bit like that. Yet whatever purposes they were designed to fit, digging holes was certainly not one of them; and I felt a longing to devise something better, the front legs ending in a sort of mattock, the back legs shaped more like a shovel. Thus would I reduce the time and effort spent on providing a safe repository for those four thousand eggs.

But on reflection I see now that I was misguided. Why should I suppose that an oil beetle would welcome my efforts to increase its efficiency? Why should I suppose it was not perfectly happy with things the way they were? What benefits would increased efficiency be likely to bring? Might not such benefits be offset by drawbacks that left the beetle worse off than before? These are the questions I now ask myself; and they ought to be the sort of questions we always ask ourselves before, in our passion for efficiency, we change people's lives—all too often for the worse.

The oil beetle can give a ready answer to our criticism. It may not manage to dig more than three holes in a season, but it lays several thousand eggs in each. A weakness in the legs is thus compensated for by magnificent ovaries.

And so it is with other creatures; and so it is with man. Efficiency and inefficiency exist happily side by side, and both have a place in our lives. We may wish to change things in order to enjoy greater comfort or greater security or in order to have more time for other desirable things. Greater efficiency may well help us toward these ends. But it should never be thought an end in itself.

Thus when I am given the task of clearing the supper things from the dining table to the kitchen, I will use my hands for the purpose, carrying, it may be, a plate in one hand and two forks in the other. Lesley points out that if instead I used a tray, I would be able to carry more things at once and so need to make fewer journeys. Maybe. But why should she assume that I wish to make fewer journeys? I enjoy walking to and fro between rooms, picking up something and putting it down. I find it physically satisfying, and a simple enough task to allow my thoughts to wander elsewhere. Whereas piling things up on a tray and fearing all the time that a cup or glass will topple over the edge requires all my care and attention.

Looking at the larger world beyond Embridge, I am becoming more and more convinced that the blind pursuit of efficiency is doing us immense harm. It has led us to specialization, which may well have been good, but it is now leading on to overspecialization, which is dangerous. It may well have been a good thing when the carpenter specialized and became a chair maker, but it became less good when the chairmaker specialized and became the man who operates the machine that cuts the dowels that pin the rails to the legs.

The supreme example of pointless overspecialization is that we now have in our world two vast groups of men who—independently of each other—are engaged in making the most highly efficient engines of destruction, whose one and only purpose is that they should never be used. If only they could look up from their work for a moment and then look around at other parts of the world and then perhaps meet and talk things over, they would surely agree what a ludicrous waste of time it all is.

Only marginally less alarming is the overspecialization and super-efficiency to be seen in our attempts to grow more food. From the minister of agriculture and the president of the National Union of Farmers down to the humblest packer of battery eggs, everyone is pursuing his task on the narrowest possible front. Looking neither to the left nor right, all forge blindly ahead. More tonnes of wheat per hectare, more sacks of fertilizer sold, more ingenious pesticides invented, more money in the bank. Success after success. Yet when it is all added up—and all the battery chickens that have managed to stay alive have come home to roost—I don't doubt that the total will be reckoned a failure.

Our world is full of holes and hole-makers. Some of the holes are brilliant feats of engineering. Others are not. It doesn't follow that the best holes are drilled for the best purposes. It is the purpose that matters. I would rather have oil beetles in my garden drilling holes for their eggs than humans drilling holes for their oil.

THIRTY-THREE

✦ ✦ ✦ ✦ ✦

The Egg, the Fox,
and the Dagger

I have been pondering on the various pleasures I enjoy as an amateur naturalist, and I have decided that they are of three different kinds; and that each kind represents a step toward a closer relationship with the natural world.

The first pleasure and the first step is that of recognition, of being able to attach a name to what I have found. It may be something I have seen often enough but whose name I have only just learned; or it may be something new that I have happened on for the first time. But more often it will be just the simple pleasure of recognizing an acquaintance: like the pleasure of being able to say, "Good morning, Mrs. Brown. Good morning, Mr. Smith," as we jostle with our fellow citizens on market day.

I first became an amateur naturalist rather than a mere nature lover when, at the age of thirteen, my father gave me a copy of Kirkman and Jourdain's *British Birds*. As a young ornithologist, keen to add to the growing list of birds I could identify, I used to spend as much time as possible out in the country with my binoculars, examining whatever I heard or saw. Then, on my return, I would thumb through Kirkman until I had matched it up. And it was not long before I could name by its song or its appearance almost any bird that came my way in the course of an afternoon's ramble.

Today, though I would still hope to be able to identify any bird I met, I no longer go searching for them. If I am searching for anything, it is now more likely to be a flower or an insect. And Fitter and Blamey's *Wild Flowers of Britain and Northern Europe* and *The Oxford Book of Insects* have become as well thumbed as my still-surviving *British Birds*.

But names, alas, are harder to remember than once they were, and I may have to remind myself more often than I would wish of the precise differences between the various hawkweeds, hawkbits, and hawkbeards.

This, the first of my three pleasures, has the particular merit that it can be enjoyed whenever I wish. At any time of the year Lesley and I can go for a walk and entertain ourselves by counting—and naming—the number of different wildflowers that we see in bloom. On our holiday last summer we named over a hundred. There is also the annual pleasure of welcoming back the first arrivals: the first celandine, the first chiffchaff, the first scarlet tiger moth. Even if we never see anything new or unusual, there is still much pleasure in greeting old friends.

Once a bird or a flower or an insect has been tracked down, the book will tell you something about its behavior; and naturally one of the things I wanted to know about my birds was when and where they built their nests. I never became an egg collector, but I most certainly became a nest seeker, and I would hunt up and down hedgerows and peer into bramble patches and work my way through reed beds, searching, searching. At Cotchford I had until the beginning of May; so mostly it was blackbirds, thrushes, hedge sparrows, and wrens, and if I was lucky, a long-tailed tit. At school I had the rest of the season, and I have memories of whitethroats and reed warblers and on one occasion a redstart. And it was then that I discovered the second of my three pleasures.

This is the pleasure of being a spectator. One can see a bird sitting in a bush or flying overhead: this, unless it is something rare, is not particularly exciting. Much more exciting is to watch it visit its nest to feed its young. One can of course remain an ornithologist, watching

and recording with scientific accuracy the number of caterpillars consumed per hour. This may well be pleasure enough for some; but not
for me. The pleasure I am thinking of is the one we share with the
audience at a theater: of watching from the shadows, of seeing without
being seen, of eavesdropping on someone's private conversation, of
taking a surreptitious glance into someone's private life. Where I live,
if you want to enjoy a few minutes of domestic bird life, a good vantage
point is the top of a cliff. Here, sitting on the short grass, you are in
the upper circle and the stage is below you; and at the right time of
year you will almost certainly be able to watch the comings and goings
of at least one pair of herring gulls together with the anxious wailings,
eager welcomings, and joyous feastings of their children.

I have used these three adjectives deliberately, and I realize that
this is something the serious ornithologist would deplore. Birds do not
have human emotions. Anthropomorphism is forbidden. But I do not
look at birds through ornithological eyes only. I am like the playgoer
who, though he knows that the actors are only actors, likes to imagine
them as the characters whose parts they are playing. Indeed the acting
can sometimes be so good that it is hard to know where truth ends and
imagination begins; and this is as true of bird as it is of man.

I remember in particular a little drama that Lesley and I watched
one afternoon many years ago from a cliff top near Start Point. There
were three actors on the stage below us: Father Herring Gull, Mother
Herring Gull, and Egg. When the curtain went up, Mother and Egg
were on the stage. Enter Father, swooping in from the sea. It was now
his turn to baby-sit while Mother stretched her wings and found something to eat. Brief duologue in which Mother gives Father his instructions and Father says, "Yes, yes, yes. Of course, dear. Of course." Exit
Mother. Father settles himself on top of Egg and fidgets his wings into
position. There. Now he can relax. No. He is not quite comfortable and
fidgets again . . . and then again. Unfortunately, the more he fidgets,
the more uncomfortable Egg becomes. Every time he moves, Egg
moves, too. Gradually it dawns on him (and we could see it dawning)
that Egg is moving nearer and nearer to the edge of the precipice. He

is now desperately trying to push it back, but alas he is only making matters worse. How easy it is for the onlooker to see what ought to be done. "Get your wing the *other* side of it." In vain. Egg is now on the verge. Nothing can save it. Over it goes, a sheer drop of some twenty feet. Smash!

And there is poor Father peering over to see what has become of it. He is still peering when Mother returns. "What are you doing? . . . *What has happened to our Egg?*"

Kirkman describes what he calls the "wild cacchination" of the herring gull thus: Head raised: "eow! eow! eow!" Head lowered: "ee-er, ee-er, ee-er." But on this occasion we had no need of Kirkman. We knew perfectly well what she with her head raised and he with his head lowered were saying to each other.

Thus my second pleasure brings the actors alive, turns them from a list of *dramatis personae* into individual characters. Yet though they perform, I merely watch. And so my third pleasure—and the final one in our relationship—is to find myself, not a spectator sitting unnoticed in the upper circle, but a fellow actor on the stage. If it was a privilege to be allowed to watch, it is an even greater privilege to be offered a part.

One becomes, I know, a fellow actor when at a picnic the wasp arrives and gets mixed up with the jam; or when, later in the evening, the mosquito settles on one's arm. But I am not thinking of those occasions when man plays his customary role—that of enemy to be avoided or supper to be eaten. I am thinking of those very much rarer occasions when, to our surprise, we are given (or appear to be given) a much more unusual and altogether more flattering part.

Yes indeed, on such occasions we are flattered; and we feel greatly honored when an animal forgets to be either afraid or fierce and comes to us for our help. Androcles, even if he had never seen his lion again after their first meeting, would still have had a story worth boasting about.

I can think of two occasions when I have been invited to become a sort of Androcles to a creature in need. On both occasions, although this was how I saw myself, I will admit that the creature I helped may have seen me rather differently. But that is no matter.

On the first occasion it was after dark on a June evening. I was in the kitchen doing the washing up when there came an unexpected and very violent battering on the window. I opened it and a large moth flew in, made for the light, and flew around it in the usual frantic mothlike manner. I reached up my hands and caught it quite easily. I held it until its flutterings had stopped and then very cautiously opened my hands to see what it was. The moth remained clinging to my finger, gently quivering. I will admit that I did not immediately recognize it. Not until later, with the help of my *Oxford Book of Insects*, did I discover it to be a female fox moth.

The fox moth likes moorland country. The female lays her eggs on the stems of heather, and in order that these eggs should be less visible to the passerby, she makes them look exactly like tiny white heather bells. I know this not only because my book told me so, but because when my moth eventually flew away into the night, I found that she had deposited on my finger in a neat line, stuck down with her own patent glue, four heather-bell eggs.

Why had she done that? No doubt an entomologist could give me the scientific reason. But I preferred to imagine that she had come from Dartmoor, had been blown south by a spell of bad weather, and had lost her way. She had searched for heather and found only grass. She had searched until she could wait no longer. Her time had come and so, seeing me, she had knocked on my window to seek my help.

I did not fail her. I was conscious of her trust and of my responsibility. I looked after her children until they were two inches long, striped black and yellow like football stockings, and well able to fend for themselves. My duties as foster parent discharged, maybe I ought to have driven them back to the moor. But my insect book assured me that they would thrive equally well on a diet of brambles. I found them a bramble bush and wished them well.

On the second occasion I played the part not of foster parent but of house agent.

It was the end of August, and Clare and I were sitting on the lawn having breakfast.

"There's a caterpillar on your shoulder," she said; and so there was.

It was about an inch-and-a-half long and gaily colored, and I didn't recognize it. I took it off and put it on the grass nearby, and at once it began to hurry toward me. I moved out of its way, and still it came toward me. I moved behind it and it turned around, raced up to me, and began to climb my trousers. I put it on a leaf and put the leaf on the flower bed. The caterpillar dropped to the ground, hurried back, and again climbed my trousers. So I left it there, settled in a fold by my pocket, while we ate our eggs. But after that I needed to go indoors for some coffee. So I put my caterpillar on the jersey I had just taken off, hoping it would be content with that while I was away. When I came back Clare told me it had left my jersey and was now somewhere under her chair. I looked but failed to find it; and we began drinking our coffee.

Then I saw the caterpillar. It had seen me and was hurrying back. It climbed quickly over the bits of breakfast that were in its way, raced up my trousers, and settled once again in a fold by my pocket.

What did it want and how could I help it? The first thing was to find out just who it was. So together we went indoors to consult my book. Luckily it was sufficiently gaudy for there to be no doubt. It was the caterpillar of the grey dagger moth, and my book told me that when they were ready to pupate, they searched for the fallen and decayed branch of a tree and either squeezed behind a piece of loose bark or else made themselves a hole in the rotting wood. That explained it! My trousers were oldish and to my caterpillar they either looked like loose bark or smelled like rotting wood. Possibly both. Nevertheless, I was not prepared to hand them over to be used as a bedroom for the next six months.

For occasions such as this I have a glass case which I can furnish within to suit most needs. I put the caterpillar inside and went off to look for some genuine rotting wood. After hunting for a while I came back with a short length of dead apple branch. It had plenty of loose bark, but the wood was rather hard. So I took it into my workshop and drilled a hole half an inch across and rather more than an inch deep. Then I offered it to my caterpillar.

It was delighted and at once began to explore the house I had made for it. It climbed the bark. It peered into possible cracks. Finally it reached the top, saw my hole, and got inside. After a moment it came out, and I feared it was dissatisfied. But no, the hole was ideal. All it lacked was a front door. For the next few minutes the caterpillar, keeping its back legs inside the hole, explored around the edge with its front legs, gathering in its jaws fragments of wood and leaf and carrying them back inside.

I left it and brought in the breakfast things, and when I next went to look, I saw that half the opening was already covered over. Soon there was not enough space left to squeeze through, and so the last of the work was done from the inside.

I left the caterpillar to sleep in peace—and hurried upstairs to record exactly what had happened.

Those, then, are my three steps toward a closer—and I believe a proper—relationship with the nonhuman world. And of course the naturalist, the biologist, will have stopped short after the first. He is quite right to do so, but he must not think that he can tell us all we need to know about nature, any more than the doctor can tell us all we need to know about humanity.

In my first step I saw the natural world through the eyes of the scientist. A plant or an animal was what my reference book said it was. I could look it up and beneath its picture read a brief description of its appearance and its habits. It is at this stage that flowers are picked and pressed, birds' eggs are blown, butterflies and moths are pinned on to a board, and animals are stuffed and put into cases in museums. Or rather this is what used to be done when I was a boy. Today this is considered cruel, and we prefer other methods of collecting and recording, such as taking photographs. But whatever method we choose, this first step is an essential one. We must start by learning what the scientist has to teach us. If I had been unable to identify my fox moth and my grey dagger, I should never have enjoyed so much pleasure in their company.

In the second stage of the relationship, creatures are no longer merely representatives of their species. They come alive. They move. They are individuals in their own right, going about their everyday affairs in their own private worlds. They are fish in a fishpond, caterpillars in a shoe box, ants in a formicarium, animals in a zoo, and flowers in a vase of water. We can watch them; but we ourselves remain outside, spectators, peering through the glass or between the bars. Their world is not our world.

In the third and final stage, the bars are pulled down. Our two worlds become one. This is the relationship we normally establish with only a few carefully selected species: our garden flowers, perhaps, and almost certainly the household cat.

As yet we are a long way from regarding every beetle as a first-class citizen or granting equal rights to every dandelion. We have, after all, only very recently reached this stage in our relationship with our fellow humans, particularly if they belong to a different race.

Very many years ago, when I was about six years old, I was walking through a wood with my parents. The track was a wide one, practically a lane, and across it, in front of us, wriggled a snake. I can still see it, and I know without any doubt that it was an adder. I bent down to stroke it, and my father, with a fierce jerk on my arm, pulled me away.

"Why did you do that?" l cried.

"It would have bitten you."

"But I was only going to stroke it. I was not going to hurt it."

"I don't think the snake could have been sure about this."

I thought for a moment. "If I had offered it some food first," I said, "would it then have been sure?"

"I don't think so. You see, if you had offered it some bread, it would have said to itself: 'Here is some bread. Let me eat it.' And when you offered it your hand, it would have said. 'Here is a hand. Let me bite it.'"

Yes, I had much to learn. And I had to start at the beginning. But though the adult has much to teach the child, the child in return has something to teach the adult. For our journey is, or should be, a circular one in which we end up where we began, returning to the world we left when first we went to school, and bringing with us the wisdom and knowledge we have gathered on our way.

The child's world is a single indivisible world in which all creatures, human and animal, live together as equals. Instinctively he feels this to be the truth—as indeed it is.

But in order to understand it, in order to learn how it works, we need to examine it bit by bit; and so we take it to pieces, separating it into its various layers—its species and subspecies, its races and classes. At school I learned how to distinguish a verb from a noun, a Cavalier from a Roundhead, a logarithm from an antilogarithm, and an atom from a molecule. When we have finished studying the world in this way and have learned all we can about it, perhaps we remember it as we once knew it. But can we ever put it together again?

This is the question that today faces not only the middle-aged adult but humanity as a whole. Can we, the human race, reassemble a world that, over the millennia, we have been taking apart? Can we put it together before it totally disintegrates?

There is not much time left. The child is waiting for us, beckoning to us. We must hurry.